T0244125

STACKPOLE BOOKS

An imprint of Globe Pequot, the trade division of
The Rowman & Littlefield Publishing Group, Inc.
4501 Forbes Blvd., Ste. 200
Lanham, MD 20706
www.rowman.com

Distributed by NATIONAL BOOK NETWORK

British Library Cataloguing in Publication Information available

Library of Congress Cataloging-in-Publication Data available

978-0-8117-7145-0 (cloth)
978-0-8117-7146-7 (electronic)

∞™ The paper used in this publication meets the minimum requirements of American National
Standard for Information Sciences—Permanence of Paper for Printed Library Materials, ANSI/
NISO Z39.48-1992.

For Hugh Higgins, who encouraged the author to write this book during lockdown

CONTENTS

List of Maps and Battle Plans

Maps

Battle Plans

The ancient Middle East.

INTRODUCTION

THE ANCIENT MIDDLE EAST WAS THE PLACE WHERE ORGANIZED WAR-fare began. Before the Sumerians fielded the world's first armies, human conflict was never conducted in a systematic fashion. Yet even the Sumerians were aghast at the casualties their battles caused, and indeed the earliest war memorial ever erected reflects this profound unease. The Stele of the Vultures, which was carved around 2460 BC after a conflict between the city-states of Lagash and Umma, is not boastful at all. If anything, it sends the message that, though a political necessity, the advent of organized warfare was a matter of regret. While King Eanna-tum of Lagash is justified in halting the encroachment of Umma on land belonging to his city-state, the real victor was the god Ningirsu, who is shown holding a net in which the bodies of the vanquished are thrown carelessly together. The implication is that the entitlement to inflict death belongs to the god, not the king.

The Stele of the Vultures functioned as a war memorial and a legal treaty defining the border between Umma and Lagash. An inscribed curse warned that anyone moving or tampering with the stele faced the anger of the gods. That Lagash had tried and failed to use diplomacy to settle the dispute with Umma only underlines the reluctance of Eanna-tum to rush into war. The Sumerians believed that at least one deity lived in each city-state and that unnecessary conflict could well trigger divine punishment. Hence Eannatum's consultation with his diviners before taking action: they assured him that "the sun god's rays will illuminate your right." Only when he was absolutely sure of divine approval would this Sumerian king commit his forces to battle.

Although the Akkadians did not share the Sumerian sense of guilt over organized conflict, their kings were equally concerned to have the support of the gods. The founder of the Akkadian dynasty, Sargon, was prepared to extend his power through extreme violence, but he was always worried about the legitimacy of his rule. His name in the Bible is indeed a corruption of *sharru kenu*, meaning "legitimate king," a title he felt it necessary to adopt. Sargon's amazing military career rested upon the first permanent army to appear anywhere in the world. Though small by later standards, it represented a turning point in interstate conflict so that Sargon's apparently endless series of campaigns became a model for the aggressive Assyrians. Sargon and his successors made war an integral part of civilization. Nothing was ever quite the same again, not least because a surge in military proficiency led to warfare on a scale unrepeated before modern times.

The Assyrian war machine in particular was a dreaded vehicle of destruction, reaching an unprecedented strength of 200,000 men in the seventh century BC. A steady increase in the size of the Assyrian army suggests that, like Napoleon, the kings of Assyria always believed in the military advantage of superior numbers. Added to this tactical edge was a deliberate policy of terror against anyone who dared to oppose Assyrian arms. For the Assyrians held that war was both just and good since it conformed to divine plans for the maintenance of the cosmic order, plans that were decreed through the omens of the gods. So sure of their right to exercise unrestrained violence were the Assyrians that there was never any hesitation on their part in recording the more gruesome aspects of war. Bas-reliefs depict the breaking and tearing of bodies, the impaling and flaying of live prisoners, and enormous piles of severed heads. Nowhere is there a hint that mercy is an obligation on the part of the victor. Honorable surrender never occurred to the Assyrians as an option: if they failed to achieve a military objective during one campaign, it simply became that of another.

Assyrian tactics are still a matter of debate, but there were standard procedures for an advance and a withdrawal, designed to protect the army from surprise attack. In 714 BC at Mount Uaush, at the end of an exhausting trek through a narrow pass, King Sargon II was confident enough to dispense with these altogether and charge the enemy head-on. He broke the enemy center and caused a general collapse of the Urartian battle line. By this period war chariots had been replaced by mounted archers, not least because the Assyrians were expanding their empire into terrain unsuited to wheeled vehicles. The great chariot battles were already a thing of the past, although the climatic clash between the Egyptians and the Hittites at Kadesh in 1274 BC was not forgotten. Then 5,000 chariots had engaged in a battle that left the young pharaoh Ramesses II in possession of the battlefield but by no means a complete winner.

The sharp decline in the number of chariots mentioned in Assyrian records from the end of the eighth century BC onward means that they no longer acted as a practical component of the Assyrian army. Henceforth the chariot had primarily a symbolic value as a conveyance that confirmed the status of kings and noblemen. Because of their great expense, they might be regarded as the ancient equivalent of the modern sports car.

Powerful though the Assyrians were for several centuries, it was the Persians who founded the first true empire in the ancient Middle East. In its extent the Persian Empire dwarfed other powers, for the interest of Persian kings in establishing a universal monarchy would have brought much of the Mediterranean under their control had not the Greeks blocked an advance westward. As it was, the Persians ruled territories stretching from the Danube to the Indus, from the Caspian Sea to the Nile. But first the mainland Greeks, then the Macedonians thwarted their imperial ambitions. Between 334 and 323 BC Alexander the Great not only defeated the Persians but also carried European arms as far east as India.

Despite Alexander the Great's successors dividing up his conquests among themselves, one of them, the Seleucid dynasty, held on to much of his Asian realm for two more centuries. Not until 126 BC were the Seleucid kings driven west of the river Euphrates, leaving them with a restricted economic base and no chance of mustering enough troops to fight back with any hope of success. The reason for this retreat westward was the Parthians, semipastoralists who led the Iranian revival. Neither the Parthians nor their Sasanian successors managed to restore Persia to its former glory, but they pressed the Romans hard on their eastern frontier. The final phase of warfare in the ancient Middle East comprised the struggle of Rome to defend its provinces there.

The Roman emperor Heraclius eventually triumphed over the Sasanians, but the victory was a hollow one because another Middle Eastern people, the Arabs, were about to set out on their world conquests. In 641 BC the Arabs destroyed Sasanid Persia and then turned their attention to the west. So impressive was the surge of Muslim power that not only was the Roman capital of Constantinople threatened, but even more Arab arms pushed along the coast of North Africa and into Spain and France. These dramatic events marked the transition from the ancient to the medieval period of world history, as religious differences came to define both political and military affairs. Already an icon of the Virgin Mary had been paraded round Constantinople's walls in order to secure divine protection against the Muslim assault.

CHAPTER ONE

Sumer and Akkad

EVER SINCE THE ENGLISH CIVIL WAR, THE BRUTAL VIEW OF HUMANITY propounded by Thomas Hobbes has cast a shadow over our ideas about warfare. Without a strong central authority, he believed, life could be nothing other than "solitary, poor, brutish and short." In his seminal work, *Leviathan*, published in 1651, Hobbes argued as a royalist exile that the state was a monster composed of people, created under pressure of human needs and dissolved by civil strife aroused by human passions. Only through ceding a degree of personal independence to a strong ruler could people enjoy a peaceful existence.

Already in 1629 Hobbes had translated Thucydides's *History of the Peloponnesian War* in order to explain the causes of political instability and armed conflict. He endeavored to show the inevitable defeat of Athens through the undue influence of demagogues in the citizen assembly; their powers of persuasion put the city-state "upon the most dangerous and desperate enterprises." With the disastrous military expedition of 415–413 BC against Syracuse in mind, Hobbes wrote that democratic government let "wicked men and flatterers" drive the Athenians "headlong into those actions that were to ruin them; and good men durst not oppose, or if they did, undid themselves." As long as Pericles was alive, Hobbes contended, Athens was a democracy in form but a monarchy in fact, because this aristocratic politician's oratorical skills ensured the safe direction of the city-state. Under stuttering King Charles I, however, England was the reverse as royal authority suffered constant challenge to the extent that, in the same year that Hobbes's translation of Thucydides appeared, the king decided "hereafter none do presume to print or publish any matter of news, relations, histories, or other things in prose or in verse that have reference to matters and affairs of state, without the view, approbation and licence" of the government.

This autocratic outlook was, however, attacked a century later by Jean-Jacques Rousseau, who put the blame for organized warfare on the state itself. The more advanced civilized arts and sciences became, the greater the damage they did to our lives. "Savage man, subject to few passions and self-sufficient" was Rousseau's ideal. His point of view would encourage many anthropologists to contend that violence hardly existed before the advent of agriculture. Because hunter-gatherers were thinly spread, were supposedly untied to territory, and held few possessions, they had no need to engage in fighting. Although there is evidence to suggest that human conflict occurred well before the Sumerians founded the first city-state in the late fourth millennium BC, it does appear to have increased in intensity among prestate agriculturalists as opposed to hunter-gatherers.

WAR BEFORE CIVILIZATION

Hunter-gatherer peoples survived undisturbed longest in Australia. Europeans arrived late in colonial times, with settlement beginning in 1788 and spreading slowly, especially in the outback. There had been no agriculturalists or pastoralists at all in Australia before the European arrival. The continent was home to about 300,000 hunter-gatherers, distributed among five hundred or so tribal groups. While European diseases took a heavy toll on Aborigines living in southern Australia, the majority of the hunter-gatherers elsewhere were able to continue their age-old way of life. As regards weaponry, the use of metal was unknown; warfare involved wooden spears, clubs, and shields as well as stone knives. So remote was Australia that the bow was never used, and the only long-range weapon in the Aboriginal armory was the boomerang. But fighting scenes depicted in ancient rock art make it clear that tribal conflict did take place.

Low hunter-gatherer population densities in poor terrain ought not cause intertribal conflict, given the ability of a group to move on to more productive areas. Yet legendary tales reflect conflict over natural resources. One of these, belonging to the Warlpiri people of central Australia, concerns the rivalry of two ancestral figures, Wardilyka, or "Bush Turkey," and Emu. During Dreamtime, when the tribal ancestors walked in Australia, Bush Turkey would collect berries and make them into fruit balls, which he stored in the ground. Having exhausted the supply of berries where he lived, Bush Turkey wandered into the preserve of Emu, picking the ripest berries he could find there. When Emu realized that his food supply would soon be exhausted as well, he flew at Bush Turkey and, with his digging stick, smashed to pieces the berries that the intruder had already collected. After a struggle, Emu managed to grab hold of Bush Turkey and fill his eyes with dirt so that a blinded Bush Turkey staggered away, dropping berries as he went. These became the rocky hills and boulders still spread across the landscape.

Alchera, or "Dreamtime," is almost synonymous with Aboriginal myth. Then the tribal ancestors formed the landscape, created plants, animals, and people, and taught language and ceremonies, putting the world in order. These chthonic spirits are believed to have returned to their underground abodes, from where they still animate the tribal lands and help sustain their descendants. That tribal ancestors are all nonhuman is probably explained by the coexistence of the Aborigines with larger versions of these creatures for millennia. Archaeological finds show that the first Aborigines traveled eastward 50,000 years ago, when the last ice age locked up so much water in ice and glaciers that the sea level was three hundred feet lower than it is today. Since the oldest stone tools of the sort necessary to make dugout canoes are only 20,000 years old, these intrepid sailors managed with rafts of lashed logs, taking advantage en route of a now invisible chain of islands.

On arrival in Australia the earliest Aborigines encountered very large animals: giant fanged kangaroos, lizards as long as buses, huge land-dwelling crocodiles, wombats the size of bears, and a fearsome marsupial lion. It was once thought that the continent's larger animals were killed through overhunting and were gone shortly after the Aboriginal arrival. But archaeological evidence has now revealed how these great creatures lived alongside human beings for up to 20,000 years. So severe changes in the environment, not human activity, seem to have led to their extermination. Hence the emphasis placed upon animals during Dreamtime.

Apart from illustrating the closeness of Aboriginal culture to the natural world, the account of the struggle between Bush Turkey and Emu suggests tribal competition over the food supply. In the initial stage of the Aboriginal occupation of Australia, it is unlikely that there was any determined attempt to defend territory or monopolize natural resources. More likely the Wardilyka myth relates to tribes bumping into each other as they regularly migrated from one place to another. The resolution of any trespass on traditional migratory routes by other tribes might bring about the hunter-gatherer equivalent of warfare, a stand-off battle in which the opposing sides positioned themselves at spear-throwing or boomerang distance. Close-quarter encounters, along with the shedding of blood, would thus have been largely avoided. Instead, an almost ritualistic approach to conflict characterized the settling of tribal differences, with a minimal loss of life. Considering how much space there was in the outback anyway, the stakes were simply not high enough to justify hand-to-hand combat. As long as one group gave ground, that was enough.

South of the Sahara the experience of African hunter-gatherers was very different from that of the Aborigines because they confronted peoples who herded animals, especially cattle. Chief among these pastoralists were the Bantu-speaking tribes that moved east and south from present-day Cameroon. These determined warriors pushed hunter-gatherers such as the Bushmen and the Hottentots into marginal terrain unsuited to herding. Perhaps the most aggressive of all Bantu-speakers were the Zulus, who later put up such a stubborn resistance to European settlement during the nineteenth century.

The 1487–1488 voyage of the Portuguese navigator Bartolomeu Dias to the Cape of Good Hope shows just how late European involvement with Africa was. Dias was not interested in Africa: the Portuguese king had sent him southward with three ships to find out where the African continent ended so that merchants from Portugal could sail directly to India in search of spices. As a result, Vasco da Gama's epoch-making voyage across the Indian Ocean to Calicut in 1498 gave the Portuguese the means of breaking the Venetian-Muslim monopoly over the supply of spices to Europe. Despite the slave trade, which the Portuguese began in 1517, the impact of Europe on traditional African society was slight before modern times.

This makes the establishment of the Zulu kingdom in southern Africa a rare example of the preurban state, although by then the Zulus were sedentary pastoralists, raising crops as well as herding cattle. The powerful kingdom that Shaka founded in the early nineteenth century may have been a relatively late creation, but it emerged before any significant contact with either Dutch or British settlers. By changing the method of Zulu fighting, replacing the metal-headed throwing spear with one more suited to thrusting at close range, King Shaka turned armed conflict into something approaching organized warfare. This new tactic terrified his opponents and allowed the Zulu kingdom to expand its territory at the expense of other tribes; the new acquisitions were secured with a standing army. Not that the Zulus could ever be described as unwarlike. Their supreme deity, the sky god Unkulungkulu, was said to have introduced marriage as a way of ensuring that brave warriors fathered children and thereby maintained the strength of the tribe. He also provided the Zulus with doctors for the treatment of wounds. Unkulungkulu embraced even fallen warriors with compassion, giving them a warm welcome in his celestial abode.

At the Battle of Isandlwana in 1879, Zulu warriors annihilated a British force of 1,200 men. Lord Chelmsford, the British commander during the invasion of the Zulu kingdom, had split his expedition into several columns so as to overcome the inherent slowness of imperial armies in the bush and to increase the chances of forcing a mobile foe to stand and fight. It proved a fatal mistake. The Zulus had every intention of seeking a decisive encounter, and by dividing his troops, Lord Chelmsford gave them an opportunity to wipe out half his army at Isandlwana. Neither breach-loading rifles nor field artillery were sufficient to repel a concentrated Zulu assault. Impressive though this triumph was for inferior arms, the success failed to prevent the British subjugation of the Zulus. Yet the Battle of Isandlwana showed how effective unity of purpose was in the Zulu kingdom in the face of a superior outside threat.

In addition to having the advantage of unity as a single tribal group, the Zulus did not suffer from the rivalry between chieftains that bedeviled so many other African tribes.

A biblical parallel of meeting such an external crisis was the election of Saul in 1020 BC as the first Jewish king, who united the various tribes in order to deal with increasingly hostile neighbors. We are told, "He took the yoke of an oxen, cut it into pieces, and sent them throughout the borders of Israel by the hand of messengers, saying, whosoever cometh not shall it be done unto his oxen. And the dread of the Lord fell on the people, and they came as one man." After thwarting the enemy, King Saul kept together a standing force of 3,000 soldiers to meet future emergencies. Indeed the steady pressure exerted by the Philistines led to the permanent Jewish adoption of a monarchy. Twenty years later David replaced Saul, and as a way of ensuring continued unity, he chose Jerusalem as the site of his capital since it belonged to no particular tribe. Under David's son Solomon, Jewish power was not inconsiderable, with an army supported by 4,000 chariots, but after this king's death in 822 BC, tension between the northern and southern tribes led to the establishment of two separate kingdoms: Judah in the south and Israel in the north. Violent disorder had already undermined Israel before the Assyrian king Sargon II abolished that kingdom altogether in 721 BC. Judah refused to assist Israel, and though it survived as an independent state for another century, the Babylonians eventually captured Jerusalem and carried prominent Jews off into captivity. As in so many other instances, an inability to stand together brought an end to the Jewish kingdom.

By the time Judah ceased to exist as an independent kingdom, the ancient Middle East was dotted with cities, the largest of which, Babylon, was regarded as a wonder of the world. The Greek historian Herodotus was amazed by its size as well as its huge fortifications, which would have impressed a visitor approaching across the open plain where Babylon stood. Rising above them was the outline of the enormous ziggurat belonging to the god Marduk. Known as Etemenaki, "the house-support of the universe," its construction is estimated to have required no less than 17 million bricks. Erected though ziggurats were in most Mesopotamian cities, it was this one, on top of which Marduk lived, that inspired

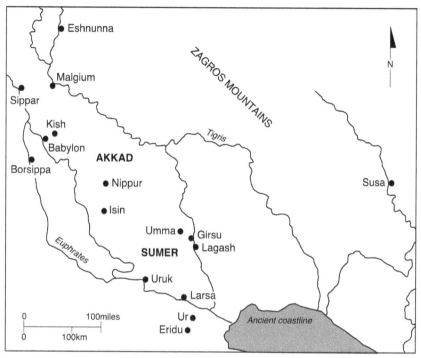

Lower Mesopotamia.

the Jewish myth of the Tower of Babel. For the Babylonians, Marduk was not simply a city god. In their view of the cosmos, they were unique, since very few Semites paid much attention to the idea of creation. But the *Enuma Elish*, a Babylonian epic dating from the late second millennium BC, provides a detailed description of the origin of the universe as well as Marduk's decisive confrontation at its inception with the forces of chaos.

A worldview placing an all-powerful deity such as Marduk in a temple at the top of an artificial mountain built in the center of a great city is a long way from the outlook of our earliest ancestors, the hunter-gatherers, who for countless generations roamed the landscape in pursuit of game and edible plants. Only between 10,000 and 5,000 years ago did humans begin to stop migrating and settle down to grow crops. Once a group started to farm, however, its members were tied to their fields as never before. Switching to agriculture involved taking on a regime of hard work as labor was necessary throughout the year, a burden echoed

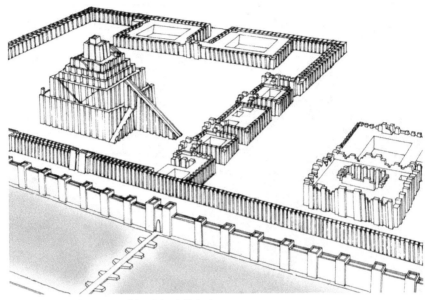

The massive ziggurat of Marduk at Babylon.

perhaps in the curse laid upon humanity on banishment from the Garden of Eden. Henceforth, Adam and Eve were told, "in the sweat of thy face shalt thou eat bread." Possibly for this reason some hunter-gatherers chose not to grow crops even when they had farmers as neighbors. And hunter-gatherers remained overall healthier than agriculturalists. Permanent settlements were dirtier places than the temporary camps of foragers, where diseases could multiply as parasites jumped from domesticated species to humans. Many of our familiar diseases, such as measles, smallpox, influenza, diphtheria, and tuberculosis, originated in animals. Carbohydrates also formed a bigger portion of the diet of farmers.

Settling down as farmers had other unplanned and unexpected consequences. Land that is farmed supports more people than land that is foraged. As the Zulus discovered, a mixture of cultivation and herding increased the population of the tribal group. There were more warriors available to fight than in the days when the Zulus were simply herders. That, in different parts of the world, people combined crop growing with animal husbandry during roughly the same period remains an unexplained mystery. But the underlying dynamic seems to have been population growth. Certainly greater numbers of people are known to have lived in locations that favored agriculture before the switch to farming.

The earliest farming was really more like gardening than full-scale agriculture. Until animal traction was available, the whole family had to take part. Even then settled cultivators were liable to face years of hunger when their key crops failed, because they were less able to diversify their diet or move on. The result of such scarcity can be seen in the graveyards that began to be laid out around villages. In the ancient Middle East, the transition from hunting-gathering to agriculture is clearly visible. Between 8500 and 6500 BC, a range of settlements appeared, from tiny hamlets to substantial villages such as Catal Huyuk in Asia Minor. The defenses of Catal Huyuk may have been intended as protection against neighboring agricultural communities, although its inhabitants already possessed cattle, a favorite target of hunter-gatherers. Crops would have always been far more difficult and dangerous to obtain by force than livestock, not least because crop raiding entailed the occupation of a settlement following a coordinated assault. Such instances of wholesale slaughter seem to have been less frequent than livestock raiding.

The most striking illustration of the threat posed by raiders is the defenses built in the eighth millennium BC at Jericho in the Jordan river valley. Even before the domestication of animals, the ten-acre site with an estimated population of 3,000 had enclosed itself with a deep moat and a high stone wall. The unusually fertile land upon which Jericho was located may be the clue to these extensive defenses: its considerable agricultural surplus would have acted as a magnet during times of famine. Another explanation for the outside threat could be the role played by Jericho as a trading center for Dead Sea minerals. In any event, as hunter-gatherers were contracting in numbers worldwide, conflict between agricultural communities became the norm.

Catal Huyuk and Jericho were exceptional. Most farmer villages had fewer inhabitants and comprised a cluster of huts built with either mudbrick and stone or timber and earth. But all these communities were bound together by kinship ties, celebrated on occasion by the consumption of fermented drinks. Beer made from cereals is mentioned on cuneiform tablets unearthed in Mesopotamia, where writing was developed to keep accurate records of what lay in temple storerooms. Around 3000 BC the Sumerians in Uruk, the earliest city to appear on the planet, hit upon the idea of creating hundreds of pictograms, plus signs for numbers and measures; these were pressed into clay tablets with a reed stylus to record temple assets. From this tentative step toward literacy evolved cuneiform, from *cuneus*, the Latin for wedge, since the script's characters were wedge shaped.

There is no doubt that without this stroke of genius, we would have no access to the events, decisions, and ideas that shaped civilization. Nor would we appreciate how, from the start, armed conflict between city-states soon became taken for granted. That the invention of writing arose from the calculation of stored food indicates how fundamental agriculture was to the advent of urban living. It also accounts for the name of the earliest city, "Uruk the enclosure," since its famous walls provided refuge for herders and cultivators in moments of danger.

THE BEGINNINGS OF ORGANIZED WARFARE

The strength of the city walls that protected Uruk is recalled in *Gilgamesh*, the world's oldest long poem. It reached its final form in the first millennium BC, in the Akkadian language, but the original Sumerian version was composed to celebrate the exploits of King Gilgamesh of Uruk. This determined ruler defended his city and built new ramparts, around which, in the first lines of the epic, he strides in triumph. These bulwarks enclosed an area of six square miles, twice the size of the first settlement there. Because the Sumerian King List, like the extended genealogy in Genesis, attributes each of the earliest kings with an incredibly long reign, it is impossible to fix precise dates for Gilgamesh, although his own rule seems to have fallen somewhere between 2800 and 2500 BC. That Gilgamesh was feared by his subjects probably reflects the fact that he had to coerce them into building the extended city walls. At nearly eleven miles in length, Uruk's defenses were so unprecedented that "there was nobody among the kings who could compare with Gilgamesh, two-thirds god and one-third man, a hero who was destined for fame."

Gilgamesh's divine inheritance derived from his mother Ninsun, whose name translates as "lady wild cow." Her cult was associated with wild cattle, the untamed animals still roaming the fringes of the Euphrates-Tigris valley. But a profound unease over his mortal inheritance obliged Gilgamesh to seek a means of securing immortality during his lifetime. It forms the subject of the *Gilgamesh* epic.

The inhabitants of Uruk begged the gods for relief from Gilgamesh's tyrannical behavior, and they sent a wild man named Enkidu who ate grasses along with animals. Stories about Enkidu reached the city, and Gilgamesh set out to capture him. The wild man was finally induced to leave the wilderness and embrace civilization by two things: a sexual encounter with a prostitute from Uruk and plenty of beer. After consuming "seven kegs," Enkidu "relaxed, cheered up, his insides felt good, his face glowed." So the wild man moved to the city and became the boon companion of the king. But after the two had a series of adventures together, the sudden death of Enkidu shook Gilgamesh, who wept over his friend's "corpse for seven days and seven nights, refusing to give it up for burial until a maggot fell from one of his nostrils." Unwilling to accept that death was the inevitable end of life, Gilgamesh then sought out his ancestor Utanapishtim, the sole survivor of the Flood.

A clay tablet of the *Gilgamesh* epic, discovered at Ur, throws a sharp light on the Sumerian fear of premature death. On his deathbed Enkidu vented his fury at the prostitute who introduced him to civilization at the very moment he was being carried off by a grim man with "hands like a lion's paws and claws like an eagle's talons." The reason for this unexpected event was Gilgamesh's rebuff of the goddess Ishtar, the Semitic equivalent of Sumerian Inanna, whose temple was in Uruk. The goddess had fallen in love with the king, but he ignored her advances, mindful of the fate suffered by her previous mortal lovers once she had become bored with them. A divine bull was dispatched to punish Gilgamesh, but he and Enkidu killed it. For this act of impiety, this lack of respect for the gods, Enkidu was condemned to die.

A more mundane explanation for the wild man's death may be his susceptibility to urban diseases. That cities were hotbeds of infection

Gilgamesh killing the Bull of Heaven.

is evident in the myth of the Flood. Due to his inability to get a good night's rest because of the hubbub arising from overcrowded Sumerian cities, the storm god Enlil decided to wipe out humanity altogether. One method of destruction that Enlil tried without success was plague, an indication that visitations by deadly viruses were not unknown. The deluge was the final resort, which Ziudsura escaped in a giant coracle, the predecessor of Noah's Ark. Translation of the cuneiform text containing this story caused a sensation in London. It was announced in 1872 at the winter meeting of the Society of Biblical Archaeology. Even Prime Minister William Gladstone was in the audience. Everyone was baffled that a clay tablet from a Mesopotamian library, inscribed centuries before the Jews arrived in Palestine, could refer to the biblical Flood. Only gradually did scholars come to realize that this myth, like so much else in the ancient world, went all the way back to the Sumerians.

It was the water god Enki who warned Ziudsura of Enlil's murderous intentions. He told Ziudsura to "build a boat and put on board the seed of all living creatures." It is hardly surprising that Enki saved the Sumerians from the Flood, as their survival depended upon the abundant supply of fresh water he provided for their fields. Irrigation was a godsend in Sumer, where little rain fell. The life-sustaining water that appeared in rivers and canals was believed to come from Abzu, a vast underground reservoir belonging to Enki. Combined with lower Mesopotamia's rich alluvial soil, the use of water substantially reduced the amount of land that was needed to feed a family. Without this productive combination there would have never been a sufficient food surplus capable of supporting urban life, the essential feature of Sumerian civilization.

First in Uruk, then in other cities, improvements in cultivation and the management of livestock allowed greater numbers of people to live together, with between 50,000 and 100,000 dwelling in Uruk itself. The invention of the seeder-plough was crucial: it minimized seed loss by placing seeds individually inside the furrow, thereby increasing the cereal yield by an estimated 50 percent. This amazing surge in productivity, not unlike the improved output resulting from the modern mechanization of agriculture, accounts for the extra grain that encouraged rapid urban development, since there was now enough food to allow specialists the time to perfect their arts and crafts without worrying about the next meal. Alongside the advance in sowing, animal traction also sped up threshing through a sledge fitted with flint blades and pulled by an ass.

The stratification of Sumerian society caused by labor specialization affected the way people looked at the world. They came to accept a pivotal role for their temples. The temple bureaucracy took care of the city-state's economic administration: it managed the movement of the agricultural surplus from villages to storerooms in the city and determined its redistribution to specialist workers. And because of its responsibility for infrastructure, such as temples, walls, and canals, the priesthood came to occupy a commanding position in daily affairs. More importantly the priestly duty to maintain good relations with the divine meant that religion securely underpinned the temple's claim to authority.

Just how respectful the Sumerians were of the gods can be seen in the central position accorded to Ningirsu, the divine patron and protector of King Eannatum of Lagash, in the Stele of the Vultures, the world's old-

King Eannatum of Lagash.

est war memorial. This monument was carved and erected around 2460 BC after the settlement of a dispute over the ownership of Quedanna, a prized tract of land situated between the city-states of Lagash and Umma. The Stele of the Vultures, currently in the Louvre, is poorly preserved. Originally it was a large, rectangular slab of limestone with a rounded top. The present-day restoration is based on seven fragments, excavated in the 1880s at the site of ancient Girsu, a small city within the borders of Lagash. Incomplete though the stele is, the figures and text carved on its two faces are an absolute revelation of the beginnings of organized warfare. Not insignificant is the trigger for the pitched battle commemorated here: competition over agricultural resources. Lagash went to war to recover territory occupied by Umma.

Sumerian city-states settled their differences on the battlefield. But it is apparent that they did not share the later Assyrian delight in violence, which was most evident in the torture of prisoners of war. On the contrary, the Sumerians were always exercised by the need to find an ethical reason for taking human life. So the Stele of the Vultures depicts the vanquished as corpses either piled in heaps over which earth is being properly spread or else trapped in a great net held by the god Ningirsu. Even though a victorious Eannatum appears as a warrior, he is not shown dealing any death blow. Yet it was Eannatum who actually led his men into combat, for the text on the stele relates how "a man shot an arrow which penetrated the king but he broke it off."

King Eannatum appears several times on the reverse side of the stele. At the top he advances at the head of his troops; lower down he looks upon naked prisoners and the dead, while behind him vultures fly off with body parts. The front of the stele is dominated by a gigantic portrait of Ningirsu, whose name means "lord of Girsu." He was worshipped in Lagash as a warrior god whose heroic deeds saved, among others, Enlil from acute embarrassment. One particular feat is recalled by the Imdugud bird, which he holds with one hand; Ningirsu forced this troublesome creature to return the "tablet of destiny" to Enlil. Possession of the tablet gave Enlil supreme power over the entire world of the gods and humanity. With his other hand Ningirsu grasps a net inside which the bodies of the Umma dead are thrown carelessly together. The message is clear. The entitlement

Reconstructed Stele of the Vultures (front).

to inflict death belongs to the god, not to the ruler. If anything, the Stele of the Vultures signifies the limits of Sumerian kingship. Before the battle, Eannatum consulted his diviners and was informed that "the sun god's rays will illuminate your right." Only when absolutely certain of divine approval did he commit his forces to battle. Even then Eannatum was encouraged to fight because the Lagash-Umma conflict was a defensive

Reconstructed Stele of the Vultures (back).

one, since Quedanna had always been part of the traditional holdings of Lagash. The implication is that the gods fixed the boundaries of city-states, which explains why Sumerian rulers conducted wars in the names of the gods who resided in their cities. To embark on a campaign without divine support was not only militarily reckless but dangerous as an offended city deity might choose to respond in an unexpected manner.

Sumerian infantry from the Stele of the Vultures.

Apart from this religious aspect, the Stele of the Vultures provides valuable detail about Sumerian military equipment. Eannatum's soldiers wore helmets and armored cloaks. The latter were secured around the neck and made of leather, covered with metal discs. Primitive as this early body armor was, it would have afforded some protection from a spear thrust. As the seriousness of combat grew and the stand-off battle gave way to riskier clashes of arms, warriors sought any means to protect themselves in hand-to-hand fighting. They also tended to bunch closer together, seeking mutual protection in the phalanx. Yet it is doubtful whether the phalanx shown on the Stele of the Vultures ever compared with its equivalent in Greece, which was reputedly introduced by the Argives. After the defeat inflicted upon them by the Argives at Hysiai in 669 BC, the Spartans made this close-knit infantry formation their own. Its strength depended above all on a single piece of equipment, a round shield three feet in diameter, the *hoplon*, from which "hoplite," the word for the Greek infantryman, derived.

That Eannatum personally fought at the head of his troops shows how he was still essentially a war leader and not yet regarded as an absolute ruler in Lagash. Despite buttressing his position with declarations of divine support, especially that of Enlil and the storm god's wife, Ninhursag, Eannatum remained the servant of Lagash's resident deities. For the Sumerians, divinity was everywhere. It might be said that they developed their pantheon in order to understand the universe, which they called *an ki*, "heaven earth." Convinced that creation could not be explained by itself and needing to give it meaning, the Sumerians envisaged supernatural beings who were responsible for creating the world and making sure that its processes continued satisfactorily. As a consequence, the divine realm came to be imagined on the model of the earthly world, so that the gods were viewed as a spiritual aristocracy of great landowners, Sumer's all-powerful upper class, dutifully served by human beings. Even the independent-minded Gilgamesh was titled *en*, or "viceroy"; his responsibilities included the welfare of Uruk's resident deities, the heavenly god An and Inanna, the goddess of fertility.

The institution of kingship must have therefore arisen from warfare. When an enemy threatened a Sumerian city-state, a young nobleman was chosen to lead the community in battle and granted total authority during the emergency. By getting involved with justice, a few of these temporary kings managed to hold on to some power afterward. They broadened their appeal by defending the underprivileged members of society. Fundamental to a Sumerian king's position was a retinue of unfree retainers, in part recruited from war captives whose lives the king had spared. These lifelong soldiers ate with him and did his bidding in war as well as peace. Confirmation of the military origin of kingship is also found in *lugal*, the title eventually used to designate all rulers. The word consists of *lu*, "man," and *gal*, "big," which points to powerful men evolving into kings.

Despite the steady growth of royal authority, Sumerian kings appreciated that in the priesthood there was a restraining influence upon their conduct, because the first duty of every monarch was ensuring the satisfaction of the gods by means of support for the temples in which they dwelt. To an extent the priesthood forfeited some of its power over everyday life, but kings could never extinguish it, as the Sumerians were a deeply religious people. When disputes took place over royal encroachment on temple property, the usual resolution was a compromise that gave no offence to city deities. So closely were cities associated with the gods that cuneiform employed the same pictogram for the name of the city and its resident deity.

Yet the most telling sign of the rise of kingship was perhaps sacred marriage. At Uruk there is compelling evidence that the king acted as an intermediary between the city and Inanna, the city goddess, through the new year rite of sacred marriage. In a temple set within a beautiful garden, the king impersonated the dying-and-rising god Dumuzi, and a high priestess stood in for Inanna. One text has the king boast how he "lay on the splendid bed of Inanna, strewn with pure plants. . . . The day did not dawn, the night did not pass. For fifteen hours I lay with Inanna." Without this sacred coupling it was believed that not only would the city experience poor harvests, but also fewer animals would be born to its flocks.

The genesis of this singular rite was Inanna's famous descent into the underworld so as to assert her power of fertility there. Then "the impetuous lady" journeyed to the land of no return to challenge her enemy and sister goddess Ereshkigal, "the mistress of death." When finally Inanna was hung like "a side of meat on a peg," all fertility ceased on earth. Only the ingenuity of the water god Enki succeeded in saving Inanna. He sent to the underworld two expert mourners to ingratiate themselves with Ereshkigal and get the chance to revive the fertility goddess with the water and grass of life. The importance of grass—fodder for the domesticated animals upon which the Sumerian cities depended—takes us back to the agricultural origin of this myth.

Though restored to life after three days and nights, Inanna could not shake off a ghastly escort of demons as she wandered from city to city. They refused to depart unless a substitute was provided. So Inanna returned to Uruk, took offense that her husband Dumuzi was enjoying himself at a feast, and let the demons take him to Ereshkigal's gloomy realm. Thereafter Dumuzi's fate was to spend half the year in the land of the living and the other half with the dead. It is tempting to see the joy of the inhabitants of Uruk during the new year festival as recognition that a new seasonal cycle was about to begin, marked by the return of Dumuzi from the underworld to Inanna's "ever youthful bed."

THE RUTHLESS ASCENDANCY OF AKKAD

Any ambiguity about the role of a king was brought to an abrupt end by Sargon, the founder of the Akkadian Empire, which fused two traditions together, one Sumerian, the other Semite. Prior to Sargon, who reigned from 2340 to 2774 BC, some of the Sumerian city-states belonged to an alliance or league whose sense of identity derived from a common religious heritage. By the time Sargon conquered its members, Nippur, the city of Enlil,

King Sargon of Akkad.

enjoyed such cultural and religious prestige that Akkadian kings always credited the storm god with their spectacular victories. Sargon placed commemorative inscriptions in Enlil's temple and presented defeated Sumerian kings there, while Naramsin, the fourth ruler of Akkad, rebuilt the temple in lavish style. He also installed his daughter, Tatanabshum, as high priestess. As the city of Nippur was never wealthy enough to be ruled by a Sumerian king, it seems likely that its administration was in the hands of temple officials. Because the assembly of the gods met there in Enlil's temple, where its decisions included the confirmation of kingship, Nippur always remained a cherished city. A Sumerian poem leaves no doubt about its importance, saying that "in his wisdom, Enlil made the city his home, the pivot of the earth and sky, where his nobility set his greatest sanctuary aglow with radiant glory."

By his personal association with Enlil's city, Sargon claimed the right to rule the Sumerians. A newcomer to the political scene and the first empire builder in the ancient Middle East, he had an urgent need for legitimacy. Sargon's background remains obscure: He was said to have been discovered, like Moses, in a basket floating down the Euphrates and raised at the royal court of Kish, where eventually he was appointed as the cupbearer of its Sumerian king. Another legend asserts he was loved and preserved by Ishtar, the Semitic name of the great Sumerian goddess Inanna. Whatever the circumstances of his seizure of power in Kish, Sargon was a Semite and therefore adopted the Akkadian title *sharru kenu*, meaning "legitimate king." In the Old Testament this was transformed into Sargon.

His meteoric rise is apparent in his own inscriptions. They are completely silent about Sargon's antecedents and rehearse instead his outstanding military achievements. The swift elevation of such an outsider facilitated an entirely new image for Mesopotamian kingship: it replaced the cultic and administrative role performed by Sumerian rulers with adulation for a war hero. Sargon was pleased to advertise above all his campaigns, during which he was "victorious in thirty-four battles." Another description boasts that he fed 5,400 troops daily, a massive increase over the personal retinues of previous kings and obviously the core of regulars who comprised the backbone of his army. This elite group alone represented the largest standing force of the time by far. And unlike earlier wars between city-states, Sargon's conquests resulted in the building of an empire that needed an even larger number of soldiers to control it. In a sense, he faced the same manpower dilemma as Alexander the Great, after the final defeat of the Persians in 331 BC. The Macedonian king solved the problem by augmenting his army with Asian recruits, who were trained to fight in the same manner as his existing Macedonian, Greek, and Balkan troops. Sargon therefore obliged the defeated Sumerian city-states to place some of their military forces at his disposal. Conquered non-Sumerian peoples would have provided yet another source of soldiers. Likewise the armies of Assyria and Persia included large contingents of former enemies within their ranks.

Yet even conscripts added to the professionals in Sargon's army would have quickly improved their fighting skills, given the almost continuous state of war that characterized his reign. We lack any details about the organization of the Akkadian war machine, but its supply of weapons and logistics would have involved considerable investment. A new weapon was the composite bow, whose introduction on the battlefield may account for Sargon's success against the Sumerian phalanx. His deployment of bowmen and light-armed troops would have helped to overcome the less mobile infantry formations favored by the Sumerians.

The Akkadian army consisted of three corps: archers, spearmen, and axe bearers for distant, close, and hand-to-hand combat, respectively. Spears could either be thrown or used for thrusting at close quarters. Spearmen were also armed with an axe or a sword. Soldiers wielding large axes comprised the biggest corps and upon their performance the outcome of a battle ultimately rested. Their task was smashing the enemy once the archers and spearmen had disordered the opposing ranks.

The most effective close-order weapon for a long time remained the battle axe. It was excellent in combat against unprotected opponents and explains why armor became steadily more important. The most obvious countermeasure was the helmet, which evolved from early experiments in Sumer to the advanced version favored by Assyrian troops. Their iron helmets were acutely angled at the top, coming almost to a point, as a means of increasing their ability to ward off blows and arrows. They also possessed an inner cap of leather or wool, which helped adsorb the impact of any blow. The Greek helmet, constructed from bronze, had cheek and face plates. The Macedonians and the Romans made use of face plates as well. Spears were never displaced by the axe, although their tendency to encourage fighting in close order led to the phalanx as the standard infantry formation until the first century BC. Then the Romans replaced the phalanx with an open, staggered formation and relied on the sword rather than the spear. That the spear had been the favored weapon of the earliest Greeks is evident from *The Iliad*, Homer's account of the Trojan War. In this epic poem the majority of fatal spear thrusts were delivered to the chest, next to the head—the same areas for most fatalities in modern wars.

Sargon's continuous use of battle-hardened soldiers set the pattern of Akkadian aggression, marked as it was by unexampled violence and exploitation. Sargon himself wished to be remembered for three things:

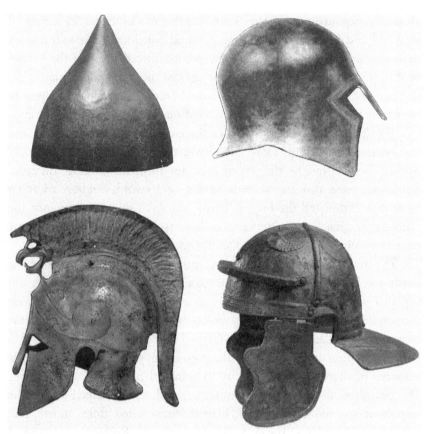

Assyrian, Corinthian, Macedonian, and Roman helmets.

installing Akkadian governors in conquered cities, bringing international trade to his capital, and having sufficient resources at his disposal
to maintain a permanent army. Sargon's far-flung campaigns were not
primarily driven by a desire for territorial aggrandizement; rather they
aimed to secure the trade routes that passed through Akkad. This concern
with trade explains Sargon's efforts to ensure that seagoing vessels could
sail upriver from the Persian Gulf and moor in the harbor of his capital,
although its exact location has yet to be identified. Inscriptions mention,
however, ships arriving from Bahrain, India, and Egypt. Long-distance
trade with India is revealed in recent archaeological discoveries in
Meluhha, as the Indus valley was known to the Akkadians. So extensive

were the commercial ventures of Indian merchants that, on the island of Bahrain, a trading center used their system of weights and not a Mesopotamian one.

Though Sumer was reorganized as an imperial province, a move designed to break down the old boundaries of the city-states, Sargon was mindful of the religious duties of Sumerian kings when he appointed his daughter Enheduanna as high priestess of the moon god at Ur. Sumerian was still the language spoken in the city, but Nanna had already become Sin, the deity's Akkadian name. The Sumerians called the moon god Nanna or Suen, which explains the change of name to Sin in Akkadian. Enheduanna composed hymns in the Sumerian language as well as an autobiographical poem in which she tells us how she prayed to Sin when rebels took control of Ur. Since the moon god did nothing to help, Enheduanna appealed to the warlike aspect of Inanna's complex nature instead, and this goddess responded with such frightening swiftness that the rebels fled the city in panic. Combined in Inanna's person were several originally distinct goddesses whose functions she discharged, including ferocity on the battlefield. Like the Greek goddess Athena, Inanna loved manly deeds and joined warriors in the thick of the fray. As Ishtar, the Akkadian version of this goddess, she was destined to receive fervent worship from the equally aggressive Assyrians, who looked back to Akkad as the perfect model for a warlike state.

The rebels who troubled Enheduanna at Ur had tried to shake off the harshness of Sargon's rule. Their local rising was followed by a more widespread rebellion on the succession of his son Rimush: it was suppressed with such severity that the Akkadians were thereafter regarded as merciless oppressors. Large numbers of Sumerians were killed or deported to forced labor camps, where many died. For the first time in Mesopotamian history, thousands were slaughtered in battle or as prisoners of war. It was therefore something of a relief when Rimush was murdered in a palace conspiracy and succeeded by his brother Manishtusu. The new king's interest was international trade, which he encouraged by friendly and unfriendly means. His army actually invaded central Iran in search of valuable materials and products, anticipating the booty-led campaigns of the Assyrians prior to Tiglath-pileser III's reform of the

Rimish stele depicting the massacre of prisoners.

Assyrian Empire. In 732 BC this energetic king substituted the collection of annual tribute from annexed lands and vassal kingdoms for the raids that had previously maintained the position of Assyrian kings.

But the surge in wealth resulting from Manishtusu's expansive policy may have wrecked Akkad in the longer term because his son Naramsin came to see divinity as his due. Not long after he ascended the throne in 2291 BC, an empire-wide rebellion almost succeeded in toppling Naramsin, but against all odds, the new king reasserted imperial authority with apparently superhuman strength. Shortly after this unexpected triumph, he adopted the title of "king of the four quarters" or, more literally, "of the four seas," for the world was then thought to comprise a great island surrounded by the ocean. To celebrate this new authority, Naramsin did two things. First, he began to rebuild Enlil's temple at Nippur, whose inhabitants were exempted from compulsory labor and military service. The reconstruction of the temple may not have progressed beyond laying the foundations during Naramsin's reign. Bricks inscribed with his name have been unearthed there, but they may have been made under his tenure and only laid by his son Sharkalisharri, who completed the project.

Naramsin's second decision was no less controversial when he assumed divine honors. Whereas Sargon had been content as the favorite of the goddess Ishtar, Naramsin wanted to be regarded as a god himself. No Mesopotamian monarch had ever dared to do this before him. The horned helmet he is shown wearing on the Victory Stele is unambiguous: such a headdress was always reserved for gods and goddesses. Carved in pink limestone, the stele records Naramsin's defeat of the Lullubi, a troublesome tribe in the Zagros mountains. The stele's unusually dramatic composition highlights and glorifies the Akkadian king as a deity. At the top the sun god beams approval of this newly won status for a war leader who readily tramples his vanquished enemies underfoot. In order

The divine king Naramsin depicted on the Victory Stele.

to emphasize the means by which Naramsin's soldiers gained this victory, the king is armed with a bow, a spear, and an axe. As the defeated Lullubi warriors have similar arms, the Akkadians enjoyed no advantage in weaponry and instead had to rely on superior tactics.

Naramsin was careful, however, in justifying his divine elevation in terms of popular demand, claiming that the people of Akkad beseeched the great deities to allow the worship of their king as a god, because he had not only preserved the Akkadian Empire but enlarged it as well. The great gods and goddesses are said to have granted this extraordinary request so that a temple was built in the king's honor. Whatever Naramsin's view of his own divinity, its assumption could have had a specific political purpose, since dissident courtiers would hardly dare to harm a god. Manishtusu, the father of Naramsin, had been the victim of yet another palace conspiracy.

The Sumerians held the decline and fall of Sargon's dynasty to have been the result of Naramsin's arrogant assumption of divinity. According to *The Curse of Akkad*, later composed in Ur as a warning to the Sumerian king Shulgi not to hanker after divine honors himself, an enraged Enlil called upon the pastoralist Gutians to descend from the Zagros mountains and punish Akkad. Knowing "no order," these hill men were "made like humans but with the brains of dogs, the shapes of apes," and "like locusts they scoured the land" so that "nothing escaped their reach." It is telling that in *The Curse of Akkad* Enlil also laments how his beloved temple "had been destroyed." This means that Naramsin's wholesale reconstruction of the temple was as much to blame for the Gutian invasion as any claim the Akkadian king made to divine status.

Sharkalisharri was actually crowned in Nippur while the temple was still under reconstruction. Although his name means "king of all kings," Sharkalisharri could not hold together the conquests of his forbears, and this fifth Akkadian monarch was also murdered by his courtiers, an action that inaugurated a period of anarchy. The Sumerian King List pointedly asks, "Who was king? Who was not king?" The last Akkadian king was Shuturul, or "the mighty one," a grandiose title belying the fact that he controlled no more than the environs of the city of Akkad.

The Sumerian King List.

That the Gutian invasion of Mesopotamia took place a century after Naramsin's reign did not invalidate Enlil's revenge in the eyes of the Sumerian priests who wrote *The Curse of Akkad*. While an epic hero such as Gilgamesh was prepared to disobey the gods, he sought for himself not divinity but rather immortality, like his ancestor Utanapishtim, the survivor of the Flood. Daring to ignore the wishes of a goddess was one thing, but setting up a temple, as Naramsin did for his own worship, was quite another. Despite the raising of former Sumerian kings to quasi-divine status after their deaths, the idea that a living ruler could become a divinity was unacceptable in Sumer. Such a lack of respect for the gods was bound to invite retribution. Among the Semites the distinction between the human and the divine was even more pronounced, which made Naramsin's elevation so unexpected. Yet even Gilgamesh's perpetual challenge to the divine order caught up with him when his close friend Enkidu suffered an early death. Fear of such a fate haunted Gilgamesh throughout his life, as he could not but notice how "the dead outnumber the living."

UR AND ELAM

When the Akkadian Empire crumbled, the Gutians to the east and the Babylonians to the north of Sumer were able to carve out kingdoms of their own. All we have now are the names of a couple of Gutian leaders. The Sumerians described the era as one of terror and preferred to concentrate in their historical record on the Third Dynasty of Ur, named from the Sumerian King List. The origins of this new dynasty remain obscure. Inscriptions indicate that moves toward claiming hegemony over the revived Sumerian city-states were initiated by Utuhegal of Uruk, credited with a seven-year reign in the Sumerian King List. He also figures as a prominent leader in the struggle to expel the Gutians. It is quite possible that Urnammu, founder of the Third Dynasty of Ur, was Utuhegal's governor of the city. He could have been a close relative of the king of Uruk, since there is no trace of any hostility toward Utuhegal in the account of Urnammu's reign, and he even built a magnificent ziggurat at Uruk for its city deities. In view of Uruk's antiquity, the new dynasty at Ur likely would have fostered a strong link between the two cities. It is indeed possible that the Uruk epics about Gilgamesh and other early kings took their classic Sumerian form at this time.

Because of his forceful foreign policy, Urnammu was called "the strongman," but whereas the kings of Akkad had assumed the herculean task of controlling "the four quarters," particularly the trade routes to the Mediterranean and Iran, both Urnammu and, later, his son Shulgi concentrated on Mesopotamia itself. The strict supervision of the cities of Sumer would have been unbearable had not their rule returned prosperity to the Sumerians. Many of Urnammu's inscriptions place emphasis on peaceful projects such as the digging of canals, the protection of villages, and the repair of temples. He hoped they would be looked upon "in wonder and preserve the name of Urnammu for ever."

It might be said that Urnammu's program of temple construction, including Ur's first ziggurat, was part of a political strategy designed to put his dynasty at a safe distance from that of Akkad. He must have witnessed the dissolution of the Akkadian Empire and noted how priests had encouraged defiance of its authority. So Urnammu's enhancement of Sumerian temples could not but conciliate the priestly establishment. That no protest met his other policies confirms the wisdom of this approach. One of these policies was the creation of the earliest known law code. Even though its laws were inspired by previous royal edicts, their collection in a single format was innovative. Its arrangement of a prologue followed by legal prescriptions anticipates the most famous Mesopotamian set of laws, the code issued by King Hammurabi of Babylon. Urnammu also standardized weights and measures.

Yet the frequency of military campaigns may reflect an urge to imitate to a lesser degree the territorial ambitions of Akkad. Urnammu soon discovered, however, the difficulty of securing firm frontiers in northern Mesopotamia and along the border with Elam. The Elamite kingdom based in southern Iran was a constant irritant, its raids having in all probability begun in preurban times. Both Eannatum and Sargon had fought the Elamites with mixed success. So involved with warfare did Urnammu become that he died from wounds sustained in battle. Only two Mesopotamian kings are recorded as war casualties: the Sumerian Urnammu and the Assyrian Sargon II. A lamentation relates of the former,

The shepherd does not give orders any more in battle and combat. The king, the advocate of Sumer, the ornament of the assembly, the leader of Sumer lies sick. His hands cannot grasp any more, he lies sick. His feet cannot walk any more, he lies sick. The trustworthy shepherd of Sumer, Urnammu was taken to the house. The king was taken to the house. The proud one lay in his palace. Urnammu, beloved by his troops, could not raise his neck any more. The wise one lay down and silence descended. He who was the vigor of the land, had fallen, and the land was demolished; like a cypress forest it was stripped bare, its appearance totally changed. As if he were a boxwood tree, they put axes against him in his joyous resting place. As if he were a cedar tree, he was uprooted in the palace. . . . His appointed time had come, and he passed away in his prime.

That Sumer "was devastated" by Urnammu's sudden death in 2095 BC must be a statement of fact because he had reestablished Sumer as a strong independent state. Uncertain of the future, Shulgi may have thought his father's deification would stabilize the dynasty. Somehow he had to repair the impression of divine disfavor that Urnammu's unexpected removal from the political scene appeared to signal.

Deification seemed a solution, and Shulgi may have tried to claim divine status for himself as well. That the cult of King Naramsin was still in existence then provides the context for the composition of *The Curse of Akkad*: it was a priestly warning to Shulgi of the danger he courted if he offended the gods. In Sumer there was no scope for royal apotheosis. Shulgi took the hint and put his energies into the development of the economy. An inscription mentions his enlargement of footpaths, straightening of roads, construction of rest houses for travelers, and protection of wayfarers from robbers.

Two sons of Shulgi, Amarsin and Shusin, who succeeded their father, were obliged to renew costly wars in northern Mesopotamia as well as block incoming Semitic pastoralists. They had to build a wall there in order to halt the Maru, or Amurru, Amorite tribesmen moving from the north into the Euphrates-Tigris valley. A second wall built by Ibbisin, the last king of the Third Dynasty of Ur, was meant to deter the restive

Elamites. The kingdom that Ibbisin inherited was the same size as at its fullest extent in Shulgi's reign, but enemies were already placing it under intense pressure, while a reduction in the flow of both the Euphrates and the Tigris may have caused problems with the irrigation system, perhaps even famine.

Despite the construction of "a long wall in front of the mountains," the Elamites looted Ur in 2004 BC. After their withdrawal, the king of Isin emerged from the strengthened fortifications that had saved his city and annexed the territory of Ur. Another settlement arose on the site of Ur, but the city never flourished as before. Its final decline coincided with the eclipse of Sumer, for in 1750 BC King Hammurabi incorporated the whole of southern Mesopotamia into the Babylonian Empire, bringing to an end a civilization that had started nearly a millennium and a half earlier with the foundation of Uruk. By the time of Hammurabi's advance southward, Sumerian speakers were in a minority, and their language had absorbed many Semitic words. Yet the Babylonians were in such awe of Sumer's heritage that, like Latin in medieval Europe, Sumerian retained an exulted position in cuneiform texts. And the cultural synthesis between Semitic and Sumerian traditions, which Akkadian kings had actively sponsored, reached its fulfilment in Hammurabi's Babylon. His own military success was short-lived, but the annexation of Sumer gave a boost to Mesopotamian culture, which was to reach maturity under the rule of Babylonian and Assyrian kings.

Chapter Two

International Rivalry

The five hundred years that separated Sargon from Hammu-rabi, founders of Mesopotamia's earliest empires, was a chaotic period in which rival city-states competed for hegemony. The Sumerian King List summarized the situation as follows: "Then who was the king? Who was not the king?" Almost at the end of the third millennium BC, a dynasty established in the city of Ur imposed a degree of order on Mesopotamia.

Two of the kings of Ur, Urnammu and his son Shulgi, were largely responsible for the return of political stability. They introduced standard weights and measures, wrote down laws, and constructed ziggurats, the monumental stepped towers upon which Sumerian deities were believed to dwell. Their copious records provide a rare glimpse of a bureaucratic kingdom whose survival depended as much on diplomatic maneuvering as on warfare. Envoys were sent to distant lands carrying letters and gifts, while closer to home princesses were married off to powerful Elam. Only after Hammurabi inflicted a severe defeat on the Elamites did they withdraw from Mesopotamia, although they remained a thorn in its side prior to the Assyrian king Ashurbanipal's overrunning the kingdom of Elam a millennium later.

HAMMURABI'S BABYLON

Despite the claim in a Babylonian inscription that "Hammurabi, the mighty one, beloved of Marduk, thanks to the sublime power of the gods, has overcome Elam," the repulse of an Elamite invasion of Mesopotamia in 1765–1764 BC was not as simple as the king of Babylon would have us believe. A letter of King Zimri-Lim of Mari mentions the assembling of 30,000 soldiers to block Elam's northern thrust. Just how vital this military assistance was can be judged from the emergency measures that Hammurabi was forced to adopt. He went beyond conscription to the extent of freeing slaves in return for joining the ranks of the Babylonian army.

At this point in Hammurabi's long reign from 1792 to 1750 BC, Babylon was not the dominant power in Mesopotamia. Even on the threshold of his great victories, Hammurabi hardly struck his contemporaries as a world conqueror. As the sixth member of the first dynasty of Babylon, he had inherited a modest city-state whose territory spread no more than fifty miles around the city. In Akkadian, the written language of the ancient Middle East after the close of the Sumerian period, the name for the city was *babilim*, meaning "the gate of god." During Hammurabi's reign, the rise of its city god, Marduk, as the supreme deity began when priests endeavored to simplify the extended pantheon they had taken over from the Sumerians. This era was noted for its bilingualism: both Sumerian and Babylonian were used. The date at which Sumerian became an extinct language is unclear, because, like Latin in medieval Europe, it retained a privileged position, not least for the reason that it had been the vehicle of the world's first advanced culture, whose ideas were translated into Semitic Akkadian. Sumer, after all, had invented civilization.

For well over a century Babylon had gone about its own business on a branch of the river Euphrates. The most formidable power on Babylon's northern border was the kingdom of Shamshi-adad I, the earliest known Assyrian ruler, while in the south Hammurabi had to placate King Rim-Sin of Larsa. Though Shamshi-adad I at first commanded the most respect, a great upheaval occurred after his death in 1781 BC with the result that Assyria suffered an assault from several directions, and even Ashur, its capital, was captured by the Babylonians. Later the Assyrians fell under the dominion of Mitanni, an entirely new kingdom founded by Hurrian invaders to their north.

Little is known about the early years of Hammurabi's reign except that on two occasions he cancelled debts, a not-unusual action when an ancient economy faltered. The repulse of the Elamites galvanized the Babylonian king into offensive action, for Hammurabi annexed Larsa, then Mari and Malgium.

The only Mesopotamian king who failed to join the struggle against the Elamites was Rim-Sin. Apparently the victory of Hammurabi and his allies did not overawe him, as time after time he raided Babylonian territory. That was what Hammurabi told Zimri-Lim in order to justify his request for military assistance from the king of Mari so as to strengthen his forces for an attack on Larsa. Initially Hammurabi had merely broken off diplomatic relations with Rim-Sin, but now he felt the moment had come to fight, since his diviners assured him of the approval of the gods. No Mesopotamian ruler would dare to undertake a military expedition without seeking the advice of the priesthood, as the outcome of all such ventures rested entirely with the gods.

Hammurabi adopted a systematic approach to consulting oracles, before and during a campaign. We are aware that his diviners always accompanied him, answering questions he put to the gods and reporting their own daily consultations with the divine realm. With the rise of Babylon, Rim-Sin might have been expected to make preparations

An incised clay liver. Priests used the livers of sheep for divination purposes.

for resisting an attack by Hammurabi. He appears to have done little, so that the city of Mashkan-shapir fell easily to the Babylonians. South of Malgium, on a canal fed by the Tigris, Mashkan-shapir could have slowed the Babylonian advance. Its garrison of several thousand soldiers under the command of Sin-Muballit, the brother of Rim-Sin, received no assistance against the attackers, and they were unable to hold out for long. Because Hammurabi insisted that mercy should be shown to the surrendered troops as well as the civilians, the march on Larsa turned into something of popular movement, with the inhabitants of southern Mesopotamia rallying to Babylon's side. The dramatic switch of loyalty must have reflected widespread discontent with Rim-Sin's rule. Reinforced by these volunteers and additional forces sent from Mari, Hammurabi laid siege to Larsa for six months. Such a long investment was unprecedented, but once the city's grain reserves were exhausted, Larsa had no choice but to give in.

"Then the Babylonian army entered Larsa," we are informed, "and the citadel was occupied." As for Rim-Sin, he was spared and removed with his sons to Babylon, where presumably they died as prisoners. Hammurabi destroyed the fortifications of Larsa, leaving the temples and houses intact. The king of Babylon later recalled how "the assistance of the gods An and Enlil" ensured this success. He had already told his men that they were marching against betrayers, who had "broken their oath to Shamash and Marduk." The expedition was in essence a holy war in which no unnecessary violence should occur, an outlook very different from that of Assyrian kings, whose absolute certainty of their right to crush opponents on behalf of the gods guided their merciless approach to warfare. As deputy of the national god Ashur, an Assyrian monarch had a duty first to protect the divinely ordered cosmos.

Next, Hammurabi conducted urgent repairs to the irrigation system, which was then unable to supply enough water for the needs of Larsa, Nippur, Eridu, Uruk, and Ur, the major cities of the south. Possibly crop failure connected with a breakdown of the economy contributed to Rim-Sin's overthrow. The prosperity of a city-state depended on its ruler, and with rainfall so unreliable in southern Mesopotamia, maintenance of canals represented a duty that no king could afford to neglect for long.

The unification of Babylon and Larsa allowed Hammurabi to style himself king of Sumer and Akkad. Mindful of the disastrous impact the same claim had on the dynasty of Sargon, following the wholesale reconstruction of Enlil's temple at Nippur, Hammurabi was keen to ascertain the attitude of its priesthood. His circumspection worked: it was reported that a meeting of the gods held in the temple there had confirmed his entitlement to rule. Despite never being the seat of any royal authority, the city of Nippur was considered to be especially holy because the storm god Enlil dwelt in its temple. His father, An, a rather remote god of heaven, had given Enlil the power to announce the legitimate king of Mesopotamia.

When Hammurabi annexed Larsa, he disrupted the balance of power in Mesopotamia. His victory over Rim-Sin obliged him to reconsider his relationship with a number of other kings. One of these was Sibi-Sin of Eshnunna, whose kingdom was centered on a tributary of the river Tigris to the north of Babylon. As no troops from Mari fought beside the Babylonians in this conflict, the war is less well known than the earlier one between Babylon and Larsa. Not only did Zimri-Lim fail to send soldiers to help Hammurabi, but he actually sent presents to Sibi-Sin as a sign of his support for Eshnunna. This breach between Hammurabi and Zimri-Lim turned into open warfare not long after the defeat of Eshnunna. We learn that the king of Babylon "was victorious in fighting the armies of Mari and Malgium. He subdued Mari and the surrounding area as well as several towns in the land of Subartum, including Ekallatum, all of Burundum and the land of Zalmaqum, from the banks of the Tigris to the Euphrates, and made them live in peace under his jurisdiction."

In 1759 BC Hammurabi sacked Mari and burned its great palace to the ground. So systematic was the destruction, another inscription tells us, that he "pulled down the walls and left no place as more than mounds and ruins." The destruction of Hammurabi also left in the palace one of the most extensive archives for ancient Middle Eastern history. The surviving 20,000 tablets were composed in the Akkadian language, mainly in a syllabic script, in which one cuneiform sign represents one syllable. The earliest use of an alphabetic system of writing evolved in Syria but only passed from the Phoenicians to the ancient Greeks in the eighth century BC.

There was no doubt in the mind of Hammurabi that his annexations and his appointment of subject kings brought peace to Mesopotamia. As he put it at the end of his famous law code, "I have embraced the people of Sumer and Akkad and they have prospered in safety. I have protected them through my wisdom." In their inscriptions, other kings tended to place emphasis on their strength, but Hammurabi wanted above all to be looked upon as a just ruler, the earthly equivalent of the sun god Shamash. At the top of the stone column on which his law code is inscribed, there is a striking scene: Shamash approves Hammurabi's introduction of a standard code of law in Mesopotamia.

Hammurabi showing reverence to the god Shamash.

As for the start of Hammurabi's reign, we lack detail about his final years on the throne other than the date of his death in 1750 BC. It appears that his son Samsuiluna was quickly assailed by enemies at home and abroad. One of Samsuiluna's victories hardly gets a mention, even though the defeated invaders were the Kassites, a people who would eventually take over the Babylonian kingdom. Hammurabi's dynasty struggled on for over another century, and then Babylon suffered a body blow in the Hittite sack of 1595 BC from which it never fully recovered.

From his capital Hattusha in central Asia Minor, a Hittite king by the name of Mursili I invaded northern Syria and, meeting virtually no opposition, swept down the Euphrates valley and fell upon Babylon. After looting the city, Mursili I withdrew homeward with his army, no doubt savoring his extraordinary triumph. But after his return home, a whole series of palace murders ensued, including his own. Conflict among the ruling class would so weaken the Hittite kingdom that Hattusha was ultimately abandoned and the remnant moved to Syria.

MITANNI AND THE CHARIOT

After the disappearance of Mari, our sources for the northern part of Mesopotamia are so scarce that there is no account of the rise of Mitanni. Nor at the moment can we firmly locate the site of its capital, Washukanni, on the upper reaches of the Tigris. The Hurrians, migrants whose language was closest to Urartian, had been moving into the area for some time before an influx of Indo-Aryans was instrumental in forming this Hurrian kingdom. There were petty Hurrian states in existence during the reign of Zimri-Lim, but they never matched the power of Mitanni, whose territory extended from the Zagros mountains to the shores of the Mediterranean. The ability of the Hurrians to push into Mesopotamia and Syria was a result of their adoption of the light horse-drawn chariot, one of the most revolutionary weapons in ancient Middle Eastern warfare.

The effectiveness of the Mitannian army rested on the war chariot, then coming into service in Asia Minor as well. Yet its charioteers enjoyed a decisive edge over their opponents because of the profound understanding of horsemanship possessed by the Indo-Aryan section of the population. Some of these people's names derived from deities mentioned in the

Rig Veda, India's oldest religious work, while others refer to horses or chariots. Biridaswa means "possessing many horses," and Sattawaza, meaning "winner of seven prizes," celebrates success in horse racing, while the name of Mitannian king Tushratta meant "having a terrifying chariot." The key document for horse training was the manual composed by Kikkuli, the "master horseman" of Mitanni. Recovered from the Hittite capital Hattusha, its text is written on four clay tablets in the Hittite language. But the technical terms and some of the numerals are not Hittite. Instead they are related to Sanskrit, the language of the Indo-Aryan invaders of India, which points to the importance of an Indo-Aryan element in Mitanni's population, which was responsible for perfecting its chariotry.

The respect accorded to Kikkuli's training manual was widespread in the ancient Middle East as contemporary kings were keen to learn about his methods. These rulers sought a foolproof way of ensuring that their chariotry was not wasted on the battlefield. They simply could not afford to commit such an expensive asset to battle unless they were certain of its quality and, in particular, the readiness of the chariot horses for the swiftness of such encounters.

An Assyrian chariot pursues fleeing enemies while a bird of prey contemplates its dinner.

45

Hence the emphasis that Kikkuli placed on continuous training, day and night. He says,

> *When midnight comes the charioteer brings the horses out of the stable and harnesses them. He drives them for over a mile, and then gallops for more than several fields. . . . When they return, he unbridles the horses and rubs them dry. In the stable they receive two handfuls of hay, one of wheat, and four handfuls of barley. When they have finished their feed, he lets them eat hay for the rest of the night.*

Exercise and nutrition, practice and reward—these are the methods by which a charioteer develops a close and trusting relationship with his team of horses. Kikkuli stresses how conscious the grooms and stable hands have to be of the horses' welfare when he insists,

> *After a long gallop a stable gets very warm. If the horses are restless, and start to sweat, their halter is removed as well as their blankets and a snaffle-bit put on them. Salt is dissolved on a fire, and after wholemeal barley has been mixed in a pitcher, they are given a bucketful, and hay to eat.*

The regime of training gradually extends the range of gallops to ten, twenty, ninety fields and even longer distances. Feeds are also varied. Sometimes little is offered to the horses, presumably because on campaign supplies could well be erratic, and at other times extensive feeding is provided to build up stamina. Attention to hygiene runs throughout Kikkuli's training manual. Horses have to be washed with warm water five times a day or bathed in a river when necessary. They always have to be rubbed down.

It goes without saying that the comprehensiveness of Kikkuli's scheme impressed everyone. The details of exercise and feeding were appreciated as vital in the successful training of chariot horses. Like racehorses, they had to be in peak form when the moment came.

Mitanni had surged to political dominance through its network of subject kings, and thanks to a decline in Hittite fortunes, it was virtually unchallenged in Syria. But the Mitannians were not to have things all their own way. Again Egypt's attention was drawn to Palestine and, in 1460 BC, culminated in the Battle of Megiddo.

EGYPTIAN EXPANSION

The Egyptians never forgot the Hyksos occupation. These Middle Eastern warriors had controlled northern Egypt between 1664 and 1555 BC. Their success depended upon the war chariot, which the Egyptians themselves adopted in the intense struggle to expel these formidable opponents. Following its liberation, Egypt decided that a more direct approach was required in Palestine in order to prevent any repeat of a Hyksos-style attack. Rather than relying on a sphere of influence, reinforced by periodic military activity, Egyptian foreign policy became more direct, with close supervision of allies, to the extent of placing Egyptian officials in loyal courts. Within this buffer zone, local kings were designated "His Majesty's tenants," swearing obedience to the will of the pharaoh. Not even succession problems in Egypt altered this new approach.

In 1504 BC Thutmose III succeeded his father at the tender age of ten years, and his stepmother, Hatshepsut, ruled in his stead, first as regent, later as pharaoh. Though Hatshepsut chose to reinvent herself as not merely a great ruler but also a renowned warrior-king, her reign was not marked by any military enterprise other than a raid on Nubia. Her deliberate nonaggressive stance put Thutmose III at a distinct disadvantage when, in 1482 BC, he gained the throne. With over thirty years of rule ahead of him, in which he effectively reasserted Egypt's authority in Palestine, Thutmose III had plenty of time to erase all trace of Hatshepsut's unusual reign by destroying her monuments. Yet he had to undertake no fewer than seventeen campaigns to regain control in Palestine, despite his stunning victory at Megiddo.

The pharaoh Thutmose III, the victor at Megiddo.

47

In 1460 BC Thutmose III could scarcely ignore the news that a large army had assembled at Megiddo, made up of troops from Palestine as well as Syria. Because his reaction was such a success, we possess a detailed account of his tactics. He led an Egyptian army of 20,000 men to Aruna, a city on the southern slope of the Carmel mountain range. Megiddo was located on its northern slope and could be reached by three routes. The most direct route, modern Wadi Ara, attracted the pharaoh's attention despite the warnings of his senior officers. At a conference he was told how dangerous it was to

> *march along a road which becomes so narrow. It is reported that the enemy is there, waiting at the other end and daily becoming more numerous. Will not horse have to follow horse, and the army likewise? Will not our vanguard be engaged in battle while there are still troops waiting to start out from Aruna? Now there are two other roads—one, to our right, comes out at Taanach, south of Megiddo, the other, to our left, comes out to its north at Djefty. Let our victorious Lord proceed on one of the easier routes rather than the difficult one in front of us.*

Not for the sake of prestige alone did Thutmose III reject their advice, though the account of the campaign, preserved on the walls of a temple in Karnak, suggests otherwise, as the pharaoh is supposed to have commented on how the rebels would scoff at him if he chose a round-about route. Thutmose III's choice of the direct route clearly had more to do with tactics than status, however. Guessing that the rebels would think like his own war council, he took the risk and ordered an advance through a pass that shrinks to a width of less than fifteen feet in places.

A whole day was needed for the Egyptian army to get through Wadi Ara, whereupon the pharaoh pitched camp. Except for a minor skirmish, the passage was as uneventful as it was unexpected. Thutmose III was right. The rebels had not anticipated his daring move and had concentrated their strength at Taanach and Djefty, leaving only a token force guarding the narrow pass. Like the English general Edmund Allenby some 3,400 years later, the pharaoh had caught his opponents off guard. Just as the advance of the Fourth Cavalry Division early one morning through the same pass totally demoralized the Turks, the sudden appearance of the Egyptian chariotry struck such fear into rebel hearts that the engagement was almost one-sided. At dawn Thutmose III rode forth in his golden chariot, spreading out his army in two great wings. If the thousand Egyptian chariots used in the battle were deployed in a single rank, the line would have extended for more than a mile. Once in motion the two wings of the Egyptian army threatened the rebels with encirclement, while the pharaoh himself charged straight into their midst. "When the rebels saw His Majesty prevailing over them," we are informed, "they fled immediately to Megiddo with faces of fear. They abandoned their horses and their chariots of gold and silver, so that they could reach the city safely. Now the people of Megiddo had shut the city gates, but they let down garments in order to hoist them over the walls."

So swift was the Egyptian attack that the opposing chariotry was possibly unable to charge at all. Enemy charioteers and chariot archers seem to have run away, leaving everything behind. But the chance of booty was too much for Thutmose III's men, depriving the pharaoh of

Egyptian foot soldiers killing Hittite charioteers.

a total victory. A short siege became necessary to reduce Megiddo to submission. Then all the rebel kings—with the exception of the ruler of Kadesh, who had rushed back to Syria from the battlefield—were made prisoner and compelled to swear eternal allegiance to Egypt. And the impressive list of loot is a reminder of how complete Thutmose III's triumph was. Carried off were

340 living prisoners and 83 hands; 2,041 horses, 191 colts, 6 stallions; a golden chariot belonging to the enemy; a fine chariot worked with gold belonging to the king of Megiddo; 892 chariots of his wretched army—in total 924; a fine bronze coat of mail belonging to the king of Megiddo and 200 leather mail coats belonging to his wretched army; 502 bows; 7 tent poles, worked with silver, belonging to the enemy.

With the rebellion thoroughly crushed, Thutmose III could move northward and reduce the influence of Mitanni, the other great power in Syria prior to the rise of Hatti, the homeland of the Hittites. He devastated the land of Kadesh, but on this occasion the city did not fall to the Egyptians. He even extended Egyptian power all the way to the Euphrates, which his forces crossed in prefabricated assault craft built from cedar wood. "At the mere sight of an Egyptian," one victory stele boasts, "the kings of Palestine flee."

At the Battle of Megiddo, Thutmose III used surprise and mobility as his main weapons. Along with his own bravery in driving straight into the enemy, these factors contributed to the swiftly won victory. As the number of hands recorded—it was an Egyptian practice to cut off one hand from the enemy dead in order to count the fallen—shows, most of the rebels ran away. The pharaoh would not have been concerned by the low figure, as he had achieved his purpose of defeating the rebellion with few casualties on his own side. His victory marks him out as a commander willing to take chances, though only after calculating the odds carefully. Thutmose III believed they were in his favor and the gain so great that he dared to reject the advice of his closest advisers. Given that the strength of the chariotry on the two sides was about equal, he knew that the concentration of his own forces at Megiddo would give him the initial advantage, as the rebels had divided their army in order to cover both the northern and southern routes of his potential advance. By the time these forces reunited, it would be too late to meet the Egyptian attack.

The apparent smallness of the Egyptian chariotry should not come as a surprise. Each chariot required two steeds to pull it, together with one or two animals in reserve for replacements. At Megiddo, 3,000 to 4,000 horses would have been needed, probably representing almost all of Egypt's trained stock. The country had no experience of large-scale horse breeding and imported most of its military requirements. Mitanni and then Hatti were better placed; they bred horses and had access to neighboring peoples expert in this difficult art. The logistical problems of moving 1,000 chariots may explain Thutmose III's desire for a quick decision on the battlefield. Apart from the maintenance of the chariots, there was the important matter of forage. So far as we are aware, the Egyptians, like other ancient peoples before the Assyrians, could only provide their army with a limited supply train, so both soldiers and horses had to live off the land.

Yet the swiftness of the Egyptian chariotry dashed rebels hopes. General Allenby's cavalry in 1918 had a similar impact on Turkish

Pharaoh Amenhotep II's target practice.

units guarding army headquarters at Nazareth. As part of the final offensive in Palestine, the Fourth and Fifth Cavalry Divisions were fed through passes in the Carmel range, while the main Turkish position was turned on the coast. When the Fourth Cavalry Division emerged from Wadi Ara,

> *a small body of Turks were surprised and rounded up . . . the advance guard of a column that was seen approaching. This was a column in six companies with twelve machine guns. It received short shrift from the leading regiment of the Division, the 2nd Lancers. Supported by the fire of an armored car, the Indian squadron were into the enemy infantry with the lance before they completed their deployment. Forty-six Turks were speared, and the remainder, about 500, surrendered. The whole action had only lasted a few minutes.*

The German general Liman von Sanders, commander of the Seventh and Eighth Turkish Armies, had sent this column to block the pass the day before. Its slowness in covering the short distance from Nazareth gave Allenby's cavalry its chance. The Fourth Cavalry Division covered an astonishing ninety miles in less than a day and a half, losing only twenty-four horses on the way. The unexpected advance beyond Megiddo amazed Allenby, who wrote to his wife that he was "almost aghast at the extent of the victory." So was Liman von Sanders: He had made a desperate escape from his quarters in Nazareth, wearing his pajamas. Street fighting saved him from capture as mounted troops were not the best equipped for this kind of combat. The unexpected advance from Megiddo effectively knocked Turkey out of World War I.

A year later Allenby told the American Egyptologist James Breasted that he had read his book and learned of "old Thutmose's experience in meeting an outpost of the enemy and disposing of them at the top of the pass leading to Megiddo." His own plan was only slightly different: instead of using a single pass, as the pharaoh had, he sent cavalry forces through two of them and also pushed another force behind the Turkish lines near the Mediterranean coast, in places employing the beach for rapid movement.

For Mitanni the Egyptian victory at Megiddo was a setback. A number of Middle Eastern kingdoms, Babylon and Hatti among them, sought in good relations with Egypt a counterbalance to Mitannian power. But once the Egyptians wound down their military ventures in Syria, a Mitannian king by the name of Shuttarna recovered the dominant position that his predecessors had enjoyed. Now Mitanni's authority reached its peak, even though Shuttarna had to keep a wary eye on Assyria. Hammurabi had thwarted Assyria's early imperial ambitions, but it was gradually becoming a threat again. Shuttarna solved the problem for a while by absorbing most of its territory within Mitanni itself.

Tushratta, the successor of Shuttarna, tried to get on friendly terms with Egypt. Surviving letters reveal how heavily he was involved in marriage negotiations and the exchange of gifts. During the reign of Amenhotep III from 1410 to 1372 BC, Egypt and Mitanni were bound by a peace treaty, which had been sealed by marriage ties. Amenhotep III had taken as wives four Middle Eastern princesses—of whom two were Babylonian and two Mitannian. But these diplomatic marriages between an Egyptian pharaoh and the daughters or sisters of foreign potentates were always a one-way arrangement: Amenhotep III bluntly said that no Egyptian princess ever married a foreigner. Both Babylon and Mitanni acquiesced but shared a concern that their prestige in Egyptian eyes was

Pharaoh Amenhotep III.

affected by their giving, not receiving, wives. Informing this reluctance to export princesses was a deep uneasiness in Egypt about the pharaoh's parity with other rulers.

Egyptian foreign policy toward Mitanni changed near the close of Amenhotep III's reign. Although an inscription claims that the pharaoh "broke Mitanni with his strong arm," the shift in attitude reflects an awareness of the coming eclipse of the Hurrians. Assyria had already regained its independence, and the Hittite king Suppiluliuma I was about to launch an invasion of Mitanni. Caught up in a civil war, Tushratta was unable to halt the Hittite advance in 1350 BC, and the Mitannian capital, Washukanni, fell to the invaders. Shortly afterward Tushratta was killed, and his son, Mattiwaza, sought asylum at Hattusha, where he was

married to one of Suppiluliuma I's daughters before being placed on the Mitannian throne as a subject king. Having dealt with Mitanni, the Hittite king conducted a lightning campaign in Syria, reducing to obedience all the former Mitannian allies except Carchemish.

No account of the chariot battles in which Mitanni was overrun exists. But the swift defeat of this once formidable kingdom meant that the remaining great Middle Eastern powers were Hatti, Assyria, and Babylon. The immediate beneficiaries were, of course, the Hittites, whose military might lay, as had the Hurrians', in chariotry. Their capital, Hattusha, east of modern Ankara, was founded in the seventeenth century BC by King Hattusili I. Hatti itself, the name by which his

A gate guardian at Hattusha, the Hittite capital.

kingdom was known, seems to have been a very ancient word connected with the district around Hattusha. With the swamping of central Asia Minor by Indo-European-speaking Hittite settlers, the original Hattian language died out. The foundation of Hattusha, a natural stronghold dominating the northern valleys, gave the Hittites a secure base from which to expand their power in Asia Minor and beyond. But Suppiluliuma I's conversion of Syria into a Hittite sphere of influence inevitably brought Hatti into conflict with Egypt. Their climatic chariot battle would take place at Kadesh in 1274 BC.

Kassite Babylon

Following King Mursili I's expedition to Babylon, Hammurabi's descendants continued to rule over a much-reduced kingdom. The situation paved the way for the rise of the Kassites, who had already attempted an invasion during the reign of Samsuiluna. The earliest known Kassite ruler of Babylon, Agum-kakrime, ensured the longevity of the new dynasty by recovering the cult statue of Marduk from the Hittites. This was a significant achievement: Nobody could legitimately claim to be king of Babylon without "grasping the hand of Marduk." Besides making arrangements for the safe journey of the cult statue back from Hattusha, Agum-kakrime was concerned about how Marduk should be received in Esagila, his temple in Babylon. The city god sat there on a cedar throne, which Agum-kakrime ordered carpenters to restore to a satisfactory condition.

That Kassite rule lasted for half a millennium is testimony to the assimilative power of Babylonian culture, which quickly made the Kassites into honorary Babylonians. Who the Kassites were remains a mystery; we know only that, like the earlier Gutians, they descended from the Zagros mountains. Similarities between the Hittites, the Hurrians, and the Kassites, however, have not escaped notice. All three peoples appeared in the ancient Middle East during the second millennium BC at a time of political confusion, and all had at their head a chariot-owning, horse-breeding aristocracy. The Hittites spoke an Indo-European language, and Indo-Aryans formed an important element among the Hurrians; there was possibly an Indo-Iranian component in the Kassite population, although this idea is not generally accepted. The equation of the Kassite sun god Suriash with the Hindu Surya is not enough to prove the case, and the fact that the Kassites have left so few inscriptions in their own language does not help either.

The practice of removing the cult statues of defeated peoples was widespread in the ancient world and continued down to the Roman period. It was believed that inducing a city god to leave its temple during a siege would hasten the fall of a city. This the Romans did by promising the deity a cult in Rome. A story about the arrival of Juno from the Etruscan city of Veii, after a protracted siege, illustrates this belief. "When as a joke, a Roman soldier asked the goddess if she wanted to move," we are told, "the goddess replied that she did. On hearing her speak, the joking turned to awe and, realising now that they were carrying not a statue but Juno herself, they joyfully installed her in Rome." Most likely the imported goddess was Uni, Juno's Etruscan equivalent. According to Tertullian, a Christian author living in Carthage, "the Romans have committed as many sacrileges as they have trophies, they have triumphed over as many gods as they have over nations. No more proof is needed than the host of captured cult statues." Assyrian bas-reliefs show similar abductions, particularly during the reign of Tiglath-pileser III, who expended much energy in restoring the Assyrian Empire. This king effectively dealt with internal and external opponents in the 730s BC.

Due to the sparseness of the Kassite record, we have to rely on outside sources such as letters exchanged with foreign kings. One in particular is quite amazing. King Kadashman-enlil I of Babylon seems to have been annoyed that foreign princesses lacked the eminence at the Egyptian court that their families expected. They certainly led luxurious lives but possessed no influence outside the pharaoh's bedroom. Just how undistinguished foreign wives were in Egypt was evident when Amen-hotep III could not confirm for the Kassite king that his daughter was still alive. She had apparently disappeared without trace among his other wives and concubines.

When Amenhotep admitted that he had forgotten which of his wives Kadashman-enlil's daughter might be, the Babylonian king sent envoys to talk to her. The scene at the Egyptian court had all the trap-pings of comic opera. As none of the envoys knew the Kassite princess personally, they were reduced to inspecting the pharaoh's entire harem, the members of which were paraded before them. As the women refused to speak, the envoys returned to Babylon none the wiser. Undoubtedly Kadashman-enlil was not satisfied with this, but Amenhotep blamed him for the confusion, saying that he should have sent from Babylon some-body who would actually recognize his daughter. Amenhotep's inability to identify his own wife as an individual, as well as his seeming lack of contrition over this, serves as proof of the limited power of foreign princesses at the Egyptian court.

Yet surviving correspondence with the Hittite court suggests an equally frustrating relationship as that with Egypt. Its subject was the physician Raba-as-Marduk, whose name means "great are the deeds of Marduk." Around 1285 BC, Raba-as-Marduk went to Hattusha at the request of the Hittite king, and Hattusili I may have detained him there against his will. As Babylon's medicine was the most advanced in the ancient Middle East, any ruler who could obtain the services of one of its doctors would have been loath to lose him. Raba-as-Marduk may also have been tempted to stay abroad by wealth, land, and even kinship ties with the royal family. That this was no isolated case is revealed by the Greek historian Herodotus, who relates how the Greek physician Democedes of Croton was kept in the Persian court after he healed King Darius I's injured leg.

There were frequent wars with a resurgent Assyria, as well as with Elam, until the latter brought to an end the Kassite dynasty in 1155 BC. Before this happened though, King Karigalzu II of Babylon defeated the Elamites and advanced as far as Susa, the Elamite capital. A record of this successful expedition was discovered on a tablet at Nippur and on another found at Susa.

The overthrow of the long-lasting Kassite dynasty was deeply resented by the Babylonians, who admired Nebuchadrezzar I, the greatest king of the next dynasty, for his chastisement of the Elamites. Nebuchadrezzar, the usual spelling of Nabu-kudurri-usur, is based on Nebuchadnezzar, a later Hebrew corruption of the name given to Nebuchadrezzar II in the Bible. Nebuchadrezzar I was the fourth king of the Isin dynasty, and he ruled Babylon for twenty-two years. By carrying off the cult statue of Marduk in the same manner as the Hittites, the Elamites had utterly humiliated the Babylonians. An outbreak of plague in Nebuchadrezzar I's army thwarted a first attempt to return the city god's cult statue to its rightful place in the Esagila temple. Having received favorable omens for a second expedition, however, the Babylonian king advanced in sweltering heat at the height of summer, and the unexpected timing of the attack caught the Elamites by surprise. In a pitched battle that "blotted out the light of day," the Babylonian chariotry decided the outcome, and in triumph Nebuchadrezzar I bore the cult statue home.

There is never any suggestion that a deity could ever be taken forcibly from one city to another. Rather, a chronicler explains how "the great god Marduk relented his anger against his land and returned to protect it once again." It may be that the crushing victory over the Elamites encouraged Nebuchadrezzar I to declare Marduk the supreme deity and, before his death in 1103 BC, raise the first ziggurat in Babylon, opposite Marduk's temple.

THE BATTLE OF KADESH

After the fall of Mitanni, the Hittites pushed into Syria and reached Kadesh but stopped there in order not to interfere too much with the Egyptian sphere of influence. The final struggle with Mitanni had already stretched Hittite military resources to their limits, so conflict with Egypt could not be readily embraced. Some clashes between the Hatti and Egypt did take place, but they were not large-scale engagements, in part because of Egypt's internal political crisis. The early death of Tutankhamun, most probably as a result of a chariot accident while hunting, had led his widow, Queen Ankhesenamun, to request a Hittite prince for a husband. In the letter she sent to the Hittite king Suppiluliuma I, she said, "I do not want to take a servant of mine and make him my husband. . . . Give me one of your sons; to me he will be husband, but in the land of Egypt he will be king!"

Suppiluliuma was at Carchemish when this extraordinary letter arrived. His initial reaction was incredulity. Surely the request hid bad intentions, since a Hittite prince would be a useful hostage during an international dispute. But finally the Hittite king came around to the view that the queen offered a way for "the land of Hatti and the land of Egypt to enjoy eternal friendship with each other." So Suppiluliuma dispatched one of his sons, Zannanza, to Egypt. The degree to which Queen Ankhesenamun had the backing of the courtiers in her bid to stay in power is now impossible to tell, but opponents of handing over the throne to a foreigner may well have ambushed the Hittite prince as he traveled through Palestine, because Zannanza never got to Egypt. A considerable delay in Tutankhamun's burial was obviously intended to give Zannanza time to arrive and be proclaimed pharaoh. With his nonarrival and no likelihood that Suppiluliuma would send another son, an Egyptian candidate came forward to play the essential role in Tutankhamun's internment and belatedly became pharaoh. This happened to be Ay, the seventy-year-old commander of Egypt's chariotry.

Whatever the cause of Zannanza's disappearance, Suppiluliuma held the Egyptians responsible, and his fury knew no bounds. Brushing aside Ay's excuses, the Hittite king attacked the subject allies of Egypt in both Syria and Palestine, carrying off many thousands of prisoners to Hatti. Ironically, they took with them a plague that ravaged the Hittites for over a generation: Among its victims were Suppiluliuma and his eldest son.

Things began to improve for Egypt when Tutankhamun's successor Ay died after a four-year reign and was replaced by another general, Horemheb. He campaigned in Syria and fought the Hittites but could not firmly secure the Egyptian position there. That was achieved by Seti I, who reigned from 1294 to 1279 BC. As Ramesses I's coregent and successor, Seti I not only helped to establish the Ramesside dynasty but, even more, reasserted Egypt's role as a great international power. Thutmose III was his model and source of inspiration. Seti I subdued Palestine and reconquered Kadesh and Amurru, a kingdom situated on the Mediterranean coast. By seizing these Hittite allies, Seti was in effect declaring war on Hatti and its king, Muwatalli II: An all-out conflict with Egypt was now inevitable. But the Hittite king did not have sufficient troops in Syria to challenge Egypt yet, and so a couple of years passed before the Hittites were ready for battle. The armies of Hatti and Egypt clashed at Kadesh, where Seti came out best. An inscription reports how "he smote the land of Hatti, causing the rebels to disperse."

Yet Muwatalli was far from finished with Egypt. His encounter with Seti was only the prelude to a second and much greater battle at Kadesh in 1274 BC. As Seti's son and successor, Ramesses II, was equally determined to hold on to Egypt's territory in Syria, he also sought a head-on conflict with the Hittites. One of the most remarkable of the pharaohs, Ramesses was only twenty-nine years old when he marched north to meet Muwatalli. Though the outcome of the Battle of Kadesh hung for a time in the balance, and it looked as if the Egyptians might be defeated, the young pharaoh rallied his men and drove off the Hittite chariotry. He saved the Egyptian army at Kadesh, an unexpected triumph that resonated for the rest of Ramesses's reign—at sixty-seven years, the second longest in Egyptian history. Celebrated as a colossus as large as his own monumental statues, the ideal warrior-king, Ramesses was in fact lucky to avoid defeat.

Moving well ahead of his army, the pharaoh was keen to camp close to the rebellious city of Kadesh because he had learned from two local inhabitants that Muwatalli had retreated northward on hearing the news of his advance. Ramesses did not realize, as the few chariots driving alongside him in the Egyptian vanguard forded a tributary of the Orontes, that the Hittite king was about to spring a trap that would lead to one of the biggest chariot battles ever fought in the ancient Middle East. The Egyptian record tells us that Muwatalli had sent two informants "to speak falsely to His Majesty in order that he might not prepare his troops for battle." But the impetuous advance of Ramesses was very much part of his character. He had set the pace for the advance from the Nile delta. "All the foreign lands trembled before him," we are told, "all their kings bringing tribute and all rebels coming in submission through fear of His Majesty."

Riding in his glittering chariot, Ramesses sped ahead of four divisions, named after the Egyptian gods: the Amun division from Thebes, the Re division from Heliopolis, the Ptah division from Memphis, and the Seth division from Tanis. These regular soldiers, numbering 20,000 in all, had mustered in the pharaoh's capital, Pi-Ramese in the Nile delta, before moving northward against the Hittites. In Syria, local allied levies, as well as a large number of mercenaries, augmented Muwatalli's forces. According to the Egyptian account of the battle, the Hittite king stripped his land of silver to hire these extra troops.

The lions decorating Ramesses's splendid chariot signaled more than the pharaoh's presence, a crucial rallying point in fast-moving, mobile engagements. So drawn to this creature was the pharaoh that he took a tame one with him on campaign. It did not, however, use its teeth or claws on his behalf: carved depictions always show the lion, lying with his front paws bound, near the pharaoh's tent. Though the old story of the lion's involvement in the battle can thus be discounted, the pairing of Ramesses with a lion is not entirely inappropriate, since the ferocity he displayed in the encounter with Muwatalli almost certainly saved the Egyptians from disaster. "A strong defence for the army," one inscription runs, "His Majesty was like a shield on the day of fighting. Braver than hundreds and thousands combined, he went first into the multitudes trusting in his strength alone."

Beneath the walls of Kadesh thousands of chariots were about to clash in a battle whose strange twists and turns are revealed in an account that Ramesses had carved on temple walls in Karnak and other religious centers. While the Egyptians may have exaggerated the numbers they faced, Muwatalli assembled a substantial force at Kadesh. His army totaled 47,000 men, including a complement of 2,500 chariots. Against this host Ramesses could not deploy so many soldiers; nor were they all available at the start of the battle: the Amun division was just behind him, the Re division was crossing the ford, and the Ptah and Seth divisions still remained south of the river. In a concealed position to the east of Kadesh, the Hittites awaited the moment to strike. It came when the Amun division was establishing a camp at a spot chosen by Ramesses on the other side of the city. "There His Majesty seated himself on a throne of gold," expecting to receive envoys from an overawed Kadesh.

Instead, Ramesses received a rude shock. Two Hittite scouts sent by Muwatalli to ascertain the exact position of the Egyptian army were captured and, after a beating, revealed where the Hittite army was hidden. "The king of Hatti," they admitted, "together with many foreign lands he has brought as allies, is armed and ready to fight behind Kadesh." The senior Egyptian officers were stunned by the news and abashed by the anger of the pharaoh over their carelessness. After a hasty conference, messengers on horseback were dispatched to hurry the two divisions still on the march. By then the Hittite chariotry had "charged the Re division, cutting through the middle, as it was not drawn up for battle."

The collapse almost engulfed the Egyptian camp when, in panic, troops from the broken Re division rushed there to escape the pursuing

Hittite chariots under fire from Egyptian archers.

Hittite chariots. A total rout seemed inevitable before Ramesses asserted his leadership. "Then His Majesty rose like his father Montu and seized his weapons of war, putting on his coat of mail." A falcon-headed god worshipped at Thebes, Montu was something of a talisman for Ramesses, and his personal identification became so strong during his lifetime that the cult statue was venerated in the pharaoh's honor. As the Hittite chariotry surrounded the Egyptian camp, Ramesses launched a desperate counterattack. First, infantrymen were sent to tackle chariots that came too close to the camp, pulling down charioteers and killing them with short swords and spears. Then, taking advantage of this confusion, the pharaoh mounted his own chariot and drove into the Hittites with tremendous force. Even though we know that Menna, his shield bearer, "saw the vast number of hostile chariots hemming the pharaoh in, and went deadly white with terror," the counterattack gave the surrounded Egyptians a respite, which Ramesses used to rally his troops. He also noticed that the eastern wing of the Hittite chariotry was the weakest, and next he turned in that direction, a switch in tactics that again disconcerted his opponents. If this move, inspired by another of Ramesses's headlong charges, was meant to convince the Egyptians of their ability to hold out until reinforcements arrived, they were right to trust the judgment of the inexperienced pharaoh.

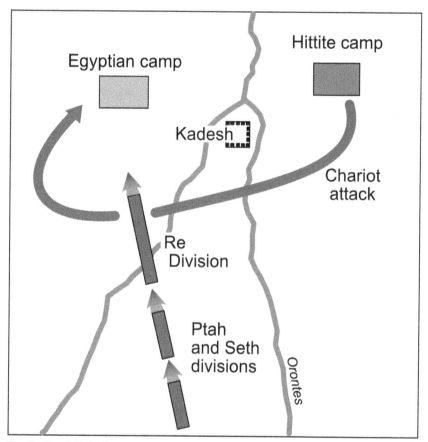

The Battle of Kadesh.

Not even a new wave of chariots sent by Muwatalli to stop this assault in its tracks could prevent Ramesses from gaining the advantage in the swirling chariot encounter. In an incredible display of courage and coolness, the pharaoh encouraged his charioteers to get the better of their foes, his own bow adding to the growing slaughter. Like all ancient armies, the Hittite one was unable to withstand the impact of such violence for long. Its chariotry was already losing cohesion when a threat developed on the western wing in the form of a column from Amurru. Perhaps its intervention had a similar effect to that on the French army of Blucher's Prussians at Waterloo, not least because the distraction may well have caused the Hittites to hesitate in driving home their attack on the hard-pressed Amun and Re divisions. When the Prussians made their dramatic flanking attack on the French columns assaulting Wellington's bloodied and thinned lines of infantry, Napoleon immediately appreciated the gravity of the situation, but there was nothing he could do to stop the final French attack of the battle from faltering. In the same manner, the Amurru column, Egyptian allies from the Mediterranean coast, relieved pressure on Ramesses's camp, leaving his charioteers free to chase the Hittites into the Orontes, where, abandoning their chariots, "they plunged like crocodiles face first into its waters."

The Egyptians were left in possession of the battlefield: prisoners were rounded up, booty collected, and a grisly count of the enemy dead made by cutting a hand from each corpse. Gathering round the triumphant pharaoh, the Egyptian soldiers "praised His Majesty, seeing what he had done to the wretched ruler of Hatti," although Ramesses scolded them severely for landing him in such a perilous predicament at the start of the battle. By this time the Ptah and Seth divisions had arrived, and the Hittites were discouraged from further action. Despite Muwatalli's losses being largely confined to his chariotry, he knew that without this mobile force his infantry was vulnerable. An inscription of Ramesses says, "Then my army came to praise me, seeing what I had done. My senior officers praised my strong arm, and my chariotry lauded my name, saying 'What a great warrior you are by vanquishing fear! You saved the infantry as well as the chariotry.'"

This is the Egyptian version of the battle. The Hittites, on the other hand, claimed to have won at Kadesh. How great Ramesses's success was is hard to judge. His account plays down the arrival of the Amurru column, as it does the belated appearance of the Ptah and Seth divisions. The Egyptians were certainly mauled until they recovered from the shock of the surprise attack and fought off the Hittite chariotry. Yet Ramesses managed to save his army and his reputation as a commander, quite an unexpected outcome in which he could have been assisted by another factor. The Hittite army was less homogeneous than the one Ramesses led, with the result that allied and mercenary troops, and possibly even Hittite regulars, may have succumbed to the temp-

Ramesses II triumphant at the Battle of Kadesh.

tation of plunder on reaching the Egyptian camp. Dismounted archers, shown struggling with foot soldiers in several depictions of the battle, might well be looters caught off guard. The Egyptian record does not enlighten us. It concludes by saying, "His Majesty turned back to Egypt together with his infantry and his chariotry, strength and power being with him, and the gods and goddesses acting as protectors of his body and his domination over the lands."

No Hittite account of Kadesh exists, but it does not seem that Muwatalli suffered a serious defeat. The Hittite king sent an envoy to propose peace, which Ramesses would only accept as a truce, because he wished to reclaim Kadesh and other Syrian cities conquered by his predecessors. That the truce held is an indication of the reluctance on the part of the Egyptians as well as the Hittites to return to the battlefield.

In the long term, however, the Hittites could justifiably be regarded as the victors in the contest, for they kept the disputed city of Kadesh until Hatti itself collapsed: Its downfall was a consequence of the great migration we call the Sea Peoples. Meanwhile, tensions continued between Hatti and Egypt, but the Battle of Kadesh had taken a heavy toll on both sides, disinclining them to engage on such a large scale again. Their great chariot engagement would remain a unique event in ancient Middle Eastern history. A peace treaty between the Egyptians and the Hittites was finally agreed in 1259 BC, its signatories Ramesses and Hattusili III, the brother and successor of Muwatalli.

THE SEA PEOPLES

Coined in the nineteenth century, the name "Sea Peoples" has been given to the perpetrators of widespread destruction in Greece, Asia Minor, Syria, and Palestine toward the end of the second millennium BC. The established centers of civilization, especially Egypt, were such tempting targets for these marauders that they literally swept over them until finally halted by Egyptian arms. Their two attacks on Egypt in 1218 and 1182 BC are described in some detail. An inscription of Ramesses III explains how in the second invasion these foreigners

> *made a conspiracy in their islands. All at once the lands were on the move, scattered in war. No country could stand before their arms, from Hatti . . . to Alashiya. . . . They were advancing on Egypt . . . the Peleset, Tjeker, Shekelesh, Denyen and Weshesh, united lands. . . . Against them I readied my troops and made the mouth of the Nile into a strong wall of ships . . . manned them with picked men. The chariotry included the best foot soldiers and every accomplished chariot warrior.*

Some of the attackers were new enemies. When in 1218 BC the Libyans had raided the Nile delta, one of their northern allies were the Shardana, some of whom served in the pharaoh's bodyguard but whose homeland is unknown. Others included the Ekwesh, Shekelesh, and Teresh. The last named came from Lydia, while the Shekelesh were most probably the Sicels, who gave their name to Sicily. The Tjeker seem to have hailed from the Troad and wore their hair in the distinctive upright fashion favored by the Peleset. The Denyen were no strangers to the Egyptians since letters refer to "the land of Danuna" in eastern Asia Minor. The homeland of the Weshesh remains a mystery.

Just how misleading the name Sea Peoples is for all the attackers is evident with the Teresh, whom the ancient Greeks called the Tyrsenoi. They lived in Lydia, a land-locked kingdom in the western part of Asia Minor, and have been linked to the Etruscans, Rome's northern neighbors. We are aware that scarcity once drove half of the Lydian population westward in search of a new place to live.

Though we can dismiss any notion of coordination among the Sea Peoples, Ramesses was convinced that in 1182 BC he faced a well-organized assault. It seems more likely that a variety of peoples were attracted by the opportunities for plunder and land that this great disturbance offered, once Hatti was overrun. Yet the Hittites were in difficulties well before this onslaught struck their kingdom. Their last ruler, Suppiluliuma II, had to cope with serious unrest in Hatti as a result of intrigue over the succession. Suppiluliuma was the brother of Amuwanda II, who in 1207 BC died after a very brief reign. Disunity at home did not assist the new king when he found himself opposed by rebellious subject allies as well. So weak had Hatti become that none of its allies could really be trusted. The sacking of Hattusha destroyed Hittite power, leaving only vestiges of its influence in Syria, where several small kingdoms continued to use the hieroglyphic script developed by the Hittites.

In Palestine the Sea Peoples destroyed the coastal city of Ashdod as well as other settlements. And after their attempted invasion of Egypt was repulsed, the retreating Sea Peoples split up, some entering the Jordan valley, where the Denyen could have become the tribe of Dan, and others like the Peleset settled on the coast. So close are the words "Peleset" and "Philistine" linguistically that there can be no doubt that the descendants of the Peleset were the Philistines, the formidable enemies of the Jews. At first the Peleset would have comprised a ruling warrior class, but by the reign of King David in the early first millennium BC, they would have become indistinguishable from the rest of the population. Under David and his son Solomon, Israel was a strong state. As David told Goliath before their famous duel, he had killed lions and bears, and the Philistine champion would die like them for having dared to taunt the ranks of an army under divine protection.

The first encounter between the Sea Peoples and the Egyptians was a land battle on the border of Palestine and Egypt. The depiction of the action, on the walls of Ramesses's memorial temple at Medinet Habu, shows a confused mass of infantrymen and chariot warriors: Egyptian troops struggle against an enemy also equipped with chariots. Yet it is not the fact that some of the Sea Peoples rode in chariots that is surprising; rather it is the ox carts loaded with women and children that seem so out of place on the battlefield. The Egyptians either fell suddenly on a camp of the Sea Peoples or caught the invaders on the march, thereby preventing them from deploying separately from their families. In the inevitable melee, the Egyptians were at a considerable advantage. The presence of two-wheeled carts drawn by oxen reveals that this southerly movement of people consisted of uprooted farmers seeking new land to cultivate. They were not raiders; nor were they pastoralists moving through settled areas on the lookout for loot. The design of the ox cart and the humped oxen point to Asia Minor as these displaced farmers' homeland.

After turning this wave of migrants back into Palestine, the Egyptians still had to confront another group of Sea Peoples moving south on water. In a sea battle, which took place in the Nile delta, the invaders were routed again. At Medinet Habu, this victory is vividly depicted with the Egyptian boats sinking enemy craft or driving them ashore, where bowmen wait to finish off the survivors. These Sea Peoples are shown sporting upright hairstyles, wearing horned helmets, and armed with swords, spears, and shields.

So complete was the defeat of the Sea Peoples that Ramesses could boast of how he "overthrew those who invaded" Egypt and "slew the Denyen, while making ashes of the Tjeker and Peleset." As Mesopotamia was spared an all-out assault, probably because the military reputation of Assyrian arms acted as a deterrent, there has been a tendency to give Egypt sole credit for containing the Sea Peoples. In some ways the vic-

An Egyptian ship battles against the Sea Peoples.

tories on land and sea marked the final glory of its power. The successors of Ramesses III were indeed hard-pressed to exercise any Egyptian influence abroad. One reason for Egyptian weakness was an increased dependence on mercenaries, which was quite as damaging as Hittite reliance on the forces of subject allies. More than a straw in the wind, therefore, was King Muwatalli II's recruitment of a such large number of mercenaries for the Battle of Kadesh.

CHAPTER THREE

The Great Mesopotamian Powers

BETWEEN THE NINTH AND SEVENTH CENTURIES BC IN THE ANCIENT Middle East, an incredible transformation took place in warfare. While in 2300 BC, Akkad, the most aggressive of the earliest states, possessed an unusually large regular army, its core only numbered 5,400 men. Even then this represented for the Akkadians a supreme effort, for at this time soldiers were only raised in any strength when circumstances demanded military action. This arrangement continued to an extent in the following millennium BC, with conscripts being called to the colors in moments of crisis, but most states maintained regular troops as well.

The majority of Ramesses II's soldiers were conscripts whose duties involved acting as garrison troops and providing labor on public works. At the Battle of Kadesh in 1274 BC between the Hittites and the Egyptians, Ramesses commanded a force of 20,000 men against a bigger Hittite army, which had been enlarged through the recruitment of mercenaries. The four divisions of infantry that Ramesses led were named after the Egyptian gods Amun, Re, Ptah, and Seth; like with present-day regiments, loyalty to the traditions of each division formed the backbone of the regular Egyptian army. That the first two divisions rallied after the surprise Hittite attack underlined this strength, even though the personal bravery of the twenty-nine-year-old pharaoh had really encouraged them.

With the Assyrian army we encounter an entirely new approach to war. Like Napoleon, who believed that it was impossible to have too many men on a battlefield, the Assyrian kings were convinced that superior numbers ensured success, with the result that the Assyrian army in the eighth century BC reached a total of some 200,000 men, the largest regular army that had ever existed. Its elite corps of 50,000 troops included infantry, chariotry, and cavalry. And it also had specialist units capable of besieging walled cities, a skill not equaled again until the Roman period.

THE RISE AND DOMINATION OF ASSYRIA

The earliest known Assyrian ruler, Shamshi-adad I, can be said to have established Assyrian power. He consolidated his position in the upper Tigris valley, enhancing the capital of Ashur, and spread his authority from the Zagros mountains all the way to the banks of the Euphrates. The kingdom of Mari fell under his direct control, and even King Hammurabi of Babylon acknowledged his suzerainty. But after the death of Shamshi-adad I in 1781 BC, a great upheaval occurred in upper Mesopotamia, with the result that the Babylonians captured Ashur and brought this early period of Assyrian power to an end. Little information about Assyria is available for the next five hundred years, although we are now aware that it was dominated by Mitanni, an ancient kingdom whose existence was only discovered in the nineteenth century. As noted in the previous chapter, the rise of Mitanni was connected with the invention of the chariot, the world's first war machine.

The revival of Assyria had to await Ashur-dan II; he reigned from 934 to 912 BC and, besides pursuing an aggressive foreign policy, built a new palace and gateway at Ashur. He claimed to have brought back and resettled families that had fled the disorder in Assyria. A fundamental feature of the Mesopotamian economy was the management of agriculture, its most critical factor being the supply of labor, not the availability of land. But there is no doubt that Ashur-dan II regained territory lost during Assyria's eclipse. His son, Adad-nerari II, gave notice of Assyrian imperial ambitions when he mounted expeditions to the north against tribal enemies, to the south against the Babylonians, and to the east against the Aramaeans. His eight assaults on the Aramaeans were of the utmost importance because they opened the way to the Euphrates, which the Assyrian king crossed in 899 BC. So successful was he on

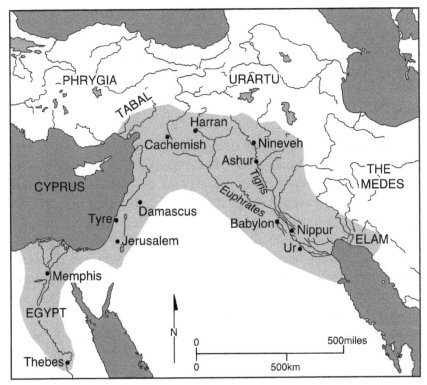

The Assyrian Empire.

the battlefield that Adad-nerari II could pass through conquered lands collecting tribute without any sign of resistance.

Although Ashur-dan II and Adad-nerari II laid the foundation of the largest empire the Middle East had yet seen, their primary aim was the recovery of territory lost to the Aramaeans. The reign of Tukulti-nin-urta II, son of Adad-nerari II, marked a pause in the expansion of Assyria, since he tended to campaign in lands already conquered by his two predecessors, which suggests that unrest among subject peoples was his chief concern. Certainly the historical record speaks for the first time of hostile action being the reason for his campaigns.

One purpose of conquest was to gain valuable goods from neighboring city-states and peoples as booty and tribute. Inscriptions dating from the reign of Ashur-dan II first mention the spoils of war, but not until the accession of Ashurnasirpal II in 883 BC do we find details of booty as well as tribute. Booty was of course taken from defeated enemies and included treasure, textiles, slaves, timber, weapons, chariots and chariot horses, other animals, wine, and foodstuffs. Another aspect of conquest was the wholesale deportation and resettlement of displaced populations. Tribute, on the other hand, comprised high-value items such as silver and gold, bronze and iron, rare wood like cedar, and luxury utensils. The systematic exploitation of the lands surrounding Assyria was a new phenomenon, but the Assyrians were not the first people to discover the economic advantages of a successful campaign: Mesopotamian kings had long looked upon spoils of war as the just reward of the gods.

Much as republican Rome sent out annual expeditions that were popular with its citizens as well as its Italian allies, the Assyrian army cheerfully marched each year to wars that were really a well-organized system of pillage that did not stop after victory on the battlefield and the capture of enemy soldiers, since Assyria added the conquered land to its empire. Ashurnasirpal II's son and successor, Shalmaneser III, was prepared to use extreme violence to intimidate his opponents during such campaigns. Dated to the late 850s BC, an inscription engraved on a large stele found in 1861 near the Tigris lists the cities Shalmaneser III subdued along the upper reaches of that river, where at the start of his reign he took the fortified city of Aridu, "massacred many of the inhabitants, carried off booty, erected towers of heads before the city, and burned young boys and girls." What we might term calculated terror at

The great Assyrian conqueror, King Shalmaneser III.

Aridu was enough to cow the entire area: tribute immediately poured in from other cities. An uncanny parallel to this harsh policy was the action of Scipio Africanus in 209 BC at New Carthage, modern Cartagena in southern Spain. On the fall of this city, he told his troops to kill everyone, to spare no one, and not to start looting until they received the order. As the Greek historian Polybius reflected, "The purpose of this custom, I suppose, was to strike terror." Brutality was, after all, a cheap tool of control. The slaughter at New Carthage was very great indeed, but there were still 100,000 survivors for the Romans to enslave.

Ashurnasirpal II's chief military target was the same as that of Adad-nerari II: the Aramaean west. He launched at least fourteen major campaigns during his twenty-five years on the throne. This energetic Assyrian king also transformed the town of Nimrud, the biblical Calah, into one of the greatest cities of the ancient world. It served as the headquarters of the Assyrian army. In building Nimrud, Ashurnasirpal II employed a large number of Assyrian workmen, in addition to subject people who were moved to Assyria to do forced labor. The new city was surrounded by a wall and a moat, while its main buildings included a palace, a fortress, and a temple dedicated to the warrior god Ninurta, the defender of the divine world order. The adoption of the Sumerian god Ninurta as the son of Ashur, the supreme deity of the Assyrians, secured his place in royal worship. At the end a campaign, the triumphant return of an Assyrian king was equated with the exploits of Ninurta, who had vanquished the forces of chaos. These monarchs were deemed the favorites of the god, "the one who controlled the four quarters with his strong might." The name Ashurnasirpal actually means "Ashur is the custodian of his son Ninurta."

Ashurnasirpal II's self-assurance of Ninurta's support is evident in the huge stone reliefs that he erected in the god's new temple at Nimrud. Not only do they praise the god "as the perfect warrior unequalled in battle," but even more they advertise the treatment that the Assyrian king meted out to his foes. For the first time in Mesopotamian warfare, we find a delight in torture, not least because the Assyrians were convinced that the only way of defeating chaos, the disorder created by human beings to subvert the divinely ordained cosmos, was the ruthless suppression of all who dared to oppose their empire.

Massacre, pillage, wholesale resettlement—these were the instruments of Assyrian domination. The prowess of their army, which increased from 60,000 during Ashurnasirpal II's reign to an amazing 200,000 men at the turn of the seventh century BC, allowed the Assyrians to behave without restraint. That the Assyrians fielded a well-organized and integrated army, led by aggressive commanders, explains their success on the battlefield. Half the army's infantry comprised bowmen; the other half, spearmen carrying large shields, behind which the bowmen could take shelter. The chief role of the spearmen, however, was to attack the enemy infantry at close quarters, in the same manner as Greek hoplites. Also deployed in the Assyrian battle line were chariots as well as cavalry. A bas-relief discovered at Nineveh depicts an engagement between King Ashurbanipal and the Arabs, who are seen to be overwhelmed by chariots and mounted archers, supporting spearmen and archers. But at the Battle of Til Tuba, in 653 BC, both the chariots and the cavalry appear to concentrate on a flanking movement. The main action of this second bas-relief focuses, however, on infantry combat.

Yet a sharp decline in the numbers of chariots mentioned in Assyrian military records from the end of the eighth century BC indicates that they were no longer seen as an indispensable component of the Assyrian army. Thus, the suggestion by some military historians that Assyria relied principally on chariots is way off the mark. Despite depictions of chariots being hauled over mountainous terrain and ferried across rivers, massed chariot charges were becoming a thing of the past. Chariots were of limited use in engagements beyond level plains and a serious shortcoming when Assyrian arms increasingly operated in hilly country as the empire pushed its borders ever forward. Another reason for the switch from chariots to cavalry was the ability of the mounted archer to control his horse through the invention of the snaffle bit, which more readily communicated a rider's intentions to his mount. True cavalry could not evolve until another critical piece of equipment arrived: the stirrup. The Romans at once adopted this Central Asian invention, which rendered mounting

Assyrian chariots struggling across hills.

easier, increased control over the horse, and resulted in a steadier seat. Then cavalry became a really powerful striking force for skirmishes, flank attacks, and hot pursuit.

One late version of the chariot developed by the Assyrians was a raised firing platform stationed alongside the infantry, possibly acting as an anchor for its ranks. These larger, heavier vehicles provided better protection for their crews by carrying more bowmen and shield bearers. But their sacrifice of speed and maneuverability, the prime advantage of the war chariot, always condemned them to a secondary role in battle.

One battle fought by Shalmaneser III is recorded in some detail. It took place in northern Syria at Qarqar in 853 BC. There the Assyrian king confronted a coalition of threatened states led by the Syrian king Ben-adad II and Ahab, his uneasy Jewish ally. Shalmaneser III explains that

> *moving from the city of Argana, I approached the city of Qarqar. I razed, destroyed and burned the city of Qarqar. . . . An alliance had been formed of . . . twelve kings: 1,200 chariots and 20,000 troops of Hadad-ezer the Damascene; 700 chariots, 700 cavalry and 10,000 troops of Irhulenu, the Hamatite; 2,000 chariots and 10,000 troops of Ahab, the Israelite; 500 troops of Byblos; 1,000 troops of Egypt; 10 chariots and 10,000 troops of the land Usunatu; 30 chariots and 10,000 troops of Adunu-baal of the land Sianu; 1,000 camels of Gindibu of the Arabs; hundreds of troops of Baasa, the man of*

Bit-Ruhubi, the Ammonite. They attacked and did battle with me. I fought them. I defeated them from the city of Qarqar as far as the city of Gilzau. I felled with the sword 14,000 troops, their fighting men, and rained arrows upon them as the god Adad would. I filled the plain with their corpses. . . . The Orontes ran red with their blood. In that battle, I took their chariots, cavalry and horses broken to harness.

As the location of Gilzau is unknown, we cannot be sure whether the Assyrian army advanced or withdrew afterward. The Syrio-Palestinians believed that they had held Shalmaneser III to a draw, which may well be the case because the Assyrian king did not cross the Euphrates river again for three years. But the two leaders of the anti-Assyrian coalition, Ben-adad II and Ahab, soon fell out, and Shalmaneser III exploited the discord, returned in 848 BC, and pushed down to the Mediterranean coast, where the cities of Byblos and Sidon both accepted Assyrian rule.

Having brought his Syrian campaign to a satisfactory conclusion, Shalmaneser III directed his forces northward, where they secured tribute from a number of kingdoms in Asia Minor. Sometimes it proved necessary to punish rebels and appoint new kings. Shalmaneser III also campaigned successfully in Urartu, a federation of tribal kingdoms centered on Lake Van to the north of Assyria. On the bank of that lake, the Assyrian king erected a stele bearing his own life-size portrait as a sign of conquest. But Urartu was not easily controlled, and both Tiglath-pileser III and Sargon II had to deal with this troublesome neighbor.

In his old age, Shalmaneser III's grip on the wheel of state weakened, and one of his sons rose in revolt. This uprising was only put down by another son, the new king Shamshi-adad V. Civil strife continued to blight the reigns of his successors down to the accession of Tiglath-pileser III in 744 BC. This determined ruler conducted a series of campaigns of exceptional intensity that reconquered the lands west of the Euphrates, intimidated Urartu, and finally placed the Babylonian crown on the Assyrian king's head. Though not in the direct line of succession, Tiglath-pileser III had taken advantage of the troubled times to stage a coup and mount the throne. It was fortunate for the Assyrians that such

King Tiglath-pileser III watching the capture of a city.

a capable man came to the fore at this juncture, since for a time their empire had appeared to be doomed.

After Tiglath-pileser III's reign, Assyria was transformed from a traditional kind of kingdom into an empire centered on a royal personage. This shift anticipated both the Persian and the Roman Empires, because Tiglath-pileser III had spectacularly altered the balance of power in the ancient Middle East. This profound change had much to do with the energy of this monarch, since he not only dealt with external enemies but reformed the army and administration as well. The Assyrian Empire was systematically organized into provinces and placed under the authority of properly appointed governors and military commanders. Trusted allies within the imperial borders were granted a degree of local autonomy, provided they delivered annual tribute, but Assyrian officials were on hand to report any sign of disobedience. By the seventh century BC, the Assyrian Empire included Egypt.

During Tiglath-pileser III's reign, Egypt remained an independent kingdom, although Assyrian power reached its border. It was a cherished ambition of Tiglath-pileser III to conquer all the territory up to this point, and his advance ended local rulers' habit of playing the Egyptians off against the Assyrians. Now acceptance of Assyrian authority meant just that: unconditional submission. Tiglath-pileser III marched as far south as Gaza, which was plundered. Its ruler, Khanunu, had fled to Egypt, but he came back and was made a subject king. The placing of a gold statue of the Assyrian king in Gaza's chief temple left no doubt as to who was in charge. A rebellion in Syria and Palestine occupied the Assyrians for two years, in 733 and 732 BC, and only finished with the capture of Damascus. This last Aramaean kingdom became an Assyrian province, while its surrendered inhabitants were deported, a standard imperial practice to forestall future attempts at rebellion; they found themselves serving the Assyrians as a small community among other deported peoples. The well-to-do sought to maintain their social position through conspicuous loyalty to Assyria, with the most ambitious joining the imperial administration. The use of large-scale population movements had unexpected linguistic consequences, leading eventually to the adoption of Aramaic as the lingua franca in the ancient Middle East. This was the tongue that Jesus spoke.

Although the Assyrian army had a permanent nucleus of full-time soldiers, the steady growth of the empire obliged Assyrian kings to leave troops in lands that were distant or hard to quell. Quite frequently these outposts were garrisoned by local contingents under their own officers. Similarly, provincial governors maintained local militias whose troops could participate in large-scale operations directed by the Assyrian king. The gradual increase of strength to some 200,000 men suggests that Assyria was always concerned to have a numerical advantage. While these large numbers were supported by supply dumps situated along the army's line of march, heavy equipment was transported by enslaved laborers. Added to this logistic advantage, which allowed a much longer campaign season, the terror practiced by Assyrian soldiers, who regularly cut off the heads and hands of the enemy as trophies, made them a formidable foe. Defeated kings, if not executed on the battlefield, were also brought back to Assyria to take part in the triumphal entry of the king and his troops into the capital, then exposed to the public gaze in humiliating situations.

Tiglath-pileser III also paid attention to internal communications, making sure there were fresh mounts at staging posts for messengers carrying official letters. The Royal Road, as it was called, connected an unprecedented expanse of territory, from the Mediterranean coast to the Zagros mountains, from the upper reaches of the Tigris to the Persian Gulf. When the Assyrian Empire disintegrated at the end of the seventh century BC, this early-warning system did not. The Babylonians and the Persians both continued to invest in the Royal Road's maintenance, so that the Greek historian Xenophon could write with admiration, "It is plain that this is the fastest land travel in the world. And it is invaluable for a ruler to learn everything as quickly as possible so he can deal with it without delay."

The fortunes of Assyria ultimately depended upon its relationship with Babylon. Tiglath-pileser III spent a great deal of time and energy on this perennial problem. In 745 BC he was obliged to intervene militarily to assist the Babylonian king, Nabonassar, against an attack by Chaldean and Aramaean tribesmen. Further interventions were required, to Tiglath-pileser III's growing frustration, and the situation was only resolved when, in 729 BC, the Assyrian king crowned himself king of Babylon. By assuming Babylonian sovereignty, Assyrian kings discovered a novel way of control, which was effective in the short term. That Assyria was always culturally dependent on Babylon goes a long way in accounting for their complex interaction. The cultural debt might well be summarized by the Roman poet Horace's comment on the Greeks: "Vanquished Greece vanquished its fierce victor and brought civilisation to the Latin peasants."

Tiglath-pileser III's successor, Shalmaneser V, had been entrusted with the administration of the Assyrian Empire in order to free his

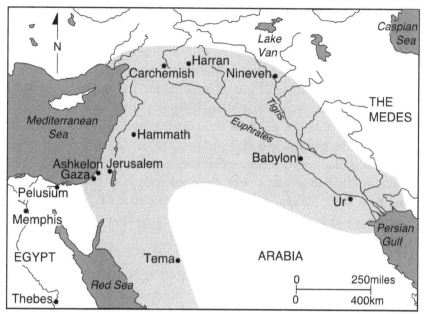

The Babylonian Empire.

father for campaigning. This role was later assigned to Sennacherib by his father, Sargon II. In 716 BC Shalmaneser V succeeded Tiglath-pileser III without any opposition. He also continued his father's Babylonian policy by ascending the throne of Babylon himself. During Shalmaneser V's five-year reign, one event stands out: the siege of Samaria, the capital of Israel. At this point, the Jewish people had split into two separate kingdoms: Israel in the north and Judah in the south, with its capital at Jerusalem. While the former fell under the Assyrian yoke, the latter managed to remain at a distance from imperial domination. When, in 722 BC, Israel rebelled on a second occasion against Assyria, Shalmaneser V put an end to the kingdom. After the capture of Samaria, the inhabitants were transported, although this operation was not completed until the reign of Sargon II.

Sargon II, another son of Tiglath-pileser III, appears to have been a usurper. We are largely in the dark about Sargon II's enthronement despite a reference to anger at the city of Ashur over Shalmaneser V's abuse of compulsory labor. It is said that the gods overthrew him and placed his younger brother Sargon II on the throne. Even then Sargon II was not the heir designate, which probably means that Ashur backed his successful bid for power. This uncertainty encouraged unrest among Assyria's subject states, and after an initial clash with Babylon and its ally Elam, Sargon II had to reassert Assyrian authority in Syria and Palestine. He even defeated an Egyptian army on the border of Egypt. Presumably the pharaoh thought intervention would then be opportune. The Syrians, the Phoenicians, and the Jews tried to use the Assyrians as allies against their neighbors and continue to appease the Egyptians. That those days were well and truly over Sargon II made abundantly clear. He established a strong point on the Egyptian border; the fortress was settled by transported peoples and put under the charge of a local Arab chieftain loyal to Assyria.

As a campaigner, Sargon II equaled the career of his father Tiglath-pileser III, but as a builder he was virtually unparalleled, for he built an entirely new Assyrian capital at Dur Sharruken. Though he did not neglect Nimrud and Nineveh, it was Dur Sharruken that held his attention. People were brought from all the areas Sargon II conquered and

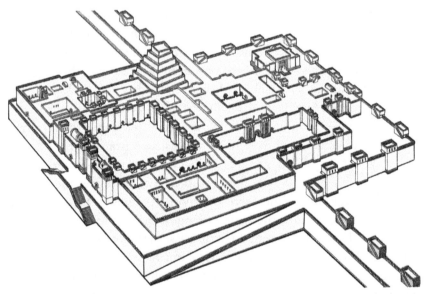

Sargon II's citadel at Dur Sharruken.

settled in the city, where they were taught to revere the Assyrian gods as well as the Assyrian king.

About two of Sargon II's victories we have some details: against the Urartians at Mount Uaush in 714 BC and, five years later, against a rebellious Babylon and its Elamite ally. According to the Assyrian record, the first battle took place in a mountainous defile because the Urartian king Rusa was sure that the limited space available for deployment would put Sargon II's larger army at a tactical disadvantage. When Rusa had gathered all his allies and formed his battle line in the pass, he sent Sargon II a formal challenge to fight. Then the Assyrian army was toiling over snowy mountains and arrived on the battlefield tired and hungry. Despite this, the Assyrians did not bother to form up the wings or wait for the rear division to arrive, as Sargon II immediately attacked. Personally leading the front division of the army, the Assyrian king struck Rusa's center "like a fierce arrow and so defeated him." The brunt of this assault was felt by a crack formation of archers and spearmen stationed, it seems, at the front of the Urartian army.

Sargon II says, "[Rusa's] warriors in whom his army trusted, carrying bows and spears, I slaughtered before his feet like lambs and cut off their heads." The effectiveness of this unexpected Assyrian advance suggests that Sargon II's cavalry then operated as bowmen. They literally crashed into the Urartian center with such force that Rusa could not hold his forces together. Rusa fell back to his camp and tried to make a stand there, but Sargon II "destroyed his chariot horses under him with arrows." So Rusa "to save his life, abandoned his chariot, mounted a mare, and led his army in flight." Although from this description of the battle it looks as if Sargon II's cavalry charge won the day, the late arriving rear division and wings likely contributed decisively to the victory, as they fed into the broken Urartian center. They finished off the best Urartian troops, which formed the enemy center, the position occupied by Rusa himself and the royal princes, many of whom Sargon II took prisoner. The flanks of Rusa's army would have been allied forces, less formidable soldiers than the crack archers and spearmen at the center.

In the event, the Battle of Mount Uaush turned on Sargon II's willingness to risk an immediate frontal attack. Assyrian military intelligence

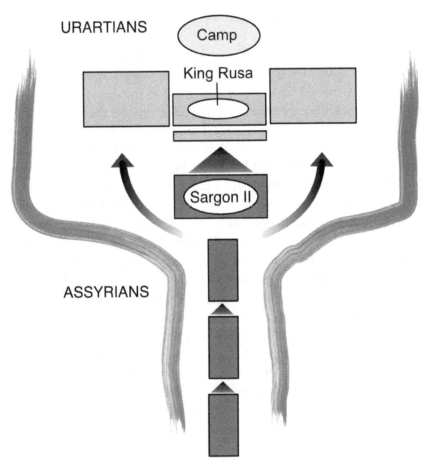

The Battle of Mount Uaush.

had given him advance warning of Rusa's intentions so that Sargon II was ready with a battle plan of his own. He did not pause to construct a camp, rest his troops, or even draw them up in a regular formation. Instead, he charged headlong with the Assyrian troops available at the Urartian center, totally disconcerting Rusa's tactics. As Sargon II reports his triumph, "I defeated him and forced him to retreat. I made carnage of him, spreading out the corpses of his warriors like malt and choking the mountain slope. I made blood flow in the chasms and gullies." Typical though this rhetoric is of Assyrian attitudes to anyone who dared to oppose them—

simply the just punishment of a dishonorable foe—there is no question that Sargon II achieved a stunning victory at Mount Uaush.

The second victory of Sargon II that we know something about occurred in 709 BC at Dur Yakin in southern Mesopotamia. Dealing with Babylon was more difficult in the reign of Sargon II than it had been in that of Tiglath-pileser III, for Assyria had lost control of the city during the confusion surrounding his succession and had not recaptured it until near the end of his reign. Possibly Sargon II intended to continue direct rule over Babylon, but he was forestalled by Merodach-baladan, the chieftain of the Chaldean tribe Bit-Yakin. Over many years the Chaldeans had been steadily moving northward from the Persian Gulf and settling in southern Mesopotamia. In either the final year of Shalmaneser V's reign or the first year of Sargon II's, Merodach-baladan claimed to have defeated the Assyrians, after which he seized Babylon. With the assistance of the Elamites, happy as ever to meddle in Mesopotamian affairs, Merodach-baladan managed to rule unchallenged until 710 BC.

That year the Assyrians launched a major offensive against Merodach-baladan and his ally King Sutur-nahhunte of Elam. Despite suffering a reverse at Der, to the northeast of Babylon, Sargon II pressed on with the campaign and stormed the nearby city of Dur Atkhara, where Merodach-baladan had installed a large garrison and strengthened its defenses by heightening the walls and flooding the plain around the city. Sargon II renamed the captured city Dur Nabu, making it the administrative center of a new Assyrian province. Large numbers of prisoners were taken in the surrounding countryside, right up to the border of Elam. When Sargon II turned against Babylon itself, Merodach-baladan fled to the Elamite court in Susa, where he offered all his possessions in a vain attempt to get Elam to attack Assyria.

Assyrian policy toward Babylon was conciliatory, as Sargon II did not hold its inhabitants responsible for the Chaldean hostility. In late 709 BC, however, the reappearance of Merodach-baladan, along with the Elamites, at Dur Yakin in the far south of Mesopotamia stirred Sargon II into action. At once he marched to confront these troublesome opponents, who had made very careful preparations to meet the Assyrian attack. Merodach-baladan had gathered his forces in the city of

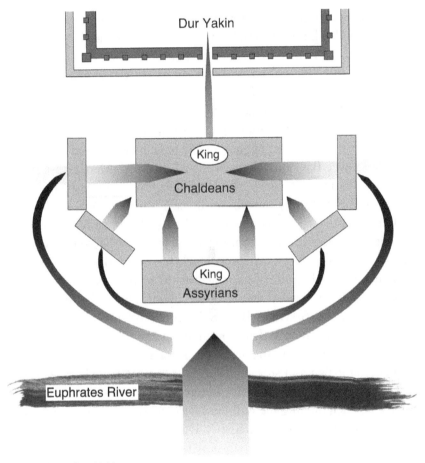

The Battle of Dur Yakin.

Dur Yakin, strengthened its fortifications, and laid in enough supplies to withstand a siege. Outside the city walls he again flooded as much land as possible in order to impede the movement of Sargon II's cavalry and chariots. Undaunted, the Assyrian king laid earthen banks across the flooded area and rushed his best divisions against Merodach-baladan's troops, who were drawn up on high ground before the city walls. A wounded Merodach-baladan slipped back inside the city and once again eluded capture. He does not appear again in the Assyrian record until the reign of Sennacherib, Sargon II's son.

Having fixed the Chaldeans with a frontal assault, Sargon II hit them on both flanks so hard that they broke and rushed, "as if they were sheep," into the city. Again it appears that the proficiency of the Assyrian archers was the decisive factor in the victory. Dur Yakin was put under a close siege and taken by the Assyrians, who tore down its fortifications. The Elamite king managed to avoid capture, and for some unknown reason, Sargon II chose not to pursue him. Even though Babylon was cowed, Elam still posed a threat to Assyria's eastern frontier, and so a number of fortresses were built along its length. Not until Ashurbanipal decided to finally settle accounts with Elam would this bellicose kingdom cease to disturb the peace of Mesopotamia.

Victorious though Sargon II was at Dur Yakin, his luck in battle ran out in Tabal, an area in Asia Minor that included several subject kingdoms in the Taurus range of mountains. This natural barrier had been fixed as part of the Assyrian Empire's northern frontier by Tiglath-pileser III. But the frontier was fluid when Sargon II began to rule, in part because of Phrygian interference. Even Urartu was drawn into the web of Phrygian intrigue before the defeat at Mount Uaush crippled it for a generation. To put an end to the unrest in Tabal, Sargon II personally led an expedition there in 705 BC. During this campaign the Assyrian king was killed, but unfortunately no details of the event are preserved. Even worse than Sargon II's death in combat was the fact that his body lay unburied on the battlefield.

Completely unaccustomed to such a disastrous event, the Assyrians wondered what the late king had done to deserve such "a divine punishment" because it was believed that the gods always determined the outcome of battle. Just as baffled was Sennacherib, who not only removed the court from Dur Sharruken, his father's newly built capital, but never mentioned his name in any of his own inscriptions. That no comet had presaged Sargon II's death, the usual signal of dynastic change, caused the Assyrian astrologers to spend years trying to make sense of the sudden event. It was finally concluded that Sargon II died due to divine abandonment. The king's acknowledged bravery was ignored despite his constant exposure to danger on the battlefield. He had always been prepared to take risks, something he obviously overdid in Tabal.

Although the sack of Babylon in 689 BC was held to be the trigger for Sennacherib's assassination at the hands of two of his sons, a curse seemed to have been laid upon the royal family as a result of Sargon II's seizure of the Assyrian throne. That Esarhaddon, the youngest son and successor of Sennacherib, had no doubt about the family's ill fortune is evident in his odd behavior. He never felt at ease, and for days at a time he would withdraw into the inner palace, rejecting food, drink, and human company. Because his subjects were more than likely to regard these disappearances as a sign of divine displeasure, Esarhaddon's condition had to be kept a state secret. On four occasions substitute kings wore his clothes, ate his meals, and slept in his bed. The execution of each substitute after one hundred days did not lesson Esarhaddon's anxieties, but at least it removed a number of political adversaries who were carefully selected for the role. The idea of a substitute's ability to ward off evil influences was deeply rooted in Mesopotamian culture, but rather than this ritual, it was the energetic crown prince Ashurbanipal who saved the situation by assuming many of the royal responsibilities. One of them was a successful completion of the Egyptian campaign, which left a compliant pharaoh to rule Lower Egypt on Assyria's behalf.

Like his father, Sennacherib was a great builder, and the work he commissioned at Nineveh surpassed that of any other Assyrian ruler. Perhaps he wished to demonstrate a dynastic break with Dur Sharruken by means of the splendor of his own palace at Nineveh, henceforth the capital of the Assyrian Empire. It was called *ekalla sa sanina la isu,* "the palace without compare." Thousands of foreign slaves toiled on the palace, the temples, and the "mountain-high" city walls. By naming the gates of Nineveh after the great gods, Sennacherib implied that the new Assyrian capital was the cosmic center of the universe and the abode of the gods themselves. As far as he was concerned, from his palace radiated outward good government, the divinely ordained peace and prosperity that would benefit every Assyrian subject and ally. For this reason Sennacherib could never tolerate disobedience of any kind: He had been charged by Ashur with ruling the Assyrian Empire, and he intended to do it in a manner pleasing to the gods.

Prisoners hauling blocks of stone at Nineveh.

Hence Sennacherib's annoyance at the unrest in Palestine and Babylon. The Assyrian king could not forgive Jewish involvement with the Chaldean rebel Merodach-baladan, who had taken advantage of the uncertainty following Sargon II's death to recapture Babylon in 703 BC. Sennacherib defeated Merodach-baladan, who again escaped capture, and continued on to the city of Babylon, where he plundered the palace but otherwise did not harm the inhabitants. On the throne of Babylon, he put Bel-ibni, a man of Babylonian descent but raised at the Assyrian court. Then in 700 BC Sennacherib advanced to the Persian Gulf and devastated the homeland of the Bit-Yakin tribe. Merodach-baladan fled again and spent his remaining years as an exile in Elam. On his way back to Assyria, Sennacherib removed the puppet king Bel-ibni and installed on the Babylonian throne his son Ashur-nadin-shumi.

But the Babylonian question was far from resolved. The final confrontation with the Chaldeans and their Elamite allies took place in 694 BC. That year Sennacherib moved to destroy the Elamite base of the fugitive Bit-Yakin on the northern shore of the Persian Gulf. Assyria had no navy at all, and so whenever the need arose to fight at sea, the Assyrians had to rely on the fleets of their seafaring subject kingdoms along the Mediterranean coast. To attack the Bit-Yakin base, therefore, Sennacherib had Syrian craftsmen construct boats to Phoenician design, to be manned by sailors from Tyre, Sidon, and Cyprus. The ships were brought down the rivers Tigris and Euphrates to the Persian Gulf, where the sailors, accustomed to the virtually tideless Mediterranean, were caught unawares by the gulf tide and forced to beach their craft. Eventually they were able to set sail, and after a difficult landing, the Assyrians routed the Chaldeans in a pitched battle. The Assyrian king himself never joined the fleet and watched its departure from the safety of the shore.

While Sennacherib had been busy on the Persian Gulf, the Elamites invaded Babylon from the north, a move that caught the Assyrians completely off guard. When the Babylonians handed over Sennacherib's son to the Elamites, the scene was set for a showdown between Assyria and Babylon. In 690 BC the enraged Assyrian king invested the city of Babylon; the siege lasted for fifteen months and caused widespread starvation and death. The destruction of the city in 689 BC was complete since Sennacherib claimed even to have diverted water from the Euphrates to flatten not only its buildings but the very mound upon which Babylon stood. Exaggerated though this boast may have been, the damage to the city was extensive as Assyrian soldiers rampaged through its streets.

Far from solving the Babylonian question, this sack left the surviving Babylonians with an abiding desire for revenge. Although Esarhaddon, Sennacherib's successor, chose appeasement and inaugurated a rebuilding program, he was unable to reduce the level of hatred for Assyria, and the breakdown of order after Ashurbanipal's death in 635 BC galvanized the Babylonians to mount a successful uprising.

Next to Babylon, the most difficult problem for Sennacherib lay in the west, especially Palestine and Egypt. According to the Bible, the Assyrian king subdued all the fortified cities of Judah except Jerusalem. In his grand palace at Nineveh, bas-reliefs record the Palestinian campaign and dwell on the siege of the Judean city of Lachish. It has been suggested that this siege was given prominence because the Assyrian king had been unable to capture Jerusalem. Sieges were regarded as a last resort and avoided whenever possible. The reasons are obvious: a direct assault often cost heavy casualties, and sometimes there was no alternative but to starve the defenders out. This tactic was tried at Jerusalem in 701 BC, but the outbreak of an epidemic among Sennacherib's soldiers forced the Assyrian army to withdraw. In light of problems in Mesopotamia, this was a sensible decision. The Jewish king Hezekiah, however, was sure that Yahweh had saved Jerusalem. As a result, the city remained independent for over a century; then, despite the warnings of the prophet Jeremiah, the king of Judah provoked the Babylonians, and in 587 BC the so-called Babylonian captivity began. In the struggle between Babylon and Egypt, Judah always sided with the latter.

Notwithstanding the failure to take Jerusalem, the Assyrian army had no trouble reducing the other Palestinian cities that defied Sennacherib. Special machines were developed to fracture city walls, and assault troops advanced under the protective fire of archers and slingers. Roofed battering rams on wheels were defended by archers positioned in turrets on top; they picked off defenders on the city wall who attempted to burn the machines with torches or dislodge the rams with chains. In addition to scaling ladders, earthen ramps were sometimes heaped against walls for battering rams to roll up and demolish the upper defenses, thereby allowing the infantry to rush up and enter the city. The Assyrians also used sappers to burrow under or through walls in addition to burning wooden gates.

Explanations for Assyrian military success that rely on the use of a particular weapon, such as the chariot or the composite bow, underestimate the integrated nature of the Assyrian army, whose different units

Assyrians checking composite bows and arrows.

combined with exceptional skill on the battlefield. Foot soldiers and mounted archers were flexible enough to adjust their tactics as circumstances demanded. Sargon II's defeat of the Urartian king Rusa depended on this ability to respond swiftly to changes in orders. His unexpected charge broke the Urartian center, where Rusa's best troops were stationed. In this respect, Assyrian tactics anticipated the form of warfare later perfected by the Romans.

The political problems of Esarhaddon were the same as those of his father, who was assassinated at Nimrud in 681 BC. It took Esarhaddon the whole of the next year to regain control of the Assyrian Empire. Relying on the support of the Assyrian nobles, who had already sworn an oath of loyalty to him as the chosen successor, the new king executed the assassins and ascended the throne without opposition. At least Esarhaddon's gentle approach toward Babylon temporarily paid off, since it allowed Assyria to crown its imperialism with the conquest of Egypt. It is reasonable to surmise that Sennacherib had intended to invade Egypt,

Assyrian foot soldiers.

and his own son wasted little time in launching an Egyptian offensive. There were several attacks before, in 671 BC, the Assyrian army crossed the Sinai desert with camels commandeered from the Arabs to carry water. Upon arrival in Egypt, it won three pitched battles and captured Memphis. Impressive though this seemed then, Egypt was able to recover sufficiently from these defeats to merit another Assyrian expedition in 669 BC. Esarhaddon died on the way to Egypt, and his son and heir, Ashurbanipal, was left to complete the conquest of Egypt.

A successful invasion of Egypt depended upon securely holding Syria and Palestine, where Esarhaddon had to reassert Assyria's authority in Phoenicia. Before he launched his major Egyptian campaign in 671 BC, the Assyrians stormed Tyre and deposed its king. Elsewhere Esarhaddon's attention was required along the Assyrian Empire's northern frontier, but it was the Elamites who once again caused the most trouble—so much so that, unusually for Assyria, a peace agreement was reached that accorded the kings of Elam and Assyria equal status. A surviving letter boldly states, "The king of Elam and the king of Assyria, after they continually listened to each other, by command of Marduk, they made peace with each other, and they made a sworn agreement with each other." This letter refers to the close relationship that evolved between the Elamite king Urtak and Esarhaddon, which is made quite clear in the repetition of "each other." Emphasis is placed here on mutual understanding and the acceptance of equality. Considering the past history of hostility between these two powers, the letter is an absolute revelation of changed political circumstances.

THE FALL OF ELAM AND ASSYRIA

Peaceful relations seem to have continued in the early part of Ashurbanipal's reign. We are told that the Assyrian king sent grain to Elam in time of famine, offered refuge to those Elamites fleeing the drought conditions, and let them return to Elam when matters improved. Everything changed, however, in 664 BC when Urtak raided Mesopotamia. Ashurbanipal drove the Elamites back to their own territory but, preoccupied with other fronts, did not cross the Elamite border. Urtak died the same year, and the flight of a number of prominent Elamite families to Nineveh points to political turmoil in Elam itself. Even the crown prince fled to Assyria.

Rebels in Egypt also troubled Ashurbanipal. He was obliged to conduct two campaigns there: the first one recaptured Memphis; the second captured Thebes. Prisoners and booty were carried back to Assyria, but the appointment of Necko as a subject pharaoh was a mistake. Necko's son Psamik I would restore Egypt's independence once Ashurbanipal decided that yet another Egyptian expedition would be unprofitable. Psamik founded the last Egyptian dynasty before the arrival of the Persians in 525 BC.

Before Ashurbanipal relinquished any ambition to rule Egypt, the expansion of the Assyrian Empire looked unstoppable, although overreach was already putting a severe strain on its military resources.

Assyrian punishment of rebels.

That is why Ashurbanipal's reign from 668 to 627 BC is regarded as the apogee of Assyria.

Shaking the base of the Assyrian Empire most was a bitter feud between Ashurbanipal and his younger brother Shamash-shuma-ukin. Esarhaddon had chosen to divide his royal powers between these two sons: whereas Ashurbanipal assumed full control of Assyria and the empire at large, Shamash-shuma-ukin became the dependent monarch of Babylon. That Shamash-shuma-ukin initially accepted this subordinate role is apparent from the letters he addressed to his older brother. But Ashurbanipal's attitude soon irked the king of Babylon; he seemed unwilling to act promptly on Shamash-shuma-ukin's behalf. The military defense of Babylon was a persistent source of friction between the two brothers, despite Ashurbanipal's claim that he had provided enough armed forces to Shamash-shuma-ukin, including infantry, cavalry, and chariots. The failure of Ashurbanipal to pursue, in 664 BC, the defeated Elamites into their homeland and punish them for invading Babylon grated on Shamash-shuma-ukin. That Babylon's defense was not always well served by Assyrian troops must account at this time for the rebuilding of the city walls. Yet, however nominal his power, Shamash-shuma-ukin presided over a period of real prosperity that derived from stable government.

It is impossible to determine Shamash-shuma-ukin's own foreign policy in the years prior to his rebellion because Ashurbanipal managed foreign relations on behalf of Babylon as well as Assyria. But it was probably realized in Babylon that Assyrian power had already begun to decline. Not only was Assyria's control over Egypt slipping, but in Asia Minor subject kingdoms had renounced their allegiance to Assyria, especially Lydia. Added to this apparent weakness was the general restlessness of the Babylonians under the Assyrian yoke ever since Sennacherib had sacked the city of Babylon. In 652 BC Shamash-shuma-ukin threw his lot in with Assyria's chief opponents in Mesopotamia, the Elamites and the Chaldeans. It took Ashurbanipal four years to restore the situation. After the defeat of the Babylonians and the Elamites, he laid siege to Babylon; its inhabitants were reduced to cannibalism, and when the city fell, Shamash-shuma-ukin, along with his closest followers, perished in the burning palace. But the city itself was not destroyed as it had been in 689 BC.

An exasperated Ashurbanipal then decided to settle the score with Elam once and for all. He also intended to win back the buffer states between Elam and Assyria as well as place a puppet king by the name of Tammaritu II on the Elamite throne. This prince had been living in exile at Ashurbanipal's court. A new Elamite king, Tepi-Huban-Insusinak, had already moved the kingdom onto a war footing. Known to the Assyrians as Teumann, he was killed at the Battle of Til Tuba in 653 BC.

At this battle the Elamites deployed hired soldiers to supplement the troops that Teumann called up. These troops were stationed along with Teumann's numerous allies at the front of the army. Whether or not the Elamite king was concerned to prevent their desertion we cannot tell, even though it was usual practice to place allied contingents on the wings. It seems they were expected to face the Assyrian infantry, while the bulk of the Elamite army was ranged behind them in a deep formation. Pre-

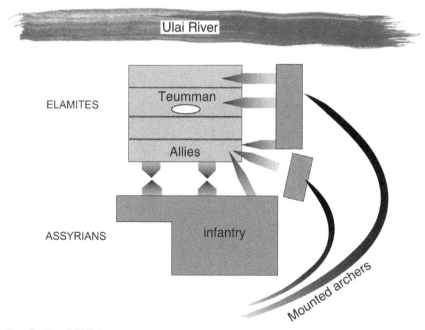

The Battle of Til Tuba.

sumably Teumann intended to preempt any advance by the Assyrians and to push their infantry back with the combined weight of his forces. Ashurbanipal frustrated this tactic by sending his cavalry to attack the Elamite left flank and roll it into the center. Surprised by this, Teumann lost his nerve and tried to escape the battlefield with his son through the Elamite right flank. But they were soon surrounded by Assyrian foot soldiers, and after a brief struggle in which Teumann's son endeavored to defend his wounded father with bow and arrows, both were killed. The Assyrians cut off their heads and hurried to carry them to Ashurbanipal. Later Teumann's severed head was publicly displayed in Nineveh before ending up as a trophy in the palace garden.

The victorious Assyrian army then advanced through Elam, taking city after city, killing, looting, and ransacking temples. But the capital, Susa, bore the brunt of the rampage, for while Ashurbanipal rested in the palace there, his men seized cult statues, set fire to temples, emptied the treasury, broke into royal tombs, and carried off the enslaved. An

The beheading of Teumann at Til Tuba.

inscription relates how at Susa the Assyrian king deliberately disturbed the enemy dead. Ashurbanipal says,

The burial places of their early and later kings, who feared not Ashur. I devastated. I exposed them to the sun and their bones I moved to Assyria. I laid restlessness on their spirits, for food-offerings and water-libations I denied them.

Despoiling the tombs of the Elamite kings was more than a final settlement of accounts with a persistent foe, because it was believed that such an action would in itself undermine Elamite strength. Bas-reliefs even appear to show Elamite prisoners being forced to grind the bones of their ancestors. Without the care of living descendants, the Mesopotamian dead were condemned to eat clay as their food, which turned them into malignant ghosts.

The devastation at Susa even entailed the spreading of salt over fields so that Ashurbanipal could boast after this symbolic act that no human voice would ever be heard again in Elam, since the kingdom had been turned into a wilderness. Some kind of diminished Elamite kingdom did survive, however, as Ashurbanipal received tribute from it after the withdrawal of the Assyrian army. And we are aware that Tammaritu II duly became its king. If anything, the final eclipse of Elam was brought about by the Medes and the Persians.

Little is known about the last twenty years of Ashurbanipal's reign despite an assumption that it was marked by unrest and dissension in Assyria. There were certainly factions among the Assyrian aristocracy that could have threatened Ashurbanipal. And it may have been the case that the transfer of the court from Ashur to Nimrud, to Dur Sharruken, and finally to Nineveh reflected a desire on the part of different kings to be with friends, or at least away from political opponents. Yet the perfect image of Ashurbanipal's final years could be the bas-relief of the king enjoying his garden in Nineveh. It reveals the king reclining in Greek fashion on a couch, but he does not drink in the company of men, as at a symposium. Only his wife, Queen Ashur-sharrat, shares the occasion with him. She sits on a low throne in front of her husband, holding a

Ashurbanipal in his cups at Nineveh, with the severed head of the Elamite king on the far left.

wine cup to her lips while gazing upon her lord and master. Servants wave fly whisks so that no insect may spoil the royal couple's relaxation. But this apparently tranquil scene still embodies the bloody nature of Assyrian domination, as the severed head of the Elamite king Teumann is suspended from the branch of a nearby tree. Birds are gathered to pluck out the eyes and pick off the flesh. In his cups Ashurbanipal may well have expected the Assyrian Empire to last forever, but within fifteen years of his death in 627 BC, it had disappeared.

A power struggle between Ashurbanipal's sons hardly helped Assyria when Babylon rose in revolt under the leadership of Nabopolassar. The suggestion that he was of Chaldean stock is now largely discounted, although the Chaldean tribes undoubtedly assisted his bid for independence. Even though he withstood Assyrian attacks, Nabopolassar's own assault on Assyria had to await the Medes, who led resistance to Assyrian expansion in the east. Ashur fell in 614 BC, Nineveh in 612 BC, and Harran in 610 BC. The last Assyrian king, Ashur-uballit II, had fled westward to Harran, where he established a government in exile. This ancient religious and commercial city, whose inhabitants enjoyed royal favors and tax exemption that ensured their loyalty, was the home of Adad-guppi, the long-lived mother of the last Babylonian monarch, Nabonidus. Possibly a distant relative of the Assyrian royal family, Adad-guppi was a priestess in the great temple there dedicated to Sin, the moon god.

Such was Egypt's concern with the threat posed by a resurgent Babylon to its ambitions in Palestine and Syria that it lent military support to its erstwhile enemy Assyria. But this was to no avail once Nebuchadrezzar II, Nabopolassar's son, forced an Egyptian withdrawal. That an ageing Ashurbanipal failed to arrange an orderly succession weakened royal authority, the very foundation of the Assyrian system of government, and only served to encourage disorder at home and rebellion abroad. But the reasons for Assyria's sudden collapse remain unclear. Possibly the cost of its armed forces had placed an unbearable strain on the royal treasury, since Egypt was the last significant input of new revenue, a source that Assyria was unable to exploit for very long. Relentless imperialism may simply have become beyond Assyria's means.

THE BABYLONIAN REVIVAL

In 612 BC the combined armies of the Medes and the Babylonians, along with their tribal allies, besieged Nineveh for three months, before inflicting "on the great people a major defeat and Sin-sharra-ukin, the king of Assyria, was slain. Then they carried off a vast amount of booty and left Nineveh a ruin." Nabopolassar followed up this unity of purpose against a common enemy with a treaty of friendship with the Medes before undertaking further military operations himself. The new Babylonian king was acutely aware of the need for peace in Mesopotamia after the prolonged struggle to overthrow the Assyrian Empire. That is why he began work at once on the renovation of the palace, ziggurat, and walls of Babylon in order to make the city of Babylon a capital worthy of a prosperous new kingdom. His son Nabu-kudurri-usur (Nebuchadrezzar, the biblical Nebuchadnezzar) was present at the foundation ceremonies, and soon afterward he was proclaimed the heir apparent. Father and son both participated in military operations at Harran, until Nabopolassar judged that, for the sake of the dynasty, his presence was necessary at Babylon.

Left to campaign on his own in Syria, Nebuchadrezzar II won a great victory over the Egyptian army at Carchemish, pursued it southward, and at Hamath scored another success in which "both sides suffered severe losses." But he was in no position to harry the Egyptians further, since news of his father's death obliged him to hasten back to the capital in order to prevent a rival's mounting the throne. That he became king in 604 BC proved to be one of the great events in the ancient Middle East as Nebuchadrezzar not only established the second Babylonian Empire but, during his forty-two-year reign, also made the city of Babylon into one of the seven wonders of the world.

Babylon was in fact the largest Mesopotamian city, exceeding even Nineveh in area. Its huge fortifications must have impressed a visitor approaching across the open plain upon which it stood. Also rising above them was the towering ziggurat of Marduk opposite Esagila, that god's temple. The second great Babylonian deity was the goddess Ishtar, after whom a famous gate was named. The processional way passed the walls of the royal palace and entered the city proper through the Ishtar Gate. Along its white limestone surface, the king of Babylon led, during the new year festival, cult statues, temple attendants, and noble citizens, followed by booty from successful campaigns. Nebuchadrezzar's partiality for blue-glazed bricks could only have made public buildings resplendent in the sunlight.

There is no mention of the Hanging Gardens in any of the inscriptions recovered from Babylon. It looks therefore as if the Greeks and Romans confused Assyrian gardens with Babylonian ones, particularly the extensive garden that Sennacherib laid out next to his palace in Nineveh. To bring water to the garden, this Assyrian king built a canal and an aqueduct. Over 2 million smooth limestone blocks were used in this unmatched feat of engineering. Most telling of all about the location of the Hanging Gardens is their absence from Herodotus's famous description of Babylon. What caught the Greek historian's eye was the city's "circuit wall of some sixty miles in length, surrounded by a broad deep moat full of water."

In Palestine the Babylonian army soon undertook military operations, bringing siege equipment to deal with pro-Egyptian cities such as Jerusalem. King Zedekiah of Judah had become the focus of opposition to Babylon, ignoring the warnings of the prophet Jeremiah. A newly agreed pact between Judah and Egypt was something Nebuchadrezzar could never tolerate. Having already subdued the rebellious Phoenician cites of Sidon and Tyre and incorporated them into a Babylonian province, he decided to conquer the remaining small kingdoms that were so tempting to Egypt.

Despite the biblical version of Jerusalem's destruction as a result of Jewish reluctance to embrace fully the commands of Yahweh, the Babylonian reaction to Zedekiah's rebellion should not be viewed as anything other than a move designed to end Judah's chronic tendency to disloyalty. Nebuchadrezzar simply wanted to create a province in Judah that would not look to Jerusalem as its capital, with all the religious tensions in that city. As a consequence of Zedekiah's stubborn refusal to listen to Jeremiah, the Bible relates, "came Nebuchadnezzar and his army against Jerusalem, and they besieged it." Though Jerusalem held out for many months in the summer of 587 BC, the walls of the starving city were eventually breached when battering rams pierced the northern defenses. The king and some of his guards "fled and went forth out of the city by night, by way of the king's garden, by the gate betwixt the walls, and he went out the way of the plain." But the Babylonians gave chase and apprehended Zedekiah on the way to Jericho. He was escorted to "Nebuchnezzar king of Babylon at Riblah in the land of Hamath, where he gave judgment upon him. Then the king of Babylon slew the sons of Zedekiah; also the king of Babylon slew all the nobles of Judah. Moreover, he put out Zedekiah's eyes, and bound him in chains, to carry him to Babylon."

Shortly after the fall of Jerusalem, the Babylonians "burnt the house of the Lord, and the houses of the people ... and broke down the walls of Jerusalem." The cause of the destruction, according to Nebuzaradin, the captain of the Babylonian king's guard, was that "the Lord thy God hath pronounced evil upon this place." Jeremiah agreed. The fall of Jerusalem was not a defeat for Yahweh but his punishment of his own people. The disobedience of the Jews, their turning to other gods, had brought about the catastrophe. Yahweh did not so much abandon the chosen people as use the Babylonians as the instrument of his anger.

The systematic destruction of Jerusalem means that Nebuchadrezzar wished to eliminate the city as a religious and political center. Additionally, the exile of many Jewish residents confirmed his policy of suppression: picked out for deportation were those likely to stir up trouble again in the new Babylonian province. Our view of this capable king is not a little influenced by the tale of his madness and William Blake's depiction of him as a haunted and terrified man crawling on all fours, his nails grown into claws, his beard dragging along the ground, and his face a study in horror. This strange image goes all the way back to the book of Daniel, which confused Nebuchadrezzar with Nabonidas. Contemporary records praise Nebuchadrezzar highly as "the king of justice," an obvious echo of Hammurabi's fame as a lawgiver. He is described as a devotee of Marduk, whose approval he sought by protecting the poor, bridling the arrogance of the rich, and preventing the bribery of officials. Above all, Nebuchadrezzar is credited with stimulating a religious revival that matched his imperial successes.

After Nebuchadrezzar's death, however, dynastic instability undermined Babylon. His own son was swept aside in a palace coup, the first of two that, in 555 BC, left Nabonidas as king. Ever since his reign, his

Nabonidas, the last Babylonian king.

conduct has baffled observers. From 551 to 541 BC Nabonidas moved the court to Tema in Arabia, leaving his son Belshazzar to administer the empire in Babylon. Even the funeral of his mother, Adad-guppi, in 547 BC failed to get him to leave Arabia, a decision that must have contributed to the story of royal madness. Possibly Nabonidas wanted to exploit the lucrative spice and incense trade, as well as the movement of gold, all of which passed through Tema. It has also been suggested that, with Persian ambitions in Syria and northern Mesopotamia becoming clear, Nabonidas may have been attempting to expand his power base into wealthy Arabia as some kind of compensation.

The ten-year voluntary exile from Babylon would probably not have mattered so much if it had not coincided with royal patronage of Sin, the moon god served by Adad-guppi. By his own fervent worship of Sin, Nabonidas was implicitly downgrading the role of Marduk, although the absent king never denied this god's importance for Babylon. In a lengthy inscription discovered at Harran, Nabonidas explains how Sin, "king of the gods, lord of the lords of the gods and goddesses, dwellers in heaven," told him to go to Tema and when to return to Babylon. But it was too late to meet the challenge of the Persian king Cyrus. The writing was already on the wall for the Babylonian Empire. The book of Daniel tells us that a lavish feast of Belshazzar was disrupted by the appearance of a strange script on the banqueting wall. Only the prophet Daniel could read the message; it warned of Belshazzar's imminent death and the Persian conquest of Babylon. At the feast Belshazzar had dared to use as drinking cups sacred vessels looted from the Temple in Jerusalem.

Cyrus attributed his capture of Babylon to the will of Marduk as punishment of a regime that had sidelined his cult. To underline the point, the Persian king immediately ordered a renovation of Marduk's temple. Yet the decline from the splendor of Nebuchadrezzar's day to the sudden collapse during the reign of Nabonidas is really a testament to the adverse effects of division among the rulers who followed him.

Chapter Four

The Persian Empire

Perhaps even more than the Assyrians, it was the Persians who founded the first true empire in the ancient Middle East. Certainly the size of their empire was something new: The conquests of Cyrus and Cambyses and then the expansion undertaken by Darius I extended its territory from the Danube to the Indus, from the Caspian Sea to the Nile. For the first time in history, almost all of West Asia was united politically. Finally, and most importantly, Europe and Asia were brought into contact in ways and with an intensity never experienced before. Greeks living in western Asia Minor came under direct Persian rule for long periods. The challenge they presented soon involved Persian kings in European affairs, both militarily and diplomatically. Twice Persian expeditions invaded the Greek mainland, and twice Persian peace settlements reordered Greek affairs.

Marked by an extraordinary ethnic diversity and by a thriving variety of forms of local government, the Persian Empire might almost be regarded as a federation, a collection of semiautonomous territories subject to the edicts of the Persian king. Under the Persians there were no more mass deportations, the instruments of imperial control favored by the Assyrians and, to a lesser extent, the Babylonians. From the start exiles were allowed to return to their homelands if they wished. Rebellions were not unknown, but apart from periodic usurpation crises, the violent repression of the Assyrians became a thing of the past. As long as they met the annual tribute imposed by the Persians and supplied troops when required, subject peoples were left largely to their own

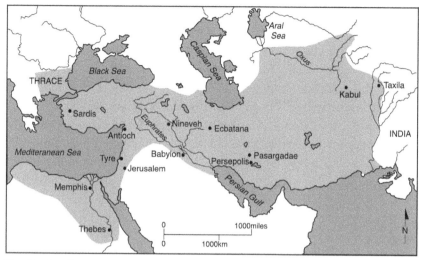

The Persian Empire.

devices. Persian rulers had little interest in internal affairs. Driving their ambition was the establishment of a universal monarchy: they intended to be "kings of the four quarters" and much more. The Persian Empire might well have reached Italy had not an inability to subdue the Greeks brought its expansion to a halt in the Mediterranean. Indeed, this conflict eventually led to the extinction of Persian power, for a determined enemy in the shape of the Macedonians would unite the Greeks in a crusade against Persia.

Despite subscribing to such a distinctive religion as Zoroastrianism, the great Persian king Cyrus was a conspicuous restorer of damaged or destroyed Mesopotamian temples, beginning in Babylon with the embellishment of Marduk's temple. A tablet recovered from its ruins relates how "Cyrus, king of all lands, loves Esagila." He understood that the cooperation of the Babylonians was essential for the establishment of his own authority on a firm basis.

THE CONQUESTS OF CYRUS THE GREAT

The ruling Persian dynasty, the Achaemenid, was named after Achaemenes, a legendary ancestor believed to have been raised by an eagle. He was likely the leader of the Persians when they finally settled in

what was once the kingdom of Elam. When the Assyrians had endeavored to expand eastward into present-day Iran, the Medes took the
lead in forming an anti-Assyrian coalition. They even combined with
the Babylonians to end Assyrian domination in 610 BC. The Persians
joined the coalition and achieved close relations with the Medes
through intermarriage. No Median inscriptions have survived, but like
the Persians, the Medes were probably Indo-European speakers. The
Persians appear to have left the Central Asian steppe much later than
the Medes, the longer sojourn on the steppe having fundamentally
influenced the Persian outlook, because there the prophet Zoroaster
gave them a singular set of beliefs. He claimed that his inspired utter-
ances were not only divine truths but divine commandments that the
worshippers of Ahura Mazda, a cosmic deity whose raiment was the
sky, had to accept if they were to be saved. Zoroaster's emphasis on
goodness as part of the divine plan was revolutionary, familiar through
it is to us now through Jewish and Christian borrowings.

Friction between the Median and Persian royal families, however,
caused a breach that was only resolved by Persian arms. When Cyrus II,
justifiably called "the Great," came to the throne in 559 BC, he may have
already decided to dominate the Medes, so that a family dispute offered
a golden opportunity for action. This proved no easy task, as the Persians
suffered three heavy defeats before overcoming the Medes. But Cyrus was
astute enough to conciliate his defeated opponents by portraying himself
as a legitimate member of their own royal house. We are told that Cyrus
entered the tent of Median king Astyages, took his place on the throne,
and grasped his scepter. The crown was then placed on Cyrus's head. More
importantly, Astyages was spared and granted a princely lifestyle.

Besides gaining control of the Iranian plateau, Cyrus acquired in the
Median royal treasure a means of financing future military operations.
Next he fought Lydia in Asia Minor, after lulling Babylon into a false
sense of security. In this war Cyrus was aided by the foolhardiness of the
Lydian king Croesus, who Herodotus says "had a craving to extend his
territories." Not only was he keen to advance his frontier eastward, but
even more he wanted to punish Cyrus for his treatment of Astyages.
Croesus's mother was the daughter of the deposed Median king. Because

Croesus "blamed Cyrus for this action, he sent to ask the oracles about his proposed attack on Persia, and, when an ambiguous answer arrived, interpreted it in his favour and began the war." Hostilities started when Croesus crossed the river Halys, which had been the boundary with the Medes. Cyrus marched to oppose the Lydian king's advance, increasing the strength of his army by levying troops from all the peoples that lay on his route. "Before setting out," adds Herodotus, "he had sent representatives to the Ionians in an attempt to detach them from Croesus, but without success." Lydia's interest in commerce pleased these Greek settlers; Lydian kings had issued the first coinage in the ancient Middle East, greatly facilitating the expansion of trade. As a result, the Greeks living in western Asia Minor were much less restive than later, under the Persians.

According to Herodotus, there was a trial of strength between Croesus and Cyrus near the river Halys. He tells us,

> *After a sharp struggle in which both sides lost heavily, night fell and the battle was broken off without a decision. Croesus laid the blame for his lack of success upon the size of his army, which in that engagement was much smaller than the army of Cyrus; so when the next day Cyrus did not advance to attack, he marched back to Sardis with the intention of calling upon the Egyptians to assist him according to the pact which he had concluded with King Amasis before the treaty of alliance with Sparta; he meant also to summon the Babylonians . . . and, lastly, to call upon the Spartans to join him on a definite date. Thus, with all these reinforcements added to his own army, he proposed to wait until winter was over, and attack the Persians in the following spring.*

Returning to his capital at Sardis, Croesus disbanded his forces, including the mercenaries hired to fight the Persians, and awaited the next campaigning season. Not for a moment did he expect, after such a close-fought contest, that Cyrus would dare to advance on Sardis. But this is exactly what the Persian king did, and after a skirmish, he besieged the city and captured Croesus. At first Cyrus prepared a pyre for the defeated monarch, but then he changed his mind; the fire was extinguished, and

A Greek vase showing King Croesus on a pyre.

Croesus was taken as a prisoner to Persia. Herodotus claims that the Lydian king blamed Apollo for his plight, since an enquiry he made at Delphi received the answer that if he attacked the Persians, he would bring down a mighty empire. "After an answer like that," comments Herodotus, "the wise thing would have been to send and enquire again which empire was meant, Cyrus's or his own. But as he misinterpreted what was said and made no second enquiry, he must admit the fault to have been his." In the end, this is what happened, as Croesus said the oracular god was innocent and he had only himself to blame.

Following the fall of Sardis, Cyrus left a general to subdue the Greek cities of Ionia, while he went to Ecbatana to prepare for the conquest of the Babylonians and the Scythians. The prolonged struggle between the Persians and the Greeks, which arose as a consequence of the latter's incorporation into the Persian Empire, was not a simple conflict between democracy and autocracy, as often contended. It should be remembered that the Ionian Greeks were themselves invaders and colonizers and not always the boon and blessing to the native inhabitants so frequently proclaimed. Added to this was the intercity rivalry, as well as the policy changes of the Greek cities planted there; they were no more satisfied with Persian rule than the Egyptians or other conquered peoples, but constant rebellion was never a feature of their behavior.

The Babylonians were now Cyrus's most formidable adversary and rival in the ancient Middle East. The last king of Babylon, Nabonidas, remains a controversial figure. Contemporaries could not understand his conduct, and subsequent generations could make no sense of his temporary abandonment of the city of Babylon. From 551 to 541 BC, Naboni-das moved his court to Tema in Arabia, leaving his son Belshazzar to run the capital city. During Nabonidas's voluntary exile, the Babylonian chronicle relates, Marduk's annual parade around the city of Babylon did not take place. Offerings "were presented to the gods," but "the king was in Tema and kept away from Babylon." This break in the traditional cycle of festivities must have worried the inhabitants because it could lead their city god, Marduk, also going into exile, with all the dreadful consequences that the withdrawal of divine protection entailed. Marduk was, after all, the supreme Babylonian deity.

Nabonidas's own relationship with the powerful priesthood of Mar-duk was complex. First of all, he was an outsider from Harran, where his long-lived mother, Adad-guppi, acted as a priestess of the moon god Sin. A second cause of his estrangement from the religious establish-ment in Babylon was the undoubted influence of Adad-guppi, about whom we know something because her biography was preserved on the underside of a paving stone used in the Great Mosque at Harran. It was discovered in 1956. Extraordinary by any standards, Adad-guppi survived four reigning monarchs in Assyria and the Babylonian-Median sack of Harran, and her life even encompassed the whole of the new Babylonian dynasty down to the ninth year of its last king, her own son Nabonidas, when she died at the advanced age of 104.

One of Nabonidas's early aims was the restoration of his mother's temple, the Ehulhul, or "the house which gives joy." Because of his concern to repair damaged temples and reinstate sacred rituals throughout his kingdom, Nabonidas has been regarded as an obsessive antiquarian. But he thought the impiety of his immediate predecessors accounted for their short reigns; he had no intention of repeating a lack of concern for Mesopotamia's pantheon.

While some argued that the strength of the moon god's worship in Arabia had attracted Nabonidas, others believed the move of the court was due to political pressure from the Persians, whose ambitions in Syria and northern Mesopotamia were becoming transparent. Nabonidas may have been attempting to expand his power base into wealthy Arabia as an alternative power base. Yet the religious argument cannot be discounted, not least because Nabonidas claimed his own elevation to the kingship was the will of Sin. That he addressed Sin as "king of the gods" and said he eventually returned to Babylon by Sin's command indicates the closeness he felt to the moon god. Indeed the theological reasons that Adad-guppi had advanced at the beginning of her son's reign had allowed Nabonidas to outmaneuver Marduk's priesthood.

During the summer of 539 BC, war clouds gathered to such an extent that the cult statues of several Mesopotamian cities were brought into Babylon for safe keeping as a precaution against a Persian invasion. Cyrus may well have been expecting Babylon to fall without too much resistance: his deliberate destruction of one Mesopotamian city was evidently intended as a brutal warning. He could have also been secretly in touch with Marduk's priests, to whom Nabonidas had given grave offence through his patronage of Sin. These priests would not have objected to a foreign dynasty, something that Babylon had experienced several times before, provided Marduk's position was not threatened. The swift and seemingly unexpected collapse of Babylon, as reflected in the Bible, could be explained by the assistance that anti-Nabonidas elements in the capital gave to the infiltrating Persians. Herodotus, on the other hand, suggests that chance played an important role. "Owing to the size of the city," he wrote, "the outskirts were captured without the people in the centre knowing about it. There was a festival going on, and they continued to dance and enjoy themselves, until they learned the news the hard way."

The cylinder describing how Cyrus captured Babylon in 539 BC.

Cyrus himself attributed his swift victory to the favor of Marduk as punishment of a regime that had tried to marginalize his cult. Even the Babylonian chronicle draws special attention to the fact that during the Persian takeover "there was no interruption of the services in the Esagila or other temples and no rite was missed." Astonishingly, too, the Jews hailed the Persian king as nothing short of a messiah. The prophet Isaiah maintained that the rise of Persia was part of a divine plan to rebuild Jerusalem, but Babylonian priests put a rather different slant on the unusual event in 539 BC. They said instead that it was Marduk who "scanned and looked through every country, searching for a king who would grace his annual procession. Then he pronounced Cyrus to be king of the world."

Immediately afterward, Cyrus was pleased to note, "all the kings of the entire world from the Upper to the Lower Sea, those who are seated in throne rooms and all the kings who live in tents, brought tribute to Babylon and kissed my feet." As he was heir to the Babylonian kings, his authority stretched from the border of Egypt to the Persian Gulf. Contemporary documents make apparent that Cyrus introduced no great changes in the economy or the customs of his new subjects, and there is no record of resistance to his rule. Just as he took care to conduct himself appropriately in Media as Astyages's successor, so in the ancient Middle East as a whole, Cyrus acted with such consideration that the political harmony he won allowed the designation of his son Cambyses as the next Persian king. Though Cambyses was Cyrus's eldest son, the Persian succession was not determined by age; the reigning king was expected to choose who would mount the throne after him.

Cambyses had already been recognized as the king of Babylon, and he may well have participated in Marduk's festival at the new year. From the Babylonian point of view, Cyrus's victory could signify the reconstruction of their empire, although Persian territorial ambitions soon revealed that Babylon was to become part of a much larger state. The resilience of the Babylonians had much to do with the lightness of the Persian yoke. Along with Greek and Phoenician cities, Babylon retained a considerable degree of autonomy, provided its financial and military obligations were fulfilled. King Darius I actually spent time in Babylon, putting down rebellions in Assyria and Media, before deciding to establish himself in the latter. Rebel leaders were usually impaled, but Fravastis the Mede suffered a more lingering punishment. His nose, ears, tongue, and one eye were cut out. Then the captured rebel was "chained under guard at the entrance of the palace so that everyone could see him."

Little is known about the last eight years of Cyrus's reign. He is assumed to have spent most of his time putting in place those governmental arrangements needed to rule so vast an empire. We are aware of his remarkable tolerance in stark contrast to the Babylonians and the Assyrians. But Cyrus did not live long enough to enjoy the benefits of this humane approach. Herodotus reports that the Persian king died fighting the Massagetae on the empire's northeastern frontier, in a battle

> *more violent than any other fought between foreign nations. . . . The engagement began by the two armies coming to a halt within range of each other and exchanging shots with bows and arrows until their arrows were used up; after which there was a long period of close fighting with spears and daggers, neither side being willing to retreat. Finally, however, the Massagetae got the upper hand, the greater part of the Persian army was destroyed where it stood, and Cyrus himself was killed.*

Herodotus adds that "in their dress and way of living the Massagetae are like the Scythians. Some ride, some do not—for they use both infantry and cavalry." Most telling of all in his description of the battle is the priority given to archery, the favorite weapon of the Persians.

From age five to twenty, when military service started, Persian boys were required to practice archery, a skill in which the Persians had been specially instructed by the Scythians—the name given by the Greeks to the people living on the northern shore of the Black Sea. Expert mounted bowmen, the Scythians dominated the steppe lands and, in the first century BC, were briefly able to rule northwestern India. Scythians and Persians spoke related languages and understood each other without interpreters.

FROM CAMBYSES TO DARIUS

The remains of Cyrus were, in 530 BC, taken to Pasargadae for burial in a tomb he had already built. The great conqueror's tomb was modest, a gabled structure set on a stepped platform of stone blocks after the style of Asia Minor. Herodotus characterizes Cyrus's successor, Cambyses, as

Cyrus the Great's modest tomb.

a madman. Whatever the truth, Cambyses's great achievement was the conquest of Egypt, an enterprise already planned during the lifetime of his father. Early in 525 BC Cambyses invaded Egypt and, after overrunning the country, was accepted as the new pharaoh. He honored Egyptian religion and kept the existing administration intact.

But Cambyses seems to have lost a degree of support through a reduction of the overly wealthy religious establishment, whose increasing domination of the economy had worried previous pharaohs. Despite Herodotus's report that Cambyses stabbed the sacred Apis bull with a sword and then laughed at the Egyptians for worshipping the animal as it bled to death, there is good evidence that the Apis bull died in 524 BC when Cambyses was actually campaigning in Nubia and that the next bull lived until the fourth year of his successor's reign. Moreover, an inscription on the coffin of the bull tells us that Cambyses ordered it to be made in honor of his father. It looks as if Herodotus obtained his poor opinion of Cambyses from Egyptian priests who resented his curtailment of temple treasuries.

Cambyses began his journey back to Persia in 522 BC, probably unaware that rebellion had broken out in the Middle East. He never arrived; on the way he succumbed to an accidental wound. That Darius I would succeed Cambyses looked by no means certain. Even though Cambyses had eliminated his brother Bardiya before he embarked on the Egyptian campaign so as to forestall any rebellion during his absence, the deed remained a state secret. Only a few of his closest companions knew that he had ordered this execution, with the result that a priest was able to declare himself Bardiya and stir the Persians into rebellion. The account of Darius's usurpation of the Persian throne is obscure, as indeed are the reasons for the widespread dislike of Cambyses. One possibility was that Cambyses's tendency to concentrate power in his own hands alienated the Persian nobility. But this does not quite fit the situation as the false Bardiya gained popular support with a moratorium of three years on the payment of taxes and the seizure of property belonging to the Persian nobility. And Darius had the support of many nobles in his overthrow of the rebellious priest, after which he restored the privileges and property of the nobility.

The entrance to Darius I's palace at Persepolis.

Skepticism has been directed at Herodotus's account of the succession of Darius from almost the moment he wrote it. Yet, in the ancient Middle East, kingship was supposed to be a matter of divine approval, and a sign from Ahura Mazda would have been required to assure the Persians of the god's will. Herodotus claimed that Darius was acknowledged as the next king because his horse neighed first after the sun rose. Apparently the contenders for power had agreed on this as an auspicious sign. So, Herodotus says,

> *Darius went to see his clever groom called Oebares. He told him of the arrangement they had come to, whereby they should sit on their horses' backs and the throne should go to the one whose horse neighed first. "Can you find a way," Darius asked, "for me to win the contest?" Oebares answered: "Well, master, if your chance of winning the throne depends upon nothing else, you may be confident that you will be king. I know a charm which will just suit your purpose." So Oebares, as soon as it was dark, took from the stable a mare which Darius' horse*

was particularly fond of, and tethered her on the outskirts of the city. Then he brought the stallion and led him round and round the mare, getting closer and closer in narrowing circles, and finally allowed him to mount her. Next morning just before dawn the six contenders, as was agreed, came riding their horses through the city, until they reached the spot where the mare had been tethered the previous night. At once Darius' horse started forward and neighed. At the same time, though the sky was clear, there was a flash of lightning and a clap of thunder. It was a sign from heaven, and the election of Darius was thus assured. His five rivals leapt from their horses and bowed to the ground at his feet.

Thus Oebares secured Darius's elevation. Only the esteem in which these ex-pastoralists still held the horse can really explain this agreed arrangement. Despite the Persians' having settled down as farmers, the horse had never lost its mystique for them.

Subject Sogdian farmers.

The false Bardiya was a Mede, which suggests that Persian domination still rankled. After all, Cyrus had deposed Astyages less than thirty years before. In addition, there may have been a religious dimension because Darius needed to restore some sanctuaries after the rebellion was crushed; a dispute over ritual or theology possibly inspired a number of the rebels. Whatever the uncertainty at the beginning of his reign, Darius did succeed in placing himself firmly on the Persian throne. Whether he could maintain his authority over the entire empire was at first unclear, since the unrest in Media and Persia encouraged revolts elsewhere. Even Babylon declared its independence a few days after the execution of the false Bardiya. By fighting a series of battles over the course of a year, Darius put down the most widespread rebellion of subject peoples ever experienced by the Persian Empire. The

Subject Saka pastoralists.

loyalty of the army, with which he had served in Egypt, was the critical factor in his success. It recognized that his abilities as a leader and a general matched those of Cyrus the Great.

Having dealt with the rebels, Darius was free to turn his attention to enlarging the empire in the east as well as the west, although toward the end of his reign, the Persian advance in Europe was, in 490 BC, temporarily checked at the Battle of Marathon. In India Darius was able to annex the whole of Sind and the greater part of the Punjab between 520 and 513 BC. We possess no details of this conquest except that the new province was so wealthy that its tribute added 360 talents of pure gold to the Persian treasury each year. Fortunately, we know a great deal about Darius's expansion of the empire in the west. In 513 BC the Persians, under the direct command of Darius, crossed the Bosporus into Europe on the way to campaign against the Scythians. The fleet used by the Persian king was provided by the Ionian Greeks, the commanders of the contingents being the rulers of the cities in the Persian interest. While Darius marched across Thrace and forced his way northward to the Danube, the ships sailed to the Danube estuary and formed a bridge two days' sail up the river. When the Persian army crossed, the Scythians sent their families away in their wagons with their herds; keeping only what they needed for food, they then withdrew in front of Darius, choking wells and springs and destroying forage. Nothing can be made of the Persian advance from Herodotus's account of it, but in the event the Scythians managed to avoid a pitched battle.

When two months had passed, a Scythian force arrived at the bridge and urged the Greeks to sail away and leave the Persians to their fate. Wisely perhaps, the Greeks merely dismantled the bridge temporarily at the north end, which allowed Darius to return across the Danube without difficulty. Despite the Scythians calling them slaves, the Ionians appreciated that peace at home depended upon Darius's goodwill, and so they chose the safest course of action. The Persian advance north of the Danube was not, as Herodotus would have us believe, a failure and nothing more than a chase of an elusive enemy, since the Scythians of this region are mentioned in the Persian records for many years afterward as a subject people. At the end of the Scythian campaign, two generals were left to continue the conquest of Thrace, which ended in Persian control of the northern Aegean coastline.

While Darius wintered in Sardis, he may have toyed with the idea of adding Greece to the Persian Empire as his ships had already reconnoitered the coasts of mainland Greece and Italy. But in the last decade of his reign, he was busy organizing his vast territories and constructing palaces worthy of such an empire. That is the reason for his surprise at the sudden outbreak of a revolt in Ionia in 499 BC.

THE GREEK CHALLENGE

Artaphernes, the half brother of Darius, had been left behind in Sardis as the principal governor of Asia Minor. In 507 BC the Athenians felt so threatened by their neighbors that they asked Artaphernes to arrange an alliance with Persia. On learning from their returning envoys that this would involve an acknowledgment of Persian suzerainty, they rejected the offer. To the Persians such an action smacked of rank disobedience, an attitude that the exiled Athenian tyrant Hippias craftily exploited. He persuaded Artaphernes to back his restoration in Athens. When the Athenians sent envoys to protest, Artaphernes told them to take him back if they wished to avoid trouble. This so incensed the Athenians, whose democracy had just been founded on Hippias's expulsion, that they offered assistance to the Ionians when they rose in revolt.

Hostilities began with a raid launched by the Ionians against Sardis itself. Unable to capture the city's acropolis, which Artaphernes defended in person, the Ionians burned the city below it and then retreated. Pursued by Persian forces, they suffered a defeat at Ephesus, upon which the Athenians recalled their ships, leaving the Ionians to continue the war on their own. The initial Persian counterattack was only partially effective, despite negotiations with individual cities to undermine the unity of the rebellion. The years 496 and 495 BC were relatively calm for the Ionians, but in 494 BC a second Persian offensive achieved its goal. Because the city of Miletus, situated on a long peninsula, was unassailable by land, the final outcome had to be decided at sea. Miletus had instigated the uprising and was the strongest remaining center of resistance. The Persians therefore assembled a large fleet from the Phoenicians, Egyptians,

Cilicians, and Cypriots, comprising 600 ships as opposed to the 359 ships mustered by the Ionians. The rebels sustained a severe blow when the Samians refused to fight and sailed home. Then the Lesbians followed their example, thanks to Persian persuasion. In the sea battle at Lade, fought near Miletus, the Ionians were completely defeated. Next the Persian fleet sailed up the coast to the Bosporus, burning rebel cities and seizing good-looking young people for eunuchs and concubines.

The Ionian revolt had failed. But it had been a tough and long, drawn-out struggle. That Darius reversed his policy toward democratic government afterward is evidence of the seriousness with which he regarded the conflict. He sent his son-in-law Mardonius with a fleet, and to the astonishment of the Ionians, the Persian general deposed compliant tyrants in favor of democratic rule. Already in 493 BC, Artaphernes was impressing on the Ionian cities the need to settle their differences amicably and carrying out a land survey that distributed taxation more fairly. Quite likely Darius was intent on conciliating the Ionians so as to ensure peace in western Asia Minor during Persian operations on the Greek mainland. The Persian king had not forgotten the naval support provided by the Athenians. Shooting an arrow into the air, he prayed to Ahura Mazda to let him punish them; he also instructed one of his servants to say before dinner each day, "Master, remember the Athenians."

The Persian Empire was becoming a family concern, like that of Ibn Saud in Arabia today. Darius tended to award commands to sons-in-law and nephews, but in this he may have been unlucky. Mardonius was an unfortunate choice, as the young commander lacked initiative and proved a second-rate general. Darius even relieved him of his command in 492 BC after an indifferent campaign in Thrace, although Herodotus admits that Persian authority in mainland Greece had been extended as far south as the border of Thessaly. King Alexander I of Macedon retained his throne but only as a subject king, liable for tribute and other services. The next year Darius sent royal heralds to demand "earth and water" from all the Greek city-states: this was the sign of submission to Persia. At the same time soldiers were being assembled in Cilicia aboard a fleet under the joint command of Datis, an experience Persian commander, and Artaphernes, son of the governor of Sardis. Herodotus records the orders given to them: "To reduce Athens and Eretria to slavery and bring the slaves before the king."

One reason for the Eretrians' support of the Ionians was a centuries-old alliance between Eretria and Miletus. We are told that "when the Athenians arrived with twenty ships, they were accompanied by five ships of the Eretrians, who came not as a favor to the Athenians but rather to the Milesians themselves, thereby repaying their debt; for earlier, the Milesians had been allies of the Eretrians in the war against the Chalcians when the Samians came to the aid of the Chalcians." Chalcis was the chief city on the island of Euboea, and its quarrel with Eretria concerned the ownership of a large area of land situated between the two city-states.

Datis and Artaphernes sailed, in 490 BC, across the Aegean to Naxos, which was taken without difficulty, its temples and city burned and its inhabitants enslaved. Then the fleet followed a course from island to island, past Delos to Euboea. Cities that resisted were harshly punished. Eretria now stood alone. Athens could not yet challenge the Persian fleet, and other Greek city-states stood aloof. The Persians assaulted Eretria for six days, many falling on both sides. On the seventh day the city was betrayed, and "the Persians pillaged the temples and set them on fire, avenging the burning of the sanctuaries in Sardis, as Darius decreed."

One target remained: Athens, Datis's most important assignment, as the presence of the deposed tyrant Hippias shows. Whether or not Datis actually intended to restore him to power—Hippias was by now an old man of nearly eighty—he was a valued adviser on the campaign. Datis rested his men for several days and gave the Athenians one more chance to surrender. His envoy told the Athenians that not a single Eretrian had escaped and warned them of a similar fate. The Athenians faced a difficult choice. Though they sent messengers to ask other Greeks for help, only Sparta and Plataea responded positively. The Spartans had over 5,000 hoplites, the best soldiers in Greece, but they lived over 150 miles from Athens. Plataea was closer, just across the border in Boeotia, but it was smaller. It could not be expected to provide more than 1,000 men.

For Athens resistance was, however, a real option. The largest of the Greek city-states, Athens could field 9,000 or 10,000 hoplites as well as 8,000 light-armed troops. When the Persian ultimatum came before the citizen assembly, Miltiades proposed that as soon as the Persians landed, the Athenians should march against them. To maximize Athenian numbers, he offered freedom to any slaves willing to fight. Miltiades had been chosen as one of the ten annually elected generals because of his knowledge of Persian tactics. While living in the Chersonesus, he had been a subject of Darius and had accompanied the Persian king on the Scythian campaign.

Perhaps fearing a betrayal of Athens, similar to that of Eretria, Miltiades was all for immediate action. He may have guessed that the Persians would land at Marathon, across the straits from Eretria, since sixty years before Hippias had landed on its beach with his father, the tyrant Peisistratus. Hippias must have hoped for a repeat performance as this earlier invasion had reestablished his family's tyranny. When he landed on the beach with the Persians, Hippias began to cough so violently that a loose tooth shot right out of his mouth. Frantically he searched in the sand, but to his dismay, he could not find it. The previous night Hippias had dreamed that he would return to Athens, recover his power, and die peacefully at home in old age. With a sigh he said, "This land is not ours. We shall never conquer it. The only part I will ever own in it my tooth now possesses."

Moving the Persian force from Eretria to Marathon, unloading men, horses, and supplies, and setting up camp took several days. Once lookouts reported this event, the Athenian generals had a trumpeter summon the army to assemble outside the city. There the citizen-soldiers swore to fight to the death, not to desert their officers, to follow their generals' commands, and to bury the dead on the battlefield. Then they marched north toward Marathon and, on arrival, camped at the sanctuary of Herakles, which had a spring. There the Plataeans joined them.

The plain of Marathon has changed a great deal since the battle took place. Then it was uninhabited, an expanse of grazing land for shepherds who lived on the hillsides surrounding the plain. Though the Athenians and the Plataeans had hurried to Marathon and secured the southern end of the plain, the Spartans had not yet arrived. The ten Athenian generals differed in their views about what to do next. Half thought their numbers were too few to fight, while the other half wanted a battle. Herodotus says Miltiades persuaded Callimachus, the commander in chief, to cast the deciding vote in favor of attacking the Persians. He warned his fellow generals, "If we fail to fight now, internal strife will convulse the Athenians and shake their resolve so violently that they will submit to the Persians."

Nevertheless, the battle did not happen at once because the ten generals took turns commanding each day, and Miltiades did not take the field until his own day came around. His greatest challenge was crossing the widest part of the plain before the Persian cavalry slowed or stopped his advance, leaving his men exposed to a rain of arrows. If Miltiades could reach the Persian infantry before the Persian cavalry intervened, then the engagement would take place on better terms. Herodotus says the Greek center was stretched thin, but the wings were strong. He also tells us that Miltiades led the troops at a run. The Persians were in fact amazed to see the Athenians and the Plataeans charging without the support of either archers or cavalry. Everyone—the hoplites, the light-armed troops, and the dismounted horsemen—charged together, armed with spears and swords.

Although delighted to see that the Greeks were going to fight, Datis thought there was plenty of time to deploy his forces. No Greek force had ever dared to charge a Persian army before. But the barrage of arrows his men loosed when the Greeks were in range merely provided an incentive to keep up the pace. Heavy as the impact was on the front ranks of the Persians, they soon rallied and pushed the Greek center back. The outcome was entirely different on the wings, where the Persians were routed. Instead of pursuing the fugitives, however, the Greek wings turned inward and attacked the Persians who had overcome the center. The battle swayed in the balance until it dawned on these Persians that, with their wings gone, they were caught in a trap. In desperation they fought their way to their ships, seven of which were captured by the Athenians. Though the suggestion that Datis had begun to withdraw before the battle started is unconvincing, the absence of the Persian cavalry in Herodotus's account of the battle remains a mystery. Either the horsemen were elsewhere, or they took too long to join the action, giving the Athenians their chance to come to grips with the Persian infantry.

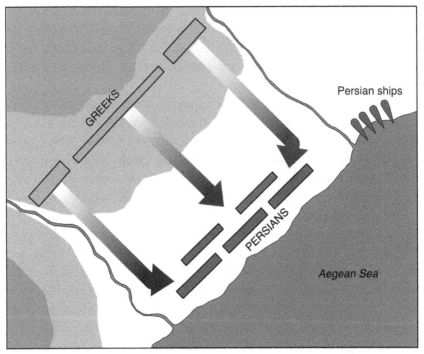

The Battle of Marathon.

Apart from the tactics adopted by Miltiades, the Persian defeat must be in part explained by a difference in equipment. The Persians may have had some hoplites in their ranks—Greeks recruited from the Aegean islands—but they relied primarily on archers and cavalry. The Athenians' thrusting spears gave them an advantage in close combat. Between seven and eight feet long, with an ash shaft about an inch in diameter, an iron spearhead, and a bronze butt spike, this weapon became rightly feared by the Persians. Hoplites also carried an iron sword.

Of all the stories told about Marathon, the most famous one relates how an Athenian ran twenty-six miles to Athens without stopping and shouted, "Rejoice, we have won!" Then he dropped dead. Though this story is probably unhistorical, though not impossible, as modern runners well know, news of the victory would have been confirmed by the army's hasty return to Athens in order to forestall Datis, who tried to get there first by

A Greek hoplite fighting a Persian soldier.

sea. He failed and returned to Asia. The Spartans arrived at Marathon too late for the battle, but they were interested to view the battlefield and learn about Persian equipment and methods of fighting before they marched home. On the Athenian side, the dead were only 192; the Persian losses were reckoned at 6,400, most of these falling in the fighting at the center. After the battle, the victors set up a trophy—a word that derives from *trope*, meaning "turn"—at the place where the enemy actually turned and ran. It consisted of captured Persian arms and was dedicated to the god to whom the victory was attributed. The Athenians later replaced this trophy with a marble column that became one of their proudest monuments.

According to Herodotus, the deity most likely to have assisted the Athenians was the goat-headed and goat-legged god Pan. He had already informed the messenger sent from Athens to request urgent military aid from Sparta that, even though the Athenians had neglected him, he was still well disposed toward them. That they did not panic at Marathon, unlike the Persians, who fled to their ships, was believed to be Pan's contribution to the overwhelming victory. When the crisis was over, a shrine was established next to the Athenian acropolis, and from that time Pan was propitiated with annual sacrifices and torch races.

To Darius the defeat meant another expedition, but after Marathon he confronted unrest within the Persian Empire, and he died in 486 BC, before he could lead an invasion of Greece himself. Along with Xerxes, his son and successor, Darius envisaged the conquest of the Greek mainland as the first stage in Europe of a holy war, part of the final conflict, foretold by the prophet Zoroaster, that would mark the end of the present world. Xerxes is supposed to have said on the eve of his own invasion, "The sun should not look down on any territory containing a city or people capable of going into battle against us." For the worshippers of Ahura Mazda, the attack on Greece constituted nothing less than a religious obligation, not unlike a Christian crusade or a Muslim jihad.

Although in military terms the Athenian repulse of Darius's expeditionary force was no more than a pinprick for the Persians, it represented an affront to their religious beliefs, with the result that Xerxes easily raised an army to avenge this defeat. Xerxes's great invasion of Greece

King Xerxes enthroned at Persepolis.

in 480 to 479 BC started a seesawing conflict between Europe and Asia that lasted into the medieval period, when both sides came to view the struggle in religious terms. The unexpected failure of Xerxes was the great event for the Greeks, but subsequent rivalry between Athens and Sparta gave the Persians a respite from a sustained counterattack, until war on the old enemy provided a useful battle cry for Alexander the Great, who in 334 BC invaded the Persian Empire.

Massive preparations for the attack on Greece were underway by 481 BC, with large numbers of troops being mustered in Asia Minor. Just how many troops there were in the Persian invading force has been a matter of much argument. Herodotus's millions are obviously an exaggeration, although at least 120,000 Persian soldiers in 480 BC crossed the Hellespont into Europe. They accomplished that crossing on two remarkable floating bridges secured by enormous ropes. Ahead of them they found abundant supplies stockpiled along the route of their march all the way to Macedon, then a subject kingdom. According to Herodotus, Xerxes conducted a review of his army at Doriscus in Thrace, next to a palace built by his father there. "The Persian king drove in his chariot past the contingents of all the various nations, asking questions, the answers to which were taken down by scribes, until he had gone from one end of the army to the other, both foot and horse."

But the invasion did not go as planned. The Persian fleet accompanying the army suffered considerable damage in a major storm and then met defeat in the narrow waters around the island of Salamis, south of the city of Athens. An abandoned Athens had already been burned by the Persians since, except for a few diehards, the Athenians had sought refuge on Salamis. Annoyed by the naval reverse, Xerxes returned to Sardis for the winter, but there is no reason to suppose anything other than that the Persian king's journey was orderly and that he had every intention of coming back to Greece in the spring, at the start of the new campaigning season.

Left behind were sufficient troops under the command of his brother-in-law Mardonius to overawe the Greek city-states. Mardonius had been given the pick of the expeditionary force and selected those men who impressed him "by their appearance or by their reputation for valor"—some 60,000 foot soldiers and perhaps 30,000 cavalry. Yet the Persian decision to retire from Attica was, in retrospect, a strategic error. So intolerable would a winter on Salamis have been for the Athenians that they could not have avoided submission to Persia or migration westward. The explanation for the Persian withdrawal to Thessaly hinged on logistics: a devastated Attica was unable to supply enough provisions for Mardonius's men.

In the event, Xerxes did not return to Greece, and the land campaign of 479 BC was the sole responsibility of Mardonius. For the deciding battle he concentrated the Persian army in Boeotia, building a strong camp close to the city of Plataea. Having got the Spartans and their Peloponnesian allies, under the command of the Spartan regent Pausanias, to join them at last, the Athenians advanced into Boeotia and camped opposite the Persians. Neither side would launch an attack on ground of the other's choice, and the two armies faced each other for a fortnight. The Persians were experimenting with the use of cavalry and discovered a weak link in the Greek line where the ground was level. Herodotus says the Megarians found themselves under such pressure there that

> they sent a messenger to the Greek generals with an urgent request for help. In response Pausanias called for volunteers and three hundred Athenians, together with a company of archers, went to their aid. During one of the cavalry charges, the horse of the Persian commander Masistius, which was ahead of the others, was shot in the side by an arrow. As it reared in agony, it pitched Masistius to the ground and he was immediately set upon by the Athenians. They seized the horse right away, but they only killed its rider after a struggle, since the armor he was wearing prevented them from dispatching him at once. Underneath his outer tunic of purple he was armed with a scaly breastplate of gold, which frustrated all attempts to pierce it. In the end, an Athenian who had carefully watched what was happening, stabbed him through the eye. Masistius fell dead. . . . Once the cavalry had returned to camp, Mardonius and the entire army went into deepest morning for Masistius. They cut their hair and the hair of the horses and baggage animals. The cry they raised was so loud and

immense that the sound of it could be heard all over Boeotia. There had died a man who ranked second only to Mardonius in the esteem of the Persians and their king. While the Persians were honouring the dead Masistius according their custom, Greek confidence was growing from the fact that they had withstood the attacks of the enemy cavalry and had driven them back. As for the corpse of Masistius, they placed it in a wagon and paraded it up and down the ranks.

This encounter with the dreaded Persian cavalry is given almost in full because it really encouraged the Greeks. Pausanias remained on the defensive, as the omens advised, but he ceased worrying about the ability of his men to withstand the cavalry probes Mardonius was making of the Greek line.

But Pausanias's attempt to readjust his dispositions one night was so badly executed that groups of troops were left isolated from each other in the morning. When reconnoitering Persian cavalry found the Spartans in an exposed position, Mardonius thought his opportunity had come, and he ordered his infantry forward to the attack. The Persians advanced within bowshot and, from their hedge of wicker shields, started to shower their arrows on the Spartan phalanx. Disregarding the intense fire, Pausanias held his ranks steady until he perceived how other enemy soldiers crowded behind them. "These men," noted Herodotus, "had no formation or discipline; each person simply ran as fast as they could. So with a great deal of shouting they surged forward in a crowd expecting to annihilate the Greeks completely." Once it was clear to Pausanias that the Persians had no room for further maneuver, he led the Spartans forward.

The fighting at first centered on the hedge of wicker shields. This breached, desperate hand-to-hand combat was the order of the day as Persian infantrymen were reduced to snapping the Spartan spears with their hands. Lacking proper armor they were no match for the finest hoplites in Greece, despite showing the courage that had made them masters of a great empire.

Fighting also occurred along the rest of the Greek line, but the impact of the Spartan phalanx proved most effective, for as soon as

Mardonius was killed, the Persians broke and fled. Because Pausanias was reluctant to take many prisoners, there was great carnage on the battlefield and in the Persian camp. How many Persians were slaughtered is uncertain, but we are aware that the Greeks lost 750 men, including 91 Spartans and 52 Athenians.

The last battle of the campaign at Mycale in Asia Minor came almost as an anticlimax. But it had far-reaching consequences. The Greeks had crossed the Aegean and raised the Ionians in revolt, thereby committing the mainlanders to the protection of the Greeks living there. From 476 BC, however, it was the Athenians who continued to confront Persia, and the Delian League they formed succeeded in reducing the last Persian possessions in the Aegean. Thucydides tells us that Sparta "no longer wanted to be burdened with the war against Persia and therefore was pleased to let the capable Athenians exercise command, at the time being on friendly relations with them." An annual contribution was fixed for league members to the satisfaction of all the city-states and the large fund that was raised paid for the expensive naval operations against the Persians.

THE TEN THOUSAND

Out of sympathy with democratic government, which was restored in Athens in 403 BC, one year after that city-state's defeat by Sparta, Xenophon went into voluntary exile and joined the Ten Thousand, Greek mercenaries recruited by Cyrus the Younger in his bid for the Persian throne. Xenophon's participation in the expedition is invaluable for the analysis of ancient warfare because he wrote a detailed account of his experience. Despite a blatant disdain for barbarians—everyone who was not a Greek—his narrative sheds light on the different approaches to warfare of the Persians and the Greeks.

In addition to numerous children born to his concubines, Darius II had several sons from his marriage to Parysatis. Most of them died prematurely, but four survived: Arses, Cyrus, Ostanes, and Oxathres. Of these four young men, Parysatis favored Cyrus, but Arses was named crown prince, in all probability because he was the oldest. Taking the name Artaxerxes II, the crown prince succeeded Darius II in 404 BC.

Cyrus's own royal ambitions had been revealed as soon as Arses was invested as crown prince, but he escaped punishment through the pleas of Parysatis. After his brother's inauguration, Cyrus returned to Sardis, the governorship of which no longer satisfied him.

"When he decided that the time had come for the march on the Persian capital," Xenophon writes, "Cyrus pretended that his purpose was to clear out the Pisidians from his province and, as though they were his objective, he assembled both local and Greek contingents of his army." On the way he collected more Greek mercenaries so that their "total number came to eleven thousand hoplites and about two thousand light-armed troops." In Cilicia, Cyrus's plans almost unraveled as the mercenaries began to suspect that they were marching against the Persian king rather than taking part in a local operation. Partially reassured that Abrocormus, the governor of Syria, was the real target, they accepted a substantial increase in pay and agreed to go further east with Cyrus.

Reaching the river Euphrates, Cyrus could no longer deceive the Greeks and admitted to their generals that he was going to march against King Artaxerxes in the direction of Babylon. He asked them to persuade their men to go with him, but Xenophon tells us,

> the soldiers were in an angry mood. They said that the generals had known this all along but kept it back, and they refused to go further unless they were given extra money. . . . The generals reported all this to Cyrus and he promised to give each man five minae of silver on their arrival in Babylon, together with full pay until he had brought the Greeks back to Ionia again. Most of the Greek army was won over by these generous terms.

Certain of his mercenaries and buoyed by a belief in divine support for his intended usurpation, Cyrus advanced quickly against his brother Artaxerxes. He had told the Greeks that he wanted them in his army because he considered them "more efficient and formidable than great numbers of natives." Further promises of reward made the mercenaries, Xenophon relates, "more enthusiastic and willing to fight on Cyrus's behalf." At the Battle of Cunaxa though, all their expectations came to nothing.

Artaxerxes II, the target of the Ten Thousand.

The engagement did not happen as Cyrus said it would; the Persian host approached in silence and not as a shouting rabble as he predicted. According to Xenophon,

> *in the early afternoon dust appeared, like a white cloud, and after some time a sort of blackness extending a long way over the plain. When they got near, then suddenly there were flashes of bronze, and the spear points and the enemy formations became visible. There were cavalry with white armor on the enemy's left. . . . Next to them were soldiers with wicker shields, and then came hoplites with wooden shields reaching to the feet. They were said to be Egyptians. Then there were more cavalry and archers. These all marched in tribes, each tribe in a dense oblong formation. In front of them, and at considerable distances apart from each, were what they called scythed chariots.*

Cyrus sent orders for the Greeks to attack the enemy's center because that was where the Persian king was. "If we win there," he said, "the whole thing is over." The advance of the Greek phalanx terrified the Persians who, "even before they were in range of the arrows, wavered and ran away. . . . The chariots rushed about, some going through the enemy's own ranks, though some, abandoned by their drivers, did go through the Greeks." Excited by the effectiveness of the mercenaries, Cyrus threw caution to the wind and charged the screen of soldiers protecting Artaxerxes. This proved a mistake. While striking the Persian king a blow on his breastplate, Cyrus received a fatal blow under his eye.

"This was the end of Cyrus," wrote Xenophon. The head and right hand of the defeated rebel were cut off. Cyrus's death came as a total surprise to the victorious Greeks, but they steadfastly refused to surrender their arms to the Persian king. After half of their generals were treacherously detained at a parley, the mercenaries elected new generals, Xenophon among them. The Persians clearly had no understanding of Greek ideas about leadership. Just as Cyrus thought that Artaxerxes's death would be enough to secure a decisive victory at Cunaxa, so the Persians believed that the leaderless Greeks would be at their mercy. Alexander the Great understood this lesson exactly. Before the Battle of Issus, in 333 BC, Alexander even mentioned the Ten Thousand to his troops and disconcerted the Persian host facing them by personally seeking out the Persian king. When in panic Darius III fled, his soldiers were not far behind him. This reliance on a single leader was the Achilles' heel of Persian arms.

Xenophon devotes the rest of his account of the Ten Thousand to their hazardous march northward to the Black Sea, where they took ship for home. What stands out most from Cyrus's recruitment of the Greeks is that soldiering had become a profession. The very existence of so many men who fought for a living was a sign of the times. The Peloponnesian War of 431 to 404 BC had stretched citizen-armies to the limit, so that even the leading city-states of Greece found mercenaries useful. They were predecessors of the Ten Thousand, the first body of mercenaries large enough to engage the forces of any single city-state.

IMPERIAL DECLINE

Though the history of the Achaemenid dynasty following the death of Xerxes in 424 BC was a tale of decline, it nevertheless took over a century to unfold. The military failure of Sparta in Asia Minor led to the peace of 387 BC and the acceptance of Persian rule over the Greeks living there.

At the time the Persian Empire still appeared secure, even though its hold over several provinces was in fact tenuous. Egypt had just revolted again shortly after the expedition of the Ten Thousand. In 374 or 373 BC an attempt to reconquer Egypt failed, but Artaxerxes IV at least had the satisfaction of restoring his authority on the island of Cyprus, where Evagoras had defied the Persians for a decade. King Evagoras of Salamis, however, did not enjoy the reasonable peace terms for long; in 374 BC he was assassinated in a palace intrigue.

The 360s and, to a lesser extent, the 350s BC were marked by the revolts of provincial governors. The western provinces seem to have risen together, and along with Phoenicia and Egypt, they united in an alliance against the Persian king. But their inability to agree on a common strategy allowed Artaxerxes to subdue them one by one, for he had the virtue of perseverance. He first overcame the Phoenicians, then defeated the western governors, and finally invaded Egypt with the aid of a large force of Greek mercenaries. Taking city after city, Artaxerxes drove the rebellious pharaoh Nektanebo II into Nubia with what treasure he could carry. By 343 BC, Egypt was back in the Persian Empire.

Not unaware of King Philip of Macedon's ambitions in Asia, Artaxerxes was glad to make an alliance with him. Like Stalin in 1939 with Hitler, the Persian king must have hoped that the nonaggression pact would last. But news of the Macedonian victory at Chaeronea in 338 BC, which made Philip master of Greece, should have signaled the likelihood of war. Assassinated later the same year, Artaxerxes was succeeded by Darius III, who was initially a puppet of his father's assassin. Even though he soon asserted his independence, Darius had little time to rule before Alexander the Great invaded the Persian Empire. Three Macedonian victories culminated in Alexander's capture of the Persian capital at Persepolis in 330 BC.

During this period of Persian decline, the situation in Greece was equally disturbed. Greek thinkers who concerned themselves not with the politics of one city-state but with the Greek world as a whole saw anarchy and disaster everywhere. In the 380s, the Athenian Isocrates observed,

Pirates command the seas and mercenaries occupy our cities. Instead
of waging war in defence of their territory the citizens fight within

their own walls against one another. Inhabitants of the cities live in greater despair than those condemned to exile, so frequent are the revolutionary changes. Some of our cities are ruled by barbarian masters. . . . [We are afflicted] by every kind of disaster . . . which we have brought upon ourselves by creating wars and revolutions, so that some are executed without respect for law, others with their wives and children are outcasts wandering foreign lands, and many enlisting as mercenaries because they lack the means of life are killed in the service of their enemies against their friends.

As the strongest city-states in Greece—Athens, Sparta, and Thebes—had all in turn failed to achieve acceptance as leaders or bring about political stability, Isocrates believed a new form of leadership was urgently required. The philosopher Plato agreed with Isocrates and tried to find it in enlightened tyranny. His abortive effort to direct Dionysius I, the tyrant of Syracuse, along these lines should have been sufficient to demonstrate the futility of such an idea.

Plato went to Syracuse in the 380s BC and criticized the way the tyrant was running the city-state. Dionysius became irate, as tyrants tend to do. He was tempted to execute Plato on the spot but settled for having him sold into slavery instead. The philosopher was finally ransomed and able to return to Athens, but, still shortsighted as regards the nature of tyranny, he returned to Syracuse to meet the tyrant's son and successor. Once again his mission ended in failure.

Isocrates finally came to appreciate that the answer might be found in kingship: except for the Spartans, the Greeks had largely discarded this archaic institution. It is not a little ironic that, from democratic Athens, a ninety-two-year-old Isocrates, in 344 BC, rebuked King Philip of Macedon for engaging in "inglorious, difficult wars" in the Balkans when he ought to be overthrowing Persia. The expedition of the Ten Thousand, in Isocrates's view, had exposed the truth about the Persian Empire. The mighty structure was crumbling: A determined Greek attack would send it crashing down in ruins. Once the Macedonians had forcibly united the Greeks, they were free to deal with the Persians, a task that fell to Philip's son Alexander, whose remarkable success entitled him to be called "the Great."

CHAPTER FIVE

The Macedonian Supremacy

THE LEAGUE THAT ATHENS FORMED IMMEDIATELY AFTER THE PERSIAN invasion of the Greek mainland in 480 to 479 BC cleared the Aegean and western Asia Minor of the Persians. From Persia's point of view, the situation was not entirely unwelcome when Spartan fears of Athenian preeminence became the focus of politics in Greece. Even though the growth of Athens's power did not affect the Spartans directly, it did affect some of their allies, and in 431 BC Sparta's invasion of Attica started the Peloponnesian War. The struggle ended with the defeat of Athens in 404 BC once Sparta gained the upper hand at sea, long an Athenian preserve. Persian gold had subsidized the Peloponnesian fleet in the mistaken belief that this policy would eliminate Greek interference along the western edge of the Persian Empire. It came as a shock, therefore, when Spartan king Agesilaus led an expedition to Asia Minor. Only Agesilaus's failure to make any permanent headway led to his recall in 394 BC and Sparta's acceptance of Persian rule over its Greek city-states. As the Greeks in mainland Greece were already growing tired of the Spartan hegemony, Agesilaus was soon involved in armed disputes there too.

In 387 BC the Spartans negotiated a settlement to which the Persian king, Artaxerxes II, only agreed on condition that the Greeks living in Asia Minor accept his authority. All the other Greek states were to remain autonomous. Although many were far from satisfied with this formula for peace, they were weary of fighting by then, and the prospect of war against the combined might of Sparta and Persia drove them to endorse the terms of the settlement. An unsettling aspect of the agreement was caused by Agesilaus's stubborn refusal to admit the claim of Theban general Epaminondas to speak on behalf of all Boeotia, a confederacy of states that acknowledged the leadership of Thebes. That a humbled Thebes had to agree to this demand only served to increase anti-Spartan sentiment. Alarmed by the growing hostility and opposed to any revival of the Boeotian confederacy, Agesilaus ordered the seizure of the Cadmeia, the Theban acropolis. The scene was set for the final reckoning between Sparta and Thebes on the battlefield at Leuctra in 371 BC.

Despite a serious manpower crisis, Sparta remained unbeaten in battle prior to the engagement at Leuctra. Its citizenry had shrunk in the century following the Persian invasion of Greece from 8,000 to under 2,000. Yet the professionalism of the Spartans disguised this weakness from their enemies until Epaminondas and his fellow general Pelopidas discovered a way to overcome superior Spartan discipline.

THEBES AND HOPLITE TACTICS

The ability of the Spartans to perform so well on the battlefield derived from their concentration on warfare to the exclusion of all else. Fear of the helots, a large population of enslaved cultivators resulting from the conquest of neighboring Messenia, was a constant reminder of the need to hone combat skills. Likewise, the defeat by the Argives in 669 BC acted as a wake-up call: this unexpected reverse at Hysiai threatened Sparta's position in the Peloponnese and encouraged a degree of social conformity unmatched among other Greeks. Loyalty and perseverance became the duty of all Spartan citizens, whose lives were henceforth dedicated to full-time military training. When at Thermopylae in 480 BC a contingent of three hundred Spartans refused to give ground to the Persian host arrayed against them, the Persian king Xerxes was utterly baffled. Herodotus tells us that Xerxes could not understand how the few Spartans holding the narrow pass would rather die than surrender or retreat. After the Spartans were finally slain, Xerxes expressed his admiration of their courage and hoped there would not be many more such men to oppose his army.

Spartan hoplites drilled in close order. The files of their phalanx were close enough together for the shields of each rank to form a continuous line, with each man protected by his right-hand neighbor's shield as well as by his own. Evidently intended to facilitate a massed attack, this compact infantry formation required a steady nerve and complete confidence in the steadfastness of one's fellow hoplites. Panic was the usual reason for the collapse of a phalanx when, for whatever reason, the rear ranks turned and fled. Anxiety could have spread backward from the front ranks where men first noticed the strength of the enemy force. The conventions surrounding hoplite engagements would have heightened the tension, since it was normal practice for both sides to be drawn up face-to-face, eyeing each other for minutes, sometimes hours, before combat commenced.

Hence the psychological advantage enjoyed by the Spartans: their scarlet cloaks and long hair always intimidated opponents. Cleon, commander of the Athenians in their defeat at Amphipolis in 422 BC, took off as soon as the Spartans approached, but this did not save his life. Xenophon relates how conscious Agesilaus was of Spartan prestige to the extent of ensuring that his men looked like "a single mass of bronze and scarlet." Plutarch adds, "It was an awesome and terrifying sight as the Spartans marched in step to the sound of pipes, leaving no gap in their line and with no uncertainty in their hearts, but calmly and cheerfully advancing into danger."

Against this formidable foe, the Thebans had to devise new tactics, a task that fell to Epaminondas and Pelopidas. These two annually elected generals were already experimenting with novel methods of fighting well before the Spartans confronted them at Leuctra. It might be argued that Agesilaus, by repeatedly taking the offensive against the Thebans, compelled them to become better-trained soldiers. During the Spartan occupation of the Cadmeia, Epaminondas had encouraged his fellow citizens to wrestle with the garrison in order to learn for themselves that they were not inferior man to man. Later he decided that "hoplites must train their bodies not just like athletes but also as soldiers. He made war on fat men, and chased one of them away from the army, saying that three or four shields would hardly cover his belly." While Epaminondas was improving the quality of the Theban infantry, Pelopidas turned the Sacred Band into shock troops. Its three hundred members comprised "lovers and their beloved." Of this close-knit group of elite soldiers, the greatest feats of arms were demanded, in particular at a critical juncture of hoplite battle. Later King Philip II of Macedon commended their bravery when he viewed their corpses after the Battle of Chaeronea in 338 BC. "A curse," he exclaimed, "on those who imagine that these men ever did or suffered anything shameful." That the Macedonian king was able to bring Theban power to an end had much to do with what he had observed as a young hostage in Thebes.

The expulsion of the Spartan garrison stationed on the Cadmeia was a result of a conspiracy between exiled Thebans and anti-Spartan politicians in Thebes itself. Of the conspirators Pelopidas is the best known, thanks to Plutarch's biography. One of the youngest exiles, he took the initiative in pressing his fellow countrymen to liberate their city. Pelopidas came to the fore during his exile in Athens, where urgent requests from the Spartans not to harbor such exiles were ignored because Thebes had been instrumental in restoring Athenian democracy following defeat in the Peloponnesian War. Offering political asylum was looked upon as a duty by Greek city-states. Having disposed of those who welcomed Spartan domination, Plutarch informs us, the conspirators called upon the citizens of Thebes to arm themselves with spears and swords taken from shops close to the Cadmeia. Had the Spartan commander of the garrison acted resolutely, the uprising would have failed, but he hesitated, probably in the hope of reinforcements arriving to overawe the Thebans. In the event, Epaminondas expelled the garrison before the second Spartan king, Cleombrotus, led an army into Boeotia. Even though no pitched battle took place, Plutarch records, the frequent "skirmishes . . . gave the Thebans invaluable training and practice and had the effect of raising their spirits, strengthening their bodies through hardship and adding to their experience and courage."

Cleombrotus carried out the invasion with such skill, however, that the Thebans could not put off battle for long. After the Spartan defeat at

The goddess Artemis with Apollo.

Leuctra, there were tales of divine warnings to the Spartans. Wolves had devoured the sacrificial animals accompanying their army, and the very battlefield itself was said to be cursed on account of a previous outrage committed against some maidens encountered there. Animal sacrifice was a normal procedure during a campaign. Greek armies marched with flocks of sheep and goats so that they could perform sacrifices before crossing a border, choosing a line of advance, building an encampment, or investing a city. Prior to an engagement, a goat was sacrificed to the goddess Artemis, the twin sister of the oracular god Apollo, in front of the battle line. A tradition recorded in the third century BC claimed this was once a human sacrifice. And it happens that vestiges of human sacrifice could still be found in Artemis's worship; her female devotees drew blood from a slight cut on the throat of a male victim. Soldiers were, of course, far more courageous when they believed they were facing danger with the backing of the gods. Favorable omens and public sacrifice united Greek armies in a way that no amount of oratory could ever match.

Despite any omens unfavorable to the Spartans, the prospects for the Thebans looked bleak. Because they were outnumbered by the Spartans and their allies, only the resolution of Epaminondas kept them together. Though he was not an elected general then, Pelopidas's support for Epaminondas helped to win the day, since he was in command of the Sacred Band. Explaining his tactics, Epaminondas caught a snake and likened it to the enemy. Then he crushed its head, which he said represented the Spartans. The Thebans immediately understood that they had only to beat the Spartans in order to sweep the field.

Today Leuctra seems admirably suited to pitched battle between hoplite armies, not least because a level plain extends for over a mile between hills that bound it on the north and south. Cleombrotus arrived first and set up camp in the steep foothills to the south of the plain, while the Thebans "encamped on the opposite ridge, leaving no great distance between them." The leaders on both sides, according to Xenophon, had good reason to risk battle. The Spartan king was under suspicion of treacherously favoring the Thebans and wanted to clear his name. On the Theban side, a refusal to fight would have undermined the restored Boeotian confederacy.

Cleombrotus's army consisted of 10,000 hoplites and 1,000 cavalry. The latter were of indifferent quality, but 700 Spartans formed the backbone of the infantry. The Thebans could only muster 7,000 hoplites and 600 cavalry.

We possess several ancient accounts of the battle. Only Xenophon's is contemporary, but it is unhelpful as it provides not a narrative but a list of reasons for the Spartan reverse. He blithely remarks, "as for the battle, everything went wrong for the Spartans, but for their opponents everything succeeded, even by chance." Plutarch says that Epaminondas, fearing some of his Boeotian allies might desert, had proclaimed that any who wished might go home. Men from nearby Thespiae left in a body. Xenophon's underestimation of the generalship of Epaminondas and his ignorance of the initiative shown by Pelopidas explain his misunderstanding of the action, for Epaminondas massed his Theban hoplites fifty shields deep opposite the Spartans, whose own depth was no more than twelve. When Cleombrotus appreciated this unusual arrangement, he endeavored to extend his line in order to encircle the Thebans and attack their flank.

"At this point," Plutarch relates, "Pelopidas charged out in front, leading the Sacred Band at the double, and anticipated Cleombrotus, before he could fully extend his wing or bring it back to the original position and close up the formation. Pelopidas struck the Spartans when they were not properly drawn up, but falling foul of one another; and yet the Spartans were such superb soldiers, and so well drilled, that when their ranks were disordered each one formed up again and fought on regardless." The impact of Epaminondas's hoplites delivered the knockout blow, but the charge of the Sacred Band, initially hidden behind the Theban phalanx, proved decisive. A new flexibility had been introduced into pitched battles.

From their encampment, the day after the battle, the Spartans sent a herald to request a burial truce. The sending of a herald was an admission of defeat. Epaminondas insisted, however, that Sparta's allies should collect their dead first so that the number of Spartan's killed would be apparent to all. As it turned out, the allies had scarcely any dead, while four hundred Spartans had lost their lives, including King Cleombrotus. They were buried on the battlefield. The Thebans may have lost as many as three hundred hoplites, but their victory was undeniable. The Battle of Leuctra broke not only the military power of Sparta but also the oligarchic order it supported. The aristocrats in the Peloponnese who had been prepared tolerate Spartan control in order to avoid popular rule were either massacred or exiled.

Epaminondas and Pelopidas used Theban power to liberate Messenia in the south and oppose Thessalian tyrants in the north. But they did not succeed in establishing a lasting hegemony. Real power, real energy had shifted to other states like Macedon, and while the Greek cities continued to squabble within and among themselves, the Macedonian king Philip and his son Alexander thrust into Greece, ushering in the twilight of democratic government.

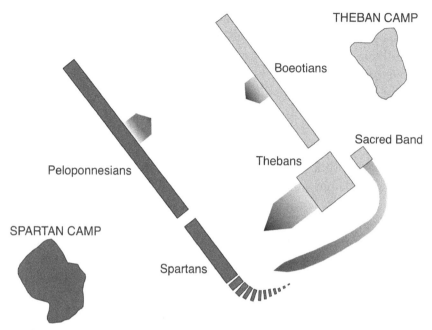

The Battle of Leuctra.

FURTHER MACEDONIAN INNOVATION

The rise of the Macedonians was not swift despite the unprecedented success of Philip and Alexander making it seem so in retrospect. A heterogeneous kingdom, Macedon forged its unity through military service: the electoral body was the army, and even though it always elected a member of the Temenid royal house as king or regent, its view could never be ignored. Feuds led to the extinction of several branches of the royal family with the result that the succession was sometimes not straightforward. Philip's own reign may have started out as a regency, but he was more than likely elected king in 359 BC at a moment of crisis. The threat of an Illyrian invasion must have focused the soldiers' minds, since 4,000 of them had just been killed by the Illyrians.

At once Philip began a long period of training and innovation designed to raise the Macedonian army to the military standard he had witnessed in Thebes. During his three years as a hostage there, he came to appreciate the training methods and tactical ideas of the two leading generals in Greece, Epaminondas and Pelopidas. The latter had taken Philip as a hostage along with the sons of aristocrats: their safety depended upon Macedon keeping out of Thessaly. Unfortunately, no ancient life of Philip has survived, and we have to rely on comments from a number of historians. Some wondered what the future Macedonian king would have become if he had been a hostage in Athens instead of Thebes, as a pupil of Plato and an observer of a sophisticated democracy at work. Plutarch sensibly sticks to the facts: Philip learned a lot from Epaminondas—a lot about war.

And of course, as an innovator Philip had an advantage as a constitutional monarch, after getting rid of three half brothers and two cousins. He possessed continuous and legitimate powers unparalleled in a democracy. He earned the devotion of his soldiers with his audacity in action and rewarded his officers with estates and his bravest men with tax exemptions. In 370 BC Epaminondas, Pelopidas, and other elected generals stood trial for retaining their offices beyond the expiration of their terms by attacking Sparta over the previous winter. In his defense Epaminondas pointed out that he and his colleagues had broken the law because it was not meant to apply in the special circumstances in which they found themselves after the Battle of Leuctra. But he admitted his guilt and said that he was prepared to accept the death sentence, provided a record of his deeds was inscribed on his tombstone: "That the Greeks should know he had compelled the unwilling Thebans to ravage Sparta, which had been free for five hundred years, that he had caused Messenia to be resettled after two hundred and thirty years, that he had gathered the Arcadians together and organized a league, and that he had given the Greeks their autonomy." On hearing this request, the case was thrown out amid laughter.

Yet another trial, instigated again by his enemies, failed to convict Epaminondas, but it did prevent him from being elected to a generalship in 368 BC. A weakness of the city-state was its bitter political rivalry, which often descended to the level of physical violence. A frustrated Xenophon, who spent his long exile from Athens in the Peloponnese, declared that after Leuctra "there was still greater indecisiveness and confusion than before in Greece." Philip would cleverly exploit this division, but first he had to strengthen his own kingdom. That he totally changed the face of his own times and provided Alexander with the means to dominate his in turn is testimony to his far-reaching achievement. By creating the first great Macedonian army, Philip enabled Macedon to subdue the Balkans, next Greece and the Aegean, and finally the Middle East, Persia, and northwestern India.

The training program that Philip introduced was particularly rigorous and designed to promote operational efficiency. We are told how, having put the military organization on a sounder footing and equipped the men with appropriate weapons of war, he held unremitting exercises in full kit as well as as well as competitive exercises. Philip also discontinued the age-old practice of allowing soldiers to take along attendants, wives, and girlfriends when they went on campaign. Under the old system, an army of 30,000 men would have dragged behind it an almost equal number of attendants, not to mention women. By forbidding the presence of all these people, Philip not only reduced the logistical burden of his army but, even more, increased its rate of march.

The decision to make maximum use of the carrying capacity of Macedonian soldiers also lessened the logistical burden. A load of between sixty and seventy pounds on each soldier's back compares favorably with the seventy-pound average carried by British soldiers at Waterloo. By requiring his men to carry their own equipment and food, Alexander the Great created the fastest army the world had ever seen. It could routinely advance by thirteen or fourteen miles a day. In times of triumph, ceremonial parades in full battle order reinforced this strict discipline and sense of corporate unity. Alexander followed this policy of Philip with great enthusiasm:

A helmet recommended by Xenophon for horsemen.

from the start of his reign, he conducted regular maneuvers. And when, after the defeat of Persia, Alexander recruited 30,000 Persian youths to augment his forces, they were subjected to the same training regime.

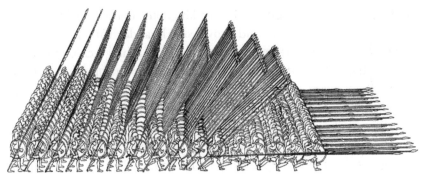

The Macedonian phalanx, the great tactical innovation of Philip.

A key weapon invented by Philip was the pike, or *sarissa*, twelve or fifteen feet long. Its iron point was so counterweighted by an iron butt that the shaft could be held close to the butt. Both hands, however, were needed to wield it. Pikemen fought in a phalanx, the depth of which was never less than ten men. Their advantage in battle was that they could present three or four pike points ahead of the front rank, while opposing hoplites' spears remained out of range. Philip had noticed the quality of Theban cavalry, and so he equipped his own horsemen with a counterweighted lance some nine feet long, which could strike an enemy horseman before he came into range with a seven-foot spear.

Such innovation involved constant experimentation and practice. Luckily for Philip, royal lands were able to furnish the best wood for the shafts of the pike and lance, while a monopoly of the crown over iron and copper production supplied the rest. Equally concerned with the capture of fortified Greek cities, he also built up a siege train. This was something new in Greek warfare, in which sieges were rare and lengthy. The catapult was developed to hurl large stones in order to achieve quicker results. It stood Alexander in good stead when confronted by stubborn defenders, as at Tyre in 332 BC. But whereas Philip tended to lead the infantry, Alexander rode with the cavalry: both knew that their conspicuous bravery was necessary to inspire their armies. Philip was badly wounded four times; his life was once saved on the battlefield by Alexander.

According to Philip, only one of his officers rated as a general, the aristocrat Parmenio. He accompanied Alexander to Asia as second in command of the army and took part in all the battles that overthrew the Persian Empire. Left behind at Ecbatana to guard the Persian treasury and the lengthening communications as the Macedonian army moved further east, Parmenio was executed after the treason of his son Philotas, who had failed to report a plot to kill Alexander. Though no accomplice himself, the distinguished soldier was seen as a threat by the young king, whose ideas for the government of Asia Parmenio thoroughly disliked. Yet, like Napoleon's marshals, Alexander inherited from Philip an impressive group of commanders, some of whom would establish their own kingdoms after Alexander's early death in 323 BC.

Notwithstanding the combat risks a Macedonian king ran, Philip owed his success as much to his diplomacy as to his bravery on the battlefield. His archcritic Demosthenes, who spent all his energy trying to keep the ear of the Athenian assembly, could only envy the unassailable position of Philip, who was "master of all things public and secret; general, ruler and treasurer all in one." It was a conclusion reached by others, who thought the success of the Macedonian monarch derived as much from his skill as a diplomat as from his leadership in war. That Philip possessed adequate funds to subvert his opponents through bribery made him notorious. Yet his strategy always remained the same: the attainment of Macedonian supremacy.

This was achieved in 338 BC at Chaeronea when the Macedonians routed an army of Thebans and Athenians despite the much better position occupied by their hoplites. Realizing that his opponents were intent on remaining on the defensive, Philip took the initiative so as to disrupt their line of battle by means of a tactical withdrawal. Apparently

Philip, with the infantry formation facing the Athenians, gave way and retired. The Athenian commander, Stratocles, shouted out, "We must not stop pressing the enemy until we drive them back to Macedon," and he did not slacken the pursuit. But Philip was retiring step by step, keeping his phalanx intact and protected with the points of its pikes. Remarking how the Athenians had no idea how to win, he gained a slight rise, exhorted his troops, and then reversed direction and powerfully charged his opponents.

This maneuver was not in itself enough to decide the outcome of battle, but it prompted the Thebans to stay linked up with the Athenians, which opened a dangerous gap in their own line: into this Alexander charged at the head of the Macedonian cavalry. His horsemen then swung round and attacked the rear of the Theban phalanx, while the troops under Philip's command were dealing with the disordered Athenians. A thousand Athenians fell, and another 2,000 were taken prisoner. Theban losses were even greater, including the total destruction of the Sacred Band.

Heavy infantry was always the mainstay of Greek military tactics, since the tightly packed phalanx made it impervious to cavalry attack. The gap into which Alexander charged at Chaeronea was fortuitous. But later in his campaigns against the Persians, he found a novel way of deploying the Macedonian phalanx. It was used to fix the center of the enemy battle line, while Alexander himself led his cavalry, armed with thrusting spears, as the primary attacking arm of the army. Except at the Battle of Gaugamela, the final defeat of the Persians, Alexander the Great always struck the enemy with his cavalry on the flank. The

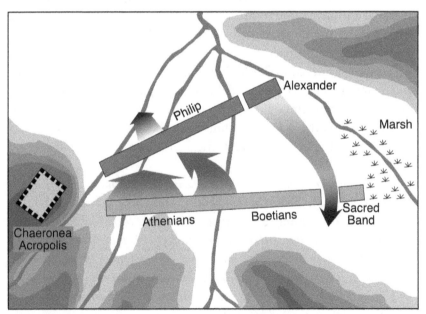

The Battle of Chaeronea.

Alexander the Great.

intention was to break the enemy flank and then envelope the main body as the Macedonian phalanx engaged its front, thereby acting as an anvil against which the cavalry could hammer the enemy.

Although the impetuosity of the Athenians contributed to the defeat at Chaeronea, it was really the preparations that Philip had undertaken to improve the quality of the Macedonian army that paid dividends. He had defeated the Greek city-states, and there was no likelihood of their raising another army. As a result, Philip did not bother to follow up the victory with further military operations; he was content to wait for the Greeks to sue for peace. And the governments of each city-state soon came to terms with him, Athens enjoying the most lenient ones. Philip's treaty with Athens provided for "friendship and alliance," leaving its democracy unchanged and Demosthenes untouched. The Macedonian king just wanted to be personally acknowledged as the leader of Greece. He was. With the notable exception of Sparta, a league of all the Greek city-states, whose purpose was to wage war against Persia, elected Philip as its head. Philip would have led the expedition eastward had he not been assassinated in Macedon. Instead, a young Alexander commanded the army that in 334 BC invaded the Persian Empire. A series of campaigns spread over more than a decade gave Alexander control of territories stretching as far east as India.

ALEXANDER THE GREAT'S CONQUEST OF PERSIA

Ever since Alexander's amazing exploits, his name has been synonymous with military glory. After his conquest of Gaul and subsequent triumph in the Roman civil war, Julius Caesar still felt the need to emulate Alexander by conducting a campaign of his own in the ancient Middle East. As it had for Philip, assassination thwarted this ambition.

From the beginning of his campaigns in Asia, however, Alexander believed he had a mission to fulfil, which worried some of his Macedonian and Greek followers. As Plutarch put it, "Alexander considered that he had come from the gods to be a governor and reconciler to the world. Using force of arms when he could not bring men together by reason, he employed everything to the same end, mixing lives, manners and customs, as it were, in a loving cup."

Possibly his followers most resented the court ceremonial that Alexander adopted, since it involved the Persian custom of prostration, which was felt to smack of divinity. But they were incorrect in thinking that the Persians ever regarded their kings as gods. Quite the contrary, kingship was bestowed upon rulers by Ahura Mazda, a cosmic deity whose raiment was the sky. Though Alexander could have practiced one form of ceremonial for Europeans and another for Asians, his insistence on the new one shows the extent to which his mind was set on treating all his subjects alike. His commitment to establishing a multiethnic kingdom had everything to do with a sense of destiny, as Alexander truly believed that he was personally empowered to reshape the ancient world.

Where, then, did he find confirmation of his entitlement to honors greater than should be paid to any man? The short answer was Egypt. In early 331 BC, he crossed the Libyan desert to the oasis of Siwah in order to consult the oracle of Ammon, an Egyptian god equated by the Greeks with their own chief deity, Zeus. He wanted to learn the truth about his supposed descent from this god. On the way to Siwah, two miracles occurred: a sudden downpour quenched Alexander's thirst, and two crows guided him when he was lost. That the chief priest at Siwah greeted Alexander as the son of Zeus seemed to satisfy his deepest desire. As a conqueror of Egypt, however, he would have been regarded as a divine incarnation, and probably Alexander went through an abbreviated pharaonic coronation before setting out for Siwah.

Yet, even Alexander's detractors were stunned by the sheer extent of his conquests. As one remarked, "There will be nothing left for him except to become a god." At Athens a lively debate took place when the assembly heard of Alexander's wish to be recognized as the thirteenth Olympian deity. Even Demosthenes, a convinced opponent of deification on principle, bent with the wind. "All right," he said, "make him the son of Zeus and of Poseidon too, if that is what he wishes." And this was exactly what Alexander desired. He had already begun minting his own coins depicting himself with divine symbols, in particular the horns worn by a Mesopotamian deity. But Alexander never lost his sense of proportion, as he firmly rejected the idea of carving his likeness Mount Rushmore–style on a cliff in Macedon.

Alexander's fame always rested on his unmatched performance in war. An enthusiasm for armed combat sprang in part from his love of Homer. He was indeed so much under the spell of this epic poet that he compared the crossing of his army from Europe to Asia with the Trojan War. On the European shore he sacrificed to Protesilaus and prayed for a happier landing than that hero's. *The Iliad* narrates that Protesilaus "was the first of the Greeks to leap ashore, but fell victim to the Trojan foe, leaving behind his wife Phylae with lacerated cheeks and a house half-built." Again the first of his own expedition to reach the Asian shore, Alexander drove his spear into the ground, marking it as a spear-won gift of the gods. It was a prophetic claim, for he intended to do much more than subdue the Persians.

After a pilgrimage to the ruins of Troy, Alexander rejoined his army and struck inland. Keen to secure a victory in order to obtain supplies, the young king met the Persians at the river Granicus, where they had taken up a strong defensive position, along with 20,000 Greek mercenaries. Alexander acted with characteristic speed and confidence, attacking without waiting for all his men to arrive. His commanders urged caution, but he told them he would be ashamed "if after crossing the Hellespont, this little stream stops us now." Again the pikes of the Macedonian phalanx gave Alexander the edge, while he, at a critical moment in the engagement, charged at the head of the cavalry. In the ferocious hand-to-hand fighting, the Macedonians gradually pushed the Persians back until they faltered and then fled, leaving the Greek mercenaries alone on the battlefield. Alexander refused to let them surrender, for he knew that they would fight once more for the Persians. So they were slaughtered, with the exception of 2,000 captives who went to Macedon to labor in chains. The punishment was justified by their treachery: he said, "Being Greek they had fought against Greece in violation of the decisions of the Greeks."

Having undermined the morale of the Persian governors of Asia Minor, Alexander was able to consolidate his position before marching into the heart of the Persian Empire. Starting with the victory at the Granicus, Alexander overthrew Persia in three pitched battles. The second one took place in 333 BC at Issus, in present-day southeastern Turkey. In comparison with the previous engagement, the scale of Issus was immense, as King Darius III assembled an enormous army, estimated at 600,000 strong. Against this formidable host Alexander could deploy less than 40,000 men, a circumstance that made tactics all important. He knew, however, that if his plan to conquer Persia was to succeed, Darius's army had to be soundly defeated, and the sooner the better. His own troops had marched for over seventy miles in two days, and at the end a violent rainstorm flattened their tents. But the confidence of Alexander was infectious, and when he addressed the troops before the battle, a reference to the Ten Thousand raised a tremendous cheer. Like Napoleon, he always ensured that his army got a good hot meal prior to engaging the enemy.

The battle order of the Persians was a mixture of mercenaries and local levies. At the center, facing the Macedonian phalanx, were stationed 30,000 Greek mercenaries, supported by some 60,000 Persian foot soldiers. Behind this line "a great number of light and heavy infantry was drawn up according to the countries of their origin" but "in greater depth than was likely to prove of much service." Because the ground over which the two armies were to fight was restricted, Alexander was pleased to discover that the two battle lines were arrayed in almost equal lengths on a three-mile front. A small river separated them without appearing to present much of an obstacle.

After a final inspection, Alexander slowly advanced in close formation until his men came within range of the Persian archers. When these loosed off "such a shower of arrows that they collided with one another in the air," the Macedonian cavalry charged over the river and dispersed the archers. Even though this encouraged Alexander, any hope of a swift victory was dashed when he noticed how the Macedonian phalanx struggled to stay in order. Negotiating the banks of the river had badly disordered this formation, which the Greek mercenaries quickly exploited to break into its ranks. Desperate fighting ensued, and relief only came after Alexander assaulted with his cavalry the flank and rear of the mercenaries. Attempts by the Persians to thwart this move were repulsed, although their own cavalry charged time and again. Seeing the sterling action of the Macedonian horsemen, the pikemen rallied and salvaged their reputation as the invincibles.

The last blow of the battle was delivered by a headlong charge toward Darius himself. Forcing his way close to the Persian king, Alexander caused Darius to turn his chariot around and flee. This precipitated a

Darius III fleeing the Battle of Issus in 333 BC.

rout, with the result that Persian losses in both cavalry and infantry were severe. Alexander pursued Darius without catching him, despite taking possession of his chariot, shield, cloak, and bow. The pursuit would have been more rapid had not Alexander waited until he was certain that the Macedonian phalanx would beat the Greek mercenaries.

"Alexander had been hurt by a sword-thrust in the thigh," according to one historian, "but this did not stop him from visiting the wounded on the day of the battle, when he gave as well a splendid military funeral to the dead in the presence of the whole army in full battle dress." Of the Macedonians 150 horsemen and 300 foot soldiers fell, while 4,500 were wounded. Alexander also extended his sympathy to Darius's mother, wife, and children, who had been taken prisoner in the Persian camp. He informed them of Darius's escape and promised that they could "retain all the marks, ceremonies, and titles of royalty, as he had not fought Darius with any personal bitterness, but for the sovereignty of Asia."

Whereas some saw the hand of providence in the narrowness of the battlefield at Issus, Plutarch dwells on the folly of Darius for giving battle there. Had the Persian king remained on a wider plain, his superior numbers would have told. Apparently Darius was worried that Alexander might slip away without a fight. Plutarch is less than sympathetic in his life of Alexander: underlying his narrative is the notion that monarchical power corrupts. At the Granicus, Alexander's charge across the river is described as "the act of a madman rather than a prudent commander." Plutarch's account of Issus is hardly more than a brief mention of how the Macedonian king "put the barbarians to flight."

To continue eastward and prevent Darius raising another army must have been a tempting prospect after the victory at Issus, but Alexander persisted in his strategy of gaining control of the Mediterranean coast and eliminating Persian power at sea. This could only be achieved by the surrender of Phoenicia, whose offshore city of Tyre had the strongest fleet. Leaving in his rear such a naval force would be dangerous: strengthened by reinforcements from Cyprus and Egypt, the Tyrians could stir up trouble in Greece with Sparta's cooperation and Athens's less than wholehearted loyalty. So Alexander constructed a causeway to reach Tyre's maritime walls and storm the city. Afterward the Macedonians marched on to Egypt, where Alexander visited the Siwah oasis and founded the city of Alexandria. Like his other foundations on the shore of the Mediterranean, Alexandria was intended as a terminal of inland trade and an exporter of goods abroad. Impressed as he undoubtedly was by his reception at Siwah, the young Macedonian king's feet remained firmly planted on the ground when it came to administration. The children of his soldiers by Asian wives were made legitimate and educated at his expense. Many of these veterans and their families were settled in the seventy new cities he founded throughout Asia; strategically sited, the fortified cities were self-governing but subject to the edicts of the king.

Representative of his foundations was Ai Khanoun in present-day Afghanistan. Located at the confluence of the river Oxus and one of its tributaries, the city was perfectly sited to manage the resources of the surrounding plain and the mountains to the south. It incorporated an acropolis that sloped down to a lower residential area. Excavations have revealed Greek temples, a theater, and a gymnasium next to a temple dedicated to a local deity. The ancient name of the city is not known; yet from its buildings and inscriptions, we can appreciate how it was a thriving urban center for well over a century. Alexander was the standard-bearer of Greek civilization in Asia.

When it became apparent that Darius would fight again, Alexander decided to advance in 331 BC. Crossing both the Euphrates and the Tigris, the Macedonians eventually caught up with the Persians at Gaugamela. The capture of Persian scouts told Alexander what he needed to know: Darius's ground-leveling operations, intended for the benefit of his chariot corps, meant that the Persian king was now determined to make a last stand. In desperation, Darius had already offered Alexander control of all the lands to the west of the Euphrates, 30,000 talents as a ransom for his mother and daughters, the hand of one daughter in marriage, and the retention of his son Ochus as a permanent hostage. An exhausted Parmenio recommended that, as no man had ever ruled from the Euphrates to the Danube, the offer be accepted. "If I were Alexander," he said, "I would accept this offer." "So would I," replied Alexander, "if I were Parmenio."

Misinformation served the Macedonians well. A false rumor of a night attack obliged the Persians to stand at arms until morning. In contrast, Alexander and his men had an untroubled sleep. So deeply did Alexander himself sleep that Parmenio had to shake him awake at breakfast time: when asked why he was so relaxed, Alexander said that Darius's preparations for a pitched battle were "exactly what I wanted."

But Gaugamela would not be as easy a fight as Issus because there were no mountains to protect the Macedonian flanks and no sea either. The Persian line overlapped his by nearly a mile, with the result that Alexander placed his wings at an angle to the main battle line, which otherwise remained the same. His tactical plan was a stroke of genius, which no general had hit upon before. To reduce the numbers directly facing him and to create an opening in the Persian line for a decisive charge, he sought to draw as many enemy units as possible away from the center and into an engagement with his flank guards. Napoleon would brilliantly employ the tactic at Austerlitz in 1805.

Given that Darius had 34,000 frontline cavalry to Alexander's 7,500, it was vital that the Persian king open the attack. Baffled by the oblique disposition of the Macedonians, who kept edging sideways toward rough ground unsuited for a chariot charge, Darius ordered the scythe chariots to immediately attack. Their razor-sharp blades attached to the turning wheels were expected to break up the Macedonian phalanx. But these vehicles did little damage, for the Macedonians had orders, whenever they were attacked, to break formation and let them pass. Meanwhile, on both flanks of Alexander's army the Persian cavalry pressed hard, feeding in squadron after squadron from the center of the Persian battle line in a determined effort to roll up the Macedonians.

This was the moment for which Alexander had been waiting. His keen eye detected a serious thinning of the Persian center and

he promptly made for the gap, and with the cavalry and all the heavy infantry in this sector of the line, drove in a wedge and, raising a battle-cry, pushed forward at the double for the point where Darius stood. A close struggle ensued, but it was soon over: for the Macedonian

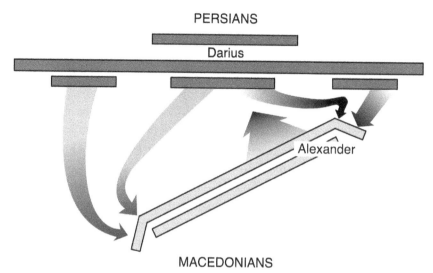

The Battle of Gaugamela.

horse, with Alexander himself at the head of them, vigorously pressed the assault, fighting hand to hand and thrusting at the Persian faces with their lances, and the infantry phalanx in close order and bristling with pikes added its irresistible weight. Darius, who had been anxious since the battle started and now saw nothing but disaster all around him, was the first to turn tail and ride for safety.

The whole of the Persian army swiftly followed his example. Alexander and Parmenio harried its fugitives continuously as their aim was to break the fighting spirit of the Persians once and for all. The extent of the casualties they inflicted made sure that Alexander would never be challenged again. Even the Persian king failed to escape, because the humiliation of another yet defeat led his closest companions to kill him. Alexander was appalled to find Darius dead. He had hoped to take the Persian king alive, since he wanted Darius and his family to continue as the royal house of the Medes and the Persians under his own authority as king of all Asia. The Macedonian king wished to conciliate Persian opinion as a means of laying a firm foundation for his new realm.

THE ADVANCE TO INDIA

Although some of the Macedonian commanders were not in favor of an advance east, Alexander appreciated that he ruled a warrior nation whose loyalty depended upon his ability to wage successful war. The best way to maintain his authority was to continue his conquests despite his Asian courtiers' warning that the vast region Alexander was about to enter comprised difficult terrain with high mountains and wide deserts and that its warlike peoples would be resolute in defense of their lands. He had seen for himself how formidable their horsemen were in the service of Darius as subject allies, particularly those of the Bactrians, Scythians, and Indians. Alexander's desire to reach India was perhaps not unreasonable as his tutor Aristotle claimed it was no more than a peninsula jutting into the circular sea that surrounded the world. The size of the subcontinent and its huge population would come as a shock to the Macedonians. Later Megasthenes, the Seleucid ambassador at the court of Candragupta Maurya, considered India unconquerable.

Alexander also thought he was following in the footsteps of his divine ancestors, simply repossessing territory that Herakles had once conquered. When in the Punjab he encountered the Sibae, a people who "clothed themselves in animal skins, carried cudgels, and branded their cattle with the mark of a club," he took them for the remnants of Herakles's invading army. And Herakles was again recalled by the worship of the Suraseni for Krishna, the charioteer of the hero Arjuna in the *Mahabharata* epic, which ends with an eighteen-day battle and general slaughter. That Krishna was able to marry 16,000 virgins held captive by a wicked king rather puts in the shade Herakles's record of satisfying fifty women in a single night. According to another myth, Herakles was the father of the Scythians. Obliged to make love to the queen of the land north of the Black Sea, a strange woman with a serpent's tail, he was asked which of the three sons she bore him should succeed her. Herakles left a bow and told her to name the boy who could draw it as her successor. Her son Scythes proved to possess this ability, and his descendants, the Scythians, became one of the strongest peoples in the ancient world.

At the river Granicus, Alexander used only Macedonian troops and some Greek horsemen. In the next two battles, his army consisted

Herakles, the hero revered by Alexander.

of Greek, Balkan, and Macedonian soldiers. Besides the Macedonian phalanx and the cavalry he personally commanded, Alexander was best served by a troop of Thessalian horsemen, without whom he would have struggled to beat mounted Persians. Once Darius was dead, Alexander turned to Asian recruits, who, with his Balkan forces, comprised half the army of 120,000 men whom he led in the invasion of India. Even though his ambition seemed to know no bounds, Alexander always believed that he acted with divine support: portents boosted his confidence throughout his Asian campaigns. While he was still in Asia Minor, a tablet was unearthed that prophesied a Macedonian victory over the Persians. At the Battle of Issus Alexander was assured that he enjoyed the protection of the gods. It was believed that they had put into Darius's mind the notion to cram his force into a confined space and leave the more open ground best suited to his larger army.

A coin showing Alexander with horns, a sign of divinity in the ancient Middle East.

An immediate problem for Alexander was Bessus, a murderer of Darius. He held out against the Macedonians until his eventual capture in the Oxus valley. Asked why he had betrayed his king, the regicide said the decision was not his alone; everyone close to Darius at the time shared in it, and their object was to win Alexander's favor. After Bessus was scourged, his nose and ears were cut off in Persian fashion, and then he was executed.

As many of his horses had died of exhaustion during the relentless pursuit of Bessus, Alexander brought his cavalry up to strength with fresh local mounts. He also had to deal with hostile tribesmen, who were only overcome with difficulty. During one engagement, an arrow shot through Alexander's leg broke his fibula. But the Macedonians prevailed and slew thousands of their attackers, who dwelt in mountain strongholds. Unrest among his Greek soldiers had already forced Alexander to release large numbers of troops with severance pay and bonuses. Those permitted to return home included the Thessalians, which made him more dependent on mounted Asian recruits. Even worse, there was division within the ranks of the Macedonians: between those who espoused nationalism and those who agreed with Alexander's orientalizing approach.

Remembering the assassination of Philip, Alexander reacted violently to the trenchant criticism of Cleitus, an experienced cavalry commander, and at a banquet ran him through with a spear. Struck with sudden remorse, he pulled the spear from Cleitus's body and would have turned it on himself, had his companions not restrained him. Though some witnesses believed that Alexander's violence was a consequence of heavy drinking, the incident nevertheless brought into the open a profound difference of outlook. The young king's refusal to enslave his Asian subjects and insistence on treating them as free people won over many hearts, despite smacking of weakness to older traditionalists. And the death of Cleitus, coming so soon after that of Parmenio, appeared to close down any possibility of a frank exchange of views in the Macedonian court. Not long afterward, Callisthenes, the court historian and philosopher, found this indeed to be the case: either he was hanged or dragged around with the army in a prison cage until he died. Callisthenes had had the temerity to suggest that oriental despotism was anathema to freedom-loving Greeks and Macedonians.

It is often speculated what would have been the result of Alexander's great multiethnic experiment had a premature death not ended it so quickly. When, at the age of thirty-three, the dying conqueror was asked to whom he left his vast kingdom, he replied, "To the strongest," correctly anticipating the prolonged struggle between his senior commanders. Their wars ensured the division of Alexander's conquests into a number of new kingdoms, one of which, founded by Seleucus at Babylon in 305 BC, stayed close to the ideal of a multiethnic society. At his eastern capital, Seleucia-upon-Tigris, a suburb was named Apamea after Seleucus's Persian wife, whom he married at Alexander's behest. This marriage lasted, unlike others between senior Macedonian commanders and Asian brides, and Apamea was the mother of Seleucus's eldest son and most able successor, Antiochus I.

Alexander's preferred Asian girl was Roxane, the beautiful daughter of a leading Sogdian family. Prior to the invasion of the Persian Empire, Alexander had neglected the advice of Parmenio to marry and beget an heir. His choice of Roxane was not only timely but also politically astute, as his love for her enhanced the affection of his Asian subjects.

When in 326 BC Alexander descended onto the north Indian plain from the mountains of Afghanistan, he thought he was entering a small extension of the Asian continent. Instead, he encountered a vast land of cities and powerful kings. Having performed sacrifices on both banks of the river Indus, Alexander marched to Taxila, "a realm as large as Egypt with good pasturage and orchards laden with choice fruit." Its ruler, Taxiles, came to terms, along with other kings, and after an exchange of gifts, Alexander pushed on with an additional 5,000 Indian troops to engage Porus, a ruler who declined to send envoys. The engagement between Alexander and Porus at the river Hydaspes was the last pitched battle of the Asian campaign, and it was fought in drenching rain. Here the Macedonians met war elephants for the first time on the battlefield.

The action was complicated by the river Hydaspes, a tributary of the Indus: it had a turbulent and swift current swollen by Himalayan snow and heavy rain. Porus was therefore taken aback by a night crossing, which one of his sons tried unsuccessfully to block. Among those who fell was Porus's son, but this did not weaken the king's resolve, and he drew his army up in the so-called Garuda formation, a standard way in which Indian generals positioned their soldiers on the battlefield. Its object in placing two hundred war elephants in front of the infantry was to scare away Alexander's cavalry, which was standing in a compact body. Both wings of Porus's army were protected by chariots and cavalry, while a screen of foot soldiers was thrown around the elephant corps to deter skirmishers. But the unexpected mobility of the Macedonians decided the outcome, as they concentrated their efforts on the left wing of the Indian battle line, making its superior numbers irrelevant. The first group of Alexander's men to engage the Indians were mounted archers who routed the charioteers and the cavalry. Into this maelstrom Alexander now sent the remainder of his horsemen, while his foot soldiers closed with Porus's infantry.

This last move, however, was not easy to achieve because of the war elephants. "These monsters," we are told, "plunged this way and that among the lines of infantry, dealing destruction to the solid mass of the Macedonian phalanx. Once again the discipline and experience of Alexander's men was crucial, for the Indians almost got the upper hand through the havoc being wrought by the war elephants. These fearful creatures trampled the Macedonians underfoot, lifting some in their trunks and bashing them on the ground, and impaling others with their tusks. But so tightly packed together did they become that they ceased to fight with any cohesion." Many of their riders were dead, with the result that riderless, often wounded war elephants set "indiscriminately upon friend and foe alike." The sign that Alexander had won happened when these tired animals "started to back away, slowly, like ships astern, with nothing worse than loud trumpetings."

Despite over 20,000 Indians being killed, the personal bravery of Porus drew Alexander's admiration because, "unlike Darius, he was not the first to flee, but so long as a single unit of his men held together, stubbornly he fought on." When Porus was finally persuaded to meet Alexander face-to-face, such was his noble bearing that he was restored to his throne by the victor. Thus at Hydaspes, Alexander demonstrated that his army could defeat any Indian ruler who dared to oppose him. But within a few months the Macedonians refused to advance into the Ganges valley, where the Nanda king reputedly could field 200,000 infantry, 20,000 cavalry, 2,000 chariots, and 4,000 war elephants. Disillusion gripped Alexander's most reliable soldiers, who were suffering from the effects of seventy days of continuous rain. They also felt that they had been misled, as the end of Asia was nowhere in sight. Alexander shared their frustration, and even though he still wished to advance farther east, he understood that this was out of the question, and so he agreed to call off the campaign.

Marching south instead of east, Alexander subdued the Indus valley and reached the ocean. There he prayed "that Poseidon would escort safely the fleet which he intended to send with Nearchus to the Persian Gulf and the mouths of the Euphrates and Tigris." The voyage was assisted by a force that was sent ahead on land to dig wells, mark water sources, dump supplies, and deal with hostile inhabitants. Alexander followed with the rest of the army, trekking across inhospitable country under a blazing sun. The troops suffered dreadfully from intense heat, shortage of water, and exhaustion. Alexander's leadership held them together. He walked in front, and when he was offered some water to drink, he poured it on the ground to show that he would only drink when all could drink.

In 323 BC Alexander reached Babylon, where he died from an incurable disease, probably a form of malaria. The thoughts of the dying king were for his Macedonian soldiers, the rank and file with whom he had endured twelve years of constant warfare. As he could not bear to die without saying farewell, they filed past him, the greatest leader of an unsurpassed warrior nation. Alexander was unable to speak, and so he welcomed each Macedonian by raising his head with difficulty and greeting them with his eyes.

A fragment of a Babylonian calendar recording Alexander's death in 323 BC.

SELEUCID ELEPHANTS

The fifty years following Alexander's death saw a protracted struggle between his leading commanders either to win overall power or to carve out for themselves separate kingdoms. This struggle ended with three major dynasties: the Antigonids in Macedon, the Seleucids in Syria and the east, and the Ptolemies in Egypt. Of these new powers, the Seleucid kingdom was the most diverse and the greatest in extent. Its founder, Seleucus, was an energetic ruler who campaigned throughout the vast area of Alexander's Asian conquests. His northern frontier was, however, too long and too inhospitable for any attempt to block it off in the same the fashion as the Great Wall of China; the only practical solution was fortresses and fortified cities, which did not stop incursions from the steppe but acted as deterrents against pastoralists and as protection for the local farmers. All the Seleucid cities were treated the same: they were taxed and expected to furnish soldiers in times of war. Most of them were, in effect, military settlements, which probably explains their longevity in comparison with those founded by the Ptolemies. The chain of new cities extending over the whole of their dominions to Bactria and Sogdiana in the east was indeed the most striking accomplishment of the Seleucid dynasty.

A core of Macedonian phalangites remained the basis of the Seleucid army, supplemented by local levies. Yet a gradual weakening of the phalanx is indicated by the adoption of new weapons: chariots and war

elephants. The latter were acquired in India, where Seleucus tried to reassert Macedonian authority over the Punjab. There is no doubt that he quickly came to appreciate the changed political situation in northwestern India, no longer a collection of rival kingdoms that could be played off against each other. Instead Seleucus encountered in Candragupta Maurya a powerful opponent who had already added the area to his own kingdom in the

King Antiochus I, the second Seleucid.

Ganges valley. Although a battle may have taken place, it appears that Seleucus and Candragupta chose to reach a peace agreement. In return for ceding the Indus valley and parts of Afghanistan, so as to establish a recognized border, the Seleucid army gained five hundred war elephants.

War elephants tended to have psychological value as a means of terrifying men and horses. Their impact on the battlefield, however, could be unpredictable, even catastrophic, particularly once the Romans learned how to deal with them. This helps to explain the growing importance of mercenaries; they had existed for centuries in Greece, but only after the breakup of Alexander's kingdom did they begin to make up such a large percentage, at times even the majority, of rival armies. The wealth of Egypt allowed the Ptolemies to recruit the greatest number of mercenaries, but the Seleucid kings were forced to employ them as well.

At the Battle of Magnesia in 189 BC, fought in the interior of Asia Minor, Antiochus III's phalanx stood up well to the Roman attack until the Seleucid war elephants, driven mad by missiles, ran amok and broke its ranks. The conflict between the Romans and the Seleucids came about through Antiochus's reassertion of a claim to Thrace. After an abortive invasion of Greece, which caused Rome to declare war, the Seleucid army returned to Asia Minor, where Antiochus at first tried to fortify the Hellespont against the expected crossing by a Roman expedition. But losing control of the Aegean, he realized that the Romans' naval supremacy enabled them to bypass his fortifications and land wherever they wished. So the Seleucid army retreated inland and prepared for a pitched battle.

The Romans defeated Antiochus III at Magnesia in 189 BC.

Knowing that winter was fast approaching and the Romans could not stay indefinitely in the field, Antiochus kept his troops within a well-fortified camp at Magnesia. As a result, Livy tells us, this reluctance to fight angered the Romans so much that they regarded their opponents "with contempt. A shout came from all sides, urging the consul to lead the army out straightaway and take advantage of the eagerness of the troops, who felt as if their task was not to do battle with so many thousands of the enemy, but to slaughter so many thousand cattle." When it was clear that the Romans would assault his camp, Antiochus brought out forces and drew them up in formation for a battle. Livy says, "The Roman battle line had a standard pattern, with the same arrangement, within limits, of types of men and equipment. There were two legions and two contingents of allies of Italian status, each consisting of 5,400 men. The Romans held the center; the Latins were on the flanks."

Light-armed troops and cavalry were stationed at the extreme ends of the battle line, with the largest concentration of horsemen on the right, where the regular Roman cavalry was augmented by a contingent from Pergamon. In all, the Romans and their allies numbered 30,000 men, half the size of Antiochus's army.

We are less certain of the Seleucid battle line, although the Macedonian phalanx, 16,000 strong at its center, comprised the main strength of the 48,000 foot soldiers that Antiochus had assembled. A contingent of 1,500 Galatians on each side of the phalanx was intended to guard its flanks. A smaller phalanx of 10,000 men was stationed opposite the Italian contingent on the Roman left. Light infantry and cavalry filled the rest of the Seleucid battle line. To underline the greater variety of Antiochus's troops, Livy mentions that in front of the cavalry there were "scythed chariots and camels of the type called dromedaries. On these were mounted Arab archers equipped with slender swords six feet in length, so that they could reach the enemy from that height." The war elephants were placed near the Macedonian phalanx.

The Seleucid right wing, under the command of Antiochus himself, charged one of the Roman legions and overwhelmed the legionaries. Even though the survivors managed to prevent an encircling move by the Seleucid cavalry, the situation on the Roman left remained dire. But the exact opposite occurred on the right, where the Seleucids also attacked. There the advance was started by chariots. It proved nothing less than a disaster; they were met with such a barrage of missiles that the charge stopped before it got up any speed. The crippled horses turned back and, reaching their own line, threw the cavalry posted there into utter confusion. As a consequence these horsemen failed to halt the Roman cavalry, which, seeing a weakness to exploit, swiftly charged. Pouring through the Seleucid disorder, the Roman cavalry was able to outflank the Macedonian phalanx, after dealing with its Galatian guards. The phalangites did not readily collapse, however, but maintained their ranks until the maddened war elephants crashed into them. The final disintegration of the phalanx marked the end of the battle, which Antiochus had to admit was lost.

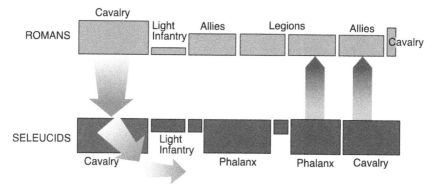

The Battle of Magnesia.

To Rome's ally Pergamon, it was obvious that the battle at Magnesia had irrevocably altered the balance of power in the eastern Mediterranean. This recently created kingdom would be content to stay in the shadow of Rome prior to its incorporation as a province of the Roman Empire in 133 BC. Fortunately for Antiochus, the defeat at Magnesia did not stop the Seleucid dynasty from ruling much of the ancient Middle East for another half century. Quite typical was the conduct of Antiochus immediately after his defeat. He went to Babylon with his wife and sons and sacrificed at the great temple of Marduk, the city's god. A local priest was pleased to note, "That day, King Antiochus entered Esagila and prostrated himself." Following the ceremony, "he went, in the afternoon, to Seleucia-upon-Tigris, the royal city."

Resilient though he undoubtedly was, Antiochus must have guessed that the Seleucid kingdom was already in terminal decline, not only in the west, as Rome flexed its muscles, but in the east too. The steady rise of the Parthians, an Iranian-speaking people living beyond the edge of Seleucid authority, now increasingly threatened its eastern possessions. The Parthian takeover of Mesopotamia was a body blow from which the Seleucids never recovered. By 126 BC they had been driven west of the Euphrates, leaving them with a restricted economic base and no chance of mustering sufficient troops to fight back with any hope of success. The extinction of this Macedonian dynasty was a foregone conclusion when, in 64 BC, the Roman general Pompey annexed Syria, observing how he found Asia a frontier but left it in the heart of Rome's empire.

CHAPTER SIX

The Iranian Revival

THE SUCCESSORS OF ALEXANDER THE GREAT PLACED ENORMOUS emphasis on war. They regarded conquest as their purpose, replied to opposition with the dispatch of armies, and took personal command of military campaigns that were viewed as critical. This warlike outlook was particularly true of Seleucid power, not least because it inherited local traditions of military glory and the quest for booty. Ever since the Assyrians had stamped the ideal of a belligerent state upon the politics of the ancient Middle East, rulers were judged by their effectiveness as war leaders. That King Seleucus conformed to this pattern can be seen in the territorial gains that he made before and after the final defeat of Antigonus at the Battle of Ipsus in 301 BC.

The defeat and death of Antigonus at Ipsus in Asia Minor ensured the permanent division of Alexander the Great's empire. From his power base in Macedon, Antigonus had endeavored to keep this empire intact, a task made an impossible by the lack of an immediately acceptable successor to Alexander. Separatist commanders worked against Antigonus and his energetic son Demetrius. Although he managed to escape after the Battle of Ipsus, which was decided by a maneuver of Seleucus's elephants, Demetrius could do little more than

Seleucus I, whose rise to power was perhaps the most spectacular among Alexander the Great's successors.

cling to power in Macedon. And because Demetrius remained a campaigner rather than a ruler, the war-weary Macedonians deserted him in 288 BC. An expedition he mounted in Asia that year with a force of mercenaries went badly wrong, and the restless Demetrius found himself the prisoner of Seleucus. "After a short confinement," Plutarch reports, "he fell sick through inactivity and overindulgence in food and wine and died in his fifty-fifth year."

As a result of Antigonus's failure to keep the empire together, Seleucus was able to consolidate his position in Asia. According to Arrian, "Seleucus was the greatest king of those who succeeded Alexander, possessing the most royal mind, and ruling over the greatest extent of territory, next to Alexander himself." Showing the magnitude of Seleucus's power, Arrian adds, "always lying in wait for neighboring nations, strong in arms and persuasive in diplomacy, he acquired Mesopotamia, Armenia, Cappadocia, the Persians, Parthians, Bactrians, Arabs, Tapyri, Sogdiani, Arachotes, Hyrcannians, and other peoples that had been subdued by Alexander, as far as the river Indus, so that he ruled a wider empire in Asia than any of his predecessors except Alexander."

Seleucus's creation of such a large realm from his original center of power in Babylon is impressive. Virtually nothing is known about this remarkable period of expansion, in which whole regions were won over, but the means seems to have been a judicious combination of military

SELEUCUS

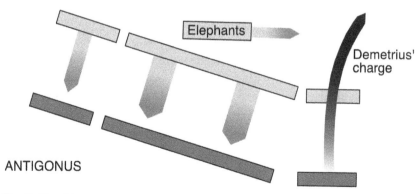

ANTIGONUS

The Battle of Ipsus.

conquest and skillful diplomacy. A factor in this success was undoubtedly the speed with which Seleucus filled the power vacuum following Alexander the Great's early death in 323 BC.

THE SHRINKING OF SELEUCID POWER

The most innovative decision that Alexander the Great made was obliging his senior commanders to marry daughters of the Persian aristocracy. But only one of the new kingdoms that emerged after the defeat of Antigonus stayed close to the ideal of the multiethnic society envisaged by Alexander. That was the one established by Seleucus, whose eastern capital, Seleucia-upon-Tigris in present-day Iraq, had a suburb named Apamea after Seleucus's Asian wife. This marriage lasted, unlike the others contracted at Alexander's behest, and Apamea was the mother of Seleucus's eldest son, the capable Antiochus I.

Well before his death in 281 BC, Seleucus had recognized the talents of Antiochus by appointing him coregent, an unusual move that ensured the dynasty's survival. Even though Antiochus was sent to take charge of the kingdom's eastern territories, there nothing formal in this division of responsibility: father and son were both monarchs with complete authority wherever they happened to be operating. The man on the spot needed to have the power of decision belonging to a ruler. From the start, Seleucus clearly appreciated the inherent difficulties of running a far-flung state.

That was most probably the reason for reaching, in 303 BC, an early agreement over the Indian border with the first Mauryan ruler, Candragupta. In return for ceding outlying areas, Seleucus received five hundred war elephants for use in the ancient Middle East. At the Battle of Ipsus, they prevented Demetrius, who commanded Antigonus's cavalry, from rejoining the infantry after a successful charge. Seeing that this left Antigonus's phalanx badly exposed, Seleucus used mounted archers to harry its unprotected flanks. Plutarch relates how Demetrius "fought brilliantly and put the enemy stationed opposite him to flight, but by pressing the pursuit too far and too impulsively he threw away the victory."

These same elephants proved equally decisive when Antiochus I had to cope with a Celtic invasion. After ravaging Greece, destroying towns and cities in search of plunder, the Celts poured into Asia Minor, but their usual ferocity was blunted by the unfamiliar war elephants. Hard fighting was still necessary before the Celts were driven into the interior, the old heartland of the Hittites near the river Halys, where they were henceforth called Galatians. Both Greek and non-Greek peoples expressed their relief at Antiochus's swift campaign by naming him *soter,* or "savior." Hemmed in though they were by Seleucid arms, the Galatians remained troublesome neighbors until the Romans conquered Galatia in 253 BC. Despite the felling of 8,000 Celts in battle then, the Senate denied the two victorious generals a triumph in Rome. Deployment of slingers to soften up the enemy prior to the legionary attack was considered unmanly. Greco-Roman disdain for missile weapons died hard.

Raids by Celtic tribesmen were not uncommon. The city of Rome itself was sacked in 387 BC, and many Celts joined Hannibal during his invasion of Italy. They took part in the Carthaginian general's great victory at Cannae in 216 BC, when he encircled two Roman armies and slew 80,000 men on a single day.

How readily Antiochus I dealt with the Celtic invasion of Asia Minor impressed the Greek world. As a cosmopolitan ruler, this Macedonian-Iranian king was prepared to be a Greek in the eastern Mediterranean, a Persian in his Asian dominions, and, of course, a Babylonian in Mesopotamia. But in Asia Minor the Seleucids had to tolerate the creation of an independent state based on the natural fortress of Pergamon, less than twenty miles from the Aegean. Attalus I was installed as its king after driving out the Celts locally. Although Pergamon developed into a power of almost equal status with Seleucid Asia, its reliance on Roman support came at a price, for Rome's defeat of the king Antiochus III at Magnesia in 189 BC turned Pergamon into little more than a pawn in Roman foreign policy.

Among the Greek cities in Asia Minor, the establishment of the Seleucid dynasty was so popular that Miletus passed decrees honoring Seleucus's queen, Apamea, and her son, Antiochus. The Milesians much appreciated the favor Apamea showed them at court and the aid she gave to the contingent they sent to fight with Seleucus in the conquest of Bactria and Sogdiana from 307 to 305 BC. Demodamas of Miletus, the commander of the force that participated in this eastern campaign, was instrumental in the passing of these decrees. Politic though it was to show generosity to cities like Miletus, both Seleucus and Antiochus knew that they had to do more than shower favors on long-established cities. So Antiochus founded new cities in order to develop the kingdom's economy, since they provided a ready market for agricultural produce. Increasingly the Seleucids sought to require tax payments in coin, which meant that farmers had to turn their surplus crops into silver. Paying for the army was always problematic, especially as larger numbers of mercenaries were recruited. The loss of Asia Minor following the Roman victory at Magnesia only compounded the problem, which could not be overcome by the collection of booty. A downward financial spiral eventually weakened the Seleucids, as insufficient revenue to maintain an adequate war machine led to the loss of more territory. The frequent squandering of military resources in internecine conflicts did not help either.

Before this decline set in, however, the Seleucid kingdom was robust enough to meet the challenges it faced. With the advantage of hindsight, the Greek historian Polybius was able to recognize that the accession, at approximately the same time, of three kings, Philip V in Macedon, Ptolemy IV in Egypt, and Antiochus III in Asia, produced an intense phase of warfare that brought about Roman intervention. Philip V ended his reign disastrously, barred from Greece and subordinate to Rome. By contrast, Antiochus III still ruled a formidable kingdom at his death in 197 BC, despite his defeat by the Romans at Magnesia.

Antiochus had ascended the throne in 223 BC as a young man, following the assassination his elder brother, Seleucus III, in Asia Minor. From the start of his reign, Antiochus III had to secure his authority in the army and the court, besides bringing to heel rebellious areas such as Media. There the Seleucid governor used Iranian troops to assert his independence and extend his power into Mesopotamia, where he captured the royal city of Seleucia-upon-Tigris. Initial expeditionary forces sent to quell the trouble proved inadequate since Antiochus had begun a campaign that would finally culminate in the conquest of southern Syria, long a bone of contention between the Seleucid and Ptolemaic kings. Like the pharaohs, the Macedonian dynasts in Egypt saw Palestine and

Syria as within their sphere of influence. Once Antiochus led his army against the rebels though, they were either defeated or persuaded to defect. With the exception of Seleucia-upon-Tigris, which failed to hold out, the other great cities remained loyal; even more importantly, none of the other Seleucid governors joined the revolt.

Probably a consequence of the apparent crisis over the succession, the Median rebellion was quite different from indigenous revolts against Seleucid rule. Much as the Persian kings had to cope with unrest during successions, the Seleucids confronted uprisings whenever there was any doubt about the position of a new ruler. But Antiochus understood how effective his own presence was in putting down the rebels. The charisma and authority of the ruler counted for a great deal in internal as well as external conflicts. With this in mind, Antiochus decided to reassert Seleucid authority throughout the 3,000-mile length of his kingdom. That he also understood the need for a pragmatic approach is clear in the treatment of Antropatene, a semiautonomous kingdom in northern Media. He left its ruler in place after a timely submission. There was no point in gratuitous violence, which would only drive indigenous communities into rebellion after Antiochus moved to another location.

Either in the 240s or 230s BC, Bactria had broken away and become a separate kingdom. It had been created by a Greek named Diodotus, the Seleucid governor who usurped power there. At the time, Seleucus II was facing a Ptolemaic invasion and strife inside the royal household, but he still managed to contain for a while the Parthians, restive Iranian pastoralists living next to the Caspian Sea. They were largely outside and beyond the control of the Seleucid kingdom, although some of them served in its army as mounted archers.

After sorting out affairs in Armenia in 212 and 211 BC, Antiochus started his eastern campaign by gathering his forces together at Ecbatana in Media. No catalogue of the expeditionary army exists, as it does for the Battle of Magnesia, but accounts of two actions give some idea of its composition. There is mention of 1,000 horsemen, 2,000 Cretan archers, the Macedonian phalanx, light infantry, pioneers, and mercenaries, though the strengths of the larger units are not given. At the Battle of the River Arios in Bactria, it would appear that Antiochus deployed some 35,000 men.

It seems that Diodotus and his son reigned for a considerable length of time, but when Antiochus arrived, he found a certain Euthydemus on the Bactrian throne. After a series of battles and sieges, including that of Bactria, present-day Balkh, the Seleucid king obliged Euthydemus to accept a subordinate role, since he recognized it was Antiochus's right to confer or refuse a royal title. Having provisioned his army at Bactria's expense and taken over its elephant corps, Antiochus then advanced into the territories ceded by Seleucus I to the Mauryan king Candragupta. Since then the Mauryan dynasty had declined in strength, and after the death of its third king, Ashoka, in 230 BC, the empire had been divided among his children and grandchildren. In the event, Antiochus's incursion had no lasting effect, and it fell to the successors of Euthydemus to gain a foothold in India, for Greeks ruled parts of northern India well into the first century BC. Eventually Central Asian invaders overthrew this outpost of the Greek world. The first of these were the Sakas, whom the Greeks knew around the Black Sea as the Scythians. Sedentary pastoralists, the Sakas had already seized Bactria, whose fertile upper Oxus valley was an irresistible place for settlement.

In summing up Antiochus's achievements in the eastern expedition, Polybius remarked that he had not only reduced its governors and kings to obedience but also reincorporated the cities founded by Alexander the Great into the Seleucid kingdom. Yet this was not enough to guarantee its longevity because the only kingdom-wide institution was the monarchy itself. The Seleucid king was the only link between the many different communities included in the kingdom: all of them possessed different customs, beliefs, and traditions, and some of them had histories of independence and resistance to outside control. This explains Seleucid dependence on the armed forces, the only really integrated element in the kingdom.

Yet earlier, in 217 BC, at the Battle of Raphia, the Seleucid army was hard put to hold off the forces assembled by Ptolemy IV. The engagement near ancient Gaza was one of the biggest to take place after the death of Alexander the Great. The key to Ptolemy IV's superiority was the surprise appearance of 20,000 Egyptians, an unexpected reinforcement on the battlefield. After indecisive charges by both sides,

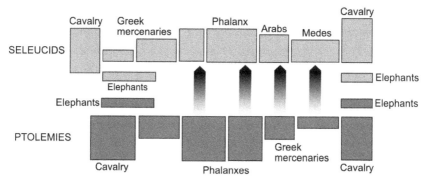

The Battle of Raphia.

the Ptolemaic cavalry dispersed two sections of the Seleucid battle line, manned by Median and Arab contingents. A swift advance by the Ptolemaic phalanx then drove home this advantage, causing the Seleucid army to fall back in disorder. Antiochus suffered 14,000 casualties, the majority of whom were killed. A truce covered more than the burial of the dead because Antiochus marched away without any interference from Ptolemy IV. A subsequent peace treaty cost the Seleucid king all his conquests in Phoenicia and Palestine, but he paid no indemnity.

King Ptolemy IV of Egypt, the victor at the Battle of Raphia in 217 BC.

Notwithstanding Antiochus's successful eastern expedition, the Seleucid kingdom had reached a state of uneasy equilibrium. Increasing Roman involvement in the eastern Mediterranean was as much a brake on Seleucid war aims as the strength of the military resources disposed by the Ptolemies. When, in 168 BC, Antiochus IV moved against Egypt

to take control of Pelusium, he was met by the Roman envoy Popilius Laenus. The king greeted him from a distance and offered him his right hand, but Popilius presented him with a tablet which contained the Senate's decree, and asked him to read it first. . . . When the king

had read it, he said he wanted to confer with his senior commanders
. . . but Popilius in reply did something which seemed insolent and
arrogant to the highest degree. With a vine stick which he had in his
hand he drew a circle around Antiochus and told him to reply before
he stepped outside the circle. The king was taken aback by this action
and after hesitating for a moment said he would do everything the
Romans asked of him. The decree of the Senate required him to put an
end at once to the war with Ptolemy.

The recent defeat of King Perseus of Macedon had given the Romans a free hand in international affairs. At the Battle of Pydna in 172 BC, the legionaries had exploited the Macedonian phalanx's loss of cohesion when it advanced over uneven ground. At close quarters they slew 20,000 Macedonians, the 3,000 men of the royal guard fighting to the last, so that Perseus had no choice but give himself up to grace the victor's march of triumph in Rome. Macedon was partitioned into four republics and made subject to Roman taxation.

THE RISE OF PARTHIA

Even more dangerous than the growth of Roman power on the western border of the Seleucid kingdom was the threat posed by the Parthians. They were the first of two Iranian groups to lead a national revival after a century and a half of Macedonian domination. Neither the Parthians nor the following Sasanians repeated the same formula of rule as had the Achaemenid Persians, but they shared the same language, religion, and culture. Their kingdoms comprised much looser arrangements, with many levels of subordination, so that some of the cities founded by Alexander the Great continued to enjoy a degree of local autonomy after the end of Seleucid rule.

Obscurity surrounds the origins of the Parthians, whose homeland was southeast of the Caspian Sea. Known as Pathava to the Achaemenid king Darius I, who incorporated the area into his empire after the Median revolt of 521 BC, it boasted a strong tradition of independence right down to Seleucid times. Whether the Parthians lived in Pathava at this period is uncertain, since they may have been later arrivals from the Central Asian steppe. All we can be sure of now is that a Parthian leader named Arshak—in Greek, Araces—set up a modest kingdom around 247 BC, which was the start of four centuries of Parthian power in the ancient Middle East. There were several attempts to restore Seleucid authority throughout the eastern provinces, including Antiochus III's expedition that reached northern India, but persistent difficulties in the west eventually obliged the Seleucid kings to recognize Parthia as an independent state.

Beginning in 171 BC, under Mithridates I, the Parthians established a power that the Seleucids were never able to match. The gradual loss of Iran to the Parthians and their attacks on Mesopotamia occurred during bitter

Mithridates I, the earliest Parthian king to place his own portrait on coinage.

internecine strife between the usurper Alexander Balas, a protégé of the Romans, and Demetrius III, who was accused of behaving with "a tyrant's lawlessness" rather than kingly authority. Civil conflict convulsed much of the western part of the Seleucid kingdom, so that "there were struggles and endless wars in Syria." Given this breakdown, the subsequent efforts of Antiochus VII to limit the growth of Parthian power were remarkable. He managed to rally the Greek and non-Greek inhabitants of Mesopotamia and Iran behind him: only his death on the battlefield in 129 BC terminated this last-gasp attempt at resistance. The reaction to the news in Antioch was extreme, since

not only did the city go into public mourning, but every house as well was dejected and filled with lamentation. Above all, the wailing of women enflamed their grief. Indeed, since 300,000 men had been lost, including noncombatants who accompanied the army, not a household could be found that was exempt from misfortune. Some were mourning the loss of brothers, some of husbands, and some of sons, while many girls and boys, left orphaned, wept for their own bereavement.

The victory left the Parthians as the main force to be reckoned with in Alexander the Great's eastern domains for the next three hundred years. Under Mithridates III, Parthian rule was extended as far west as the

Euphrates, a move that soon brought the Parthians into direct contact with the expanding Roman Empire.

Losing control of Mesopotamia, a region critical for any power with pretentions to rule the ancient Middle East, meant that the last Seleucid kings had no possibility of raising enough money or troops to fight back against the Parthians. The extinction of the dynasty was a foregone conclusion when, in 64 BC, the Roman general Pompey dethroned its last king and annexed Syria to the Roman Empire. The Seleucid kingdom was simply too weak to be of any conceivable use to Rome as a client state.

The first major clash between the Parthians and the Romans took place in 53 BC at Carrhae, where the legionaries discovered to their horror that they could not long withstand a sustained assault by mounted archers. The saying "a Parthian shot" recalls exactly the frustration felt by these Roman foot soldiers in northern Mesopotamia. The ill-fated

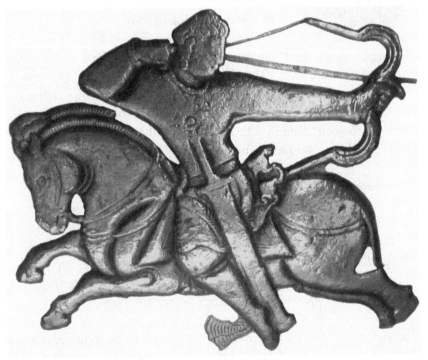

A Parthian shot. The semipastoralist Parthians totally outmaneuvered the Romans at Carrhae, taking 10,000 legionaries prisoner.

expedition resulted from Marcus Licinius Crassus's ambition to emulate the eastern conquests of Alexander the Great. Though part of the so-called First Triumvirate, a gang of three devoted to nothing more than the exercise of political power in Rome, Crassus felt himself militarily inferior to both Pompey and Caesar, its other members. It still rankled that he was denied a triumph for overcoming the slave revolt of Spartacus in 71 BC; he'd had to make do with the minor honor of a procession on foot, rather than a ride in a chariot, because of the unworthiness of his foe. The pursuit of glory on the battlefield was a reflection of the militarism of Roman society during the late republic, and it was something from which a successful general like Caesar was not entirely immune. Neither the conquest of Gaul nor his triumph in the civil war quite satisfied the ageing dictator, for Caesar still dreamed of marching his legions in the footsteps of Alexander the Great as late as 45 BC, just a year before his assassination.

Hardly surprising then was the impatience of the sixty-six-year-old Crassus to win greater military honors. In his life of this Roman politician, Plutarch says "there was considerable opposition to the idea of a man going out to make war on a people who, so far from having done the Romans any harm, were bound to them by treaties of friendship." One of the tribunes, by the name of Aetius, threatened to stop Crassus from leaving the city of Rome to take up his command. As he could not achieve this by force, at the city gate Aetius

> threw incense and libations on the brazier and called down on Crassus curses which were more dreadful by the names of certain strange and terrible deities whom he called upon in his invocation. The Romans believe that these mysterious and ancient curses are so powerful that no one who has had them laid upon him can escape their effect—and that an evil fate will also be in store for the man who utters them; consequently they are seldom made use of at all, and never lightly.

Undeterred, Crassus went on his way to Brundisium, and disregarding winter storms and rough seas, he sailed eastward. The loss of a large number of ships did not worry him in the least.

Arriving in Syria, the base for his advance against the Parthians, Crassus brushed aside any suggestions about the weakness of his cavalry, even though he would have to advance across open plains most suited to its use. It proved a fatal mistake because the Parthian army was essentially a cavalry force. Another error he committed at the start of the invasion was to take up winter quarters in northern Mesopotamia, since, as Plutarch points out, "he should have gone forward and made contact with the cities of Babylon and Seleucia-upon-Tigris, which had always been hostile to the Parthians; but instead of doing this he gave the enemy time to make his preparations." As the campaign season was about to begin in 53 BC, the Parthian king sent ambassadors with this message:

> *If the army had been sent by the Roman people, then it meant war to the bitter end and with no question of negotiations. But if, as they had been informed, the fact was that Crassus, for his own private purpose, had invaded Parthia and occupied Parthian territory, then its king was prepared to adopt a reasonable attitude: he would take pity on Crassus as an old man, and as for his soldiers, who were rather in the position of Crassus's prisoners than his protectors, he would allow them to go back to Rome.*

Marcus Crassus, the would-be Alexander, fell at the Battle of Carrhae in 53 BC.

Rejecting this offer, Crassus said he would fight. Crossing the Euphrates, he marched along the eastern bank of the river with 40,000 legionaries, nearly 4,000 cavalry, and about the same number of light-armed troops. But when he moved away from the Euphrates, striking farther eastward toward the Tigris, he suddenly encountered "a Parthian force in very great numbers and showing every sign of confidence."

Ignoring portents and refusing advice, Crassus impulsively continued the advance. The tactic seemed at first not to be unwise: few Parthian horsemen were in sight, because the Parthian general "Surena had hidden his main force behind this screen and ordered them to cover themselves with coats and skins so as to conceal their glittering armor." Once the Romans were close, however, "the whole plain was filled with a deep and terrifying sound. For the Parthians, instead of having horns and trumpets sound the attack, made use of hollow drums of stretched hide to which bronze bells are attached."

Before the Romans recovered from the shock of this din, the main force of the Sasanians dropped the coverings over their body armor and moved to the attack. At first Surena intended to charge with lances, but seeing the depth of the shields, he switched to archery. Plutarch relates how

> the Parthians spread out and began to shoot their arrows from all sides. There was no attempt at marksmanship, since the Romans were so densely crowded together that it was impossible to miss the target even if one wished to do so. They merely kept on shooting arrows with their strong bows, curved so as to give the maximum impetus to the arrows, and the blows fell powerfully and heavily upon the Romans.

Desperate though the situation was, Crassus still believed that, once the Parthians had used up their arrows, they would either break off the engagement or come to close quarters. But the arrival of camels loaded with extra arrows dashed this hope. It did not help that the Parthians were ready to retreat wherever Roman detachments tried to engage them: by apparently riding away, they lured their pursuers far from the Roman lines and then turned to beat them in detail. The readiness of the Parthians to retreat suggests a pastoralist ancestry, which seems confirmed by their hairstyles: they wore their hair "bunched over their heads in the Scythian fashion to make themselves look more formidable."

Toward the end of the battle, the Parthian light cavalry continued to ride around the Roman flanks firing arrows, while the armored cavalry attacked with their lances, driving the legionaries closer and closer together. Darkness halted the action, and during the night the Romans stole away. But it was to no avail, for the next day Crassus was beheaded, and 10,000 Roman soldiers were taken prisoner. Thus the would-be Alexander met his abject end. Many of the prisoners of war were settled on Parthia's eastern frontier, where, near the Central Asian city of Turfan, they may have faced Chinese opponents. A Chinese record mentions the surrender in 36 BC of a Hunnish chieftain whose followers included a group of mercenaries who sound suspiciously like ex-Roman legionaries from the description of their drill.

Armies older than Roman ones deployed chariotry to protect infantry against archers, as can be seen in the Hittite king Muwatalli II's unwillingness to fight on at the Battle of Kadesh after his own chariotry was routed by Ramesses II. In order to minimize the impact of arrows on the Macedonian phalanx at the Battle of Ipsus, Alexander the Great sent part of his cavalry forward to disperse Persian archers before the main infantry engagement began. The effect of chariotry, as of fully fledged cavalry, was moral as much as physical. It served to spread panic on the battlefield, but at Carrhae the indifference shown by Crassus to this arm exposed his foot soldiers to unnecessary casualties as well as capture.

Despite his delivering such a decisive victory at Carrhae, Surena's reward was execution on the order of Orodes I, the Parthian king. The energies of the Parthian monarchy were always directed at self-preservation rather than imperial expansion. Nonetheless, Orodes was murdered around 40 BC by his own son Phraates, whom he had already appointed as his successor. Phraates IV took preventive measures to ensure that the same fate did not happen to him, executing his own brothers as well as his son. Even so, Phraates IV was obliged to concentrate his attention on diffusing the grievances of the restive Parthian aristocracy.

In addition, when Rome emerged with a united empire after years of civil war, Parthia found itself again the subject of interference along its western border. Yet an amicable arrangement was reached in 20 BC with the first Roman emperor Augustus: in return for acknowledging the Euphrates as the Parthian border, the legionary standards that the Parthians had held since the Battle of Carrhae were returned to Rome. The Parthians also agreed that Armenia was a Roman client kingdom. Perhaps as a sign of good faith or possibly as a

The Parthian king Phraates IV, who reached a peace agreement with Augustus, the Roman emperor.

way of thwarting parricide, Phraates IV sent his sons to Rome as guarantors of the peace. With mischief in mind, Augustus may have sent a beautiful Italian ex-slave girl named Musa to Ctesiphon, the Parthian capital in the lower Euphrates-Tigris valley. She made an immediate impression as the queen and favorite wife of Phraates IV, giving birth to a son. In 2 BC she poisoned her old husband and raised her son to the Parthian throne. For two years she seems to have ruled alongside her son, as coins struck during their brief reign feature Phraates V on one side and Musa on the other. The legend around her portrait labels Musa as "heavenly." Both mother and son were forced to flee to Rome after being deposed by the Parthian aristocracy, which crowned Orodes II as king. But the new monarch was also replaced two years later by Vonones I, the eldest son of Phraates IV. Again the Parthian nobles were quickly dissatisfied with the new ruler, who fled to safety in Armenia.

This period of turmoil at court came to an end with the elevation in AD 10 of Artabatus II. His eighteen years on the throne were not without their troubles, since Artabatus II attempted to consolidate power in his hands, much to the annoyance of most prominent Parthian nobles. The determined king was once exiled, then allowed to return to the capital and resume his reign when no suitable successor was found. Internal discord continued to plague the Parthian kingdom down to the invasion of the Roman emperor Trajan. The specific cause of the renewal of conflict was Parthian intervention in the affairs of Armenia. Few in Rome believed that this was an adequate reason for war, despite an appreciation of Trajan's delight in campaigning. His most notable campaign so far was the conquest of Dacia, present-day Romania. Two motives in fact underlay the decision of the Roman emperor to attack Parthia; the first was strategic, the second economic.

Tidying up the Roman Empire's eastern frontier made sense. In 106 Trajan had annexed Arabia Petraea, the final piece of territory in securing Rome's control right round the Mediterranean. Following the demise of the Nabatean kingdom, a single legion plus recruited auxiliaries with specialist local skills were enough for its occupation. Then the Roman army topped 400,000 regulars, including 180,000 legionaries and 220,000 auxiliaries recruited in the provinces. Yet the thirty legions at the core of the Roman army were no longer predominantly Italian, since they consisted mostly of provincial volunteers. The attractiveness of military life was not restricted to the prospect of Roman citizenship at the end of twenty-five years' service. Once a volunteer was enrolled, his duties gave him a regime of fresh air and regular exercise. He also enjoyed good accommodation, excellent and varied food, clean water, and good preventive medicine. It was not accidental that despite the risk of death and injury in war, the average Roman soldier lived longer than the average Roman civilian, a longevity that speaks volumes about the attention paid by the military authorities to health. The bas-reliefs on Trajan's column in Rome reveal the care that army doctors took of the wounded on the battlefield and afterward in hospitals. That these men wore full combat gear suggests that their primary task, as for modern paramedics, was to reach the injured as quickly as possible and administer lifesaving first aid even in the thick of the fighting. Until World War I no army used combat orderlies as a way of reducing casualties like the Romans did during Trajan's reign. Each legionary fortress had its own hospital, and settlements behind the front line acted as convalescent centers.

If strengthening Rome's eastern frontier was one of the reasons for the invasion of Parthia, another was an urgent need to address a devastating imbalance in foreign trade. As the Roman Empire developed into a money economy, eastern spices and perfumes were purchased in large quantities, but the bulk of the imports remained raw silk thread. Stoic commentators lamented extravagant tastes and deplored the passing of a simpler Roman way of life. "I see garments," wrote the moralist Seneca, "if one may call them garments, in which there is nothing to cover either the wearer's body or shame." The squeeze the Parthians put on products passing through their kingdom exaggerated the drain of precious metals to India and China.

That Trajan himself eschewed luxurious living could well have prompted him into military action. In early 116 he marched from Syria to Mesopotamia, where at Dura Europos, a city located on the western bank of the Euphrates, a commemorative arch was erected in his honor. From there he moved eastward and captured Seleucia-upon-Tigris, the old capital of the Seleucids. Crossing the Tigris unopposed, he marched south, entering Ctesiphon without a fight. The Parthian king and his court had already abandoned the capital, leaving behind his daughter and golden throne to be captured by Trajan. It was personal triumph for the emperor who could now add Parthicus to his imperial titles. Trajan intended to carry on campaigning but was dissuaded by ill health. A remarkably well-preserved bust of the emperor carved about this time shows him with hollow cheeks and a receding hairline. He had already suffered a stroke, which left him partially paralyzed, but his refusal to slow down finally undermined his constitution.

When he died in late 117, Trajan had certainly emulated his hero Julius Caesar's foreign conquests, although his successor, Hadrian, reversed Trajan's foreign policy in the eastern Mediterranean, evacuating Mesopotamia and reverting to a buffer zone of client kingdoms.

An ageing Trajan shortly before his invasion of Mesopotamia.

Hadrian's concern with consolidating the empire's defenses came from a conviction that Trajan's eastern advance of the imperial frontier had overstretched its military resources. On the northern frontier, he confirmed the annexation of Dacia, a rich supplier of slaves and valuable metals, but in Britain he abandoned most of the conquests made by Trajan's predecessors and built a wall between Wallsend and Barrow-on-Solway. Some fifteen feet high, excluding battlements, Hadrian's wall was in places fronted by a defensive ditch twenty-six feet wide and fifteen feet deep. A series of forts acted as vantage points and gateways through the wall, which was manned against the unconquered peoples to the north, notably the Novantae and Selgovae. These peoples had caused considerable disturbances in 118, so that the chief purpose of the new line of defense was to separate the Novantae and Selgovae from their cousins, the Brigantes, who dwelt to the south in Roman territory.

The enormous booty from Trajan's wars, such as the half-million captives taken in Dacia, enabled Trajan to initiate vast public works,

Dacian heads being offered to Trajan on his column in Rome.

including a new forum and shopping center in Rome. It also gave him scope for relief measures aimed at poor children. And taxation was eased in the provinces, a move that gained Trajan the accolade of being the first of five "good emperors." This golden era in Roman history came to an end with Commodus, Marcus Aurelius's wayward son, who believed he was an incarnation of the legendary hero Herakles and decided to become a gladiator. Commodus's assassination in 192 led to the establishment of the Severan dynasty by Septimus Severus, who hailed from Lepcis Magna in North Africa.

Considering the military prowess of the Parthians, their inability to stand up to the Romans must be put down to chronic disunity. Fierce feuds were typical, as were sudden executions, as the fate of Surena after his stunning victory at Carrhae testifies. It would appear that the Parthians never shook off pastoralist ways, as they were incapable of forming anything that approached a centralized realm. Outlying areas even dared to send envoys to Rome, so fragmented was the Parthian political system. Recovery from Trajan's invasion was never complete enough to ensure Parthia's independence. Widespread rebellion and succession movements weakened royal authority to such an extent that King Artabanus V could not handle the revolt of Ardashir, who defeated and killed the king in 226. The remaining Parthian forces fled to the mountains, where Artabanus's son held out for a few years; eventually taken prisoner, he was executed in Ctesiphon, now the capital of a new Iranian power, the Sasanians.

King Ardashir I, founder of the Sasanian dynasty in Iran.

ROME VERSUS THE SASANIANS

Of the many military challenges faced by the later Roman Empire, the most persistent was that presented by Sasanid Iran. After the overthrow of the Parthian kingdom, the Sasanians—an aristocratic family from southern Iran—quickly established themselves as a force to be reckoned with, until they in turn succumbed to the Arab invasions of the 630s and 640s. The Sasanian kings were able to pose a more serious threat to the Romans compared with the Parthians because they more effectively harnessed the economic resources at their disposal. Improved irrigation schemes greatly increased food production, allowing families to expand and provide more recruits for the army, while active promotion of trade in the Indian Ocean stimulated the economy and increased the flow of tax revenue into the royal treasury. But, above all else, an end to the internal conflict that had handicapped the Parthian throne ensured there was no check on a Sasanian king's freedom of action.

The founding of the Sasanian dynasty is distinguished from that of the Parthian takeover of Iran by the fact that it was an uprising against fellow countrymen rather than a revolt against foreign intruders. Even though both the Parthians and the Sasanians were Zoroastrian, the latter were more aggressive proselytizers of that religion. So intent were Sasanian kings on religious conformity that they permitted the priesthood to exercise a role similar to that of Iranian mullahs today. Violent suppression of heterodoxy best characterizes the difference between the Parthian and Sasanian kingdoms. Ardashir himself introduced the assault on idolatry: cult statues were outlawed and fire promoted as the appropriate object of worship. Under Ardashir's successor, Shapur I, the name Kartir became synonymous with religious persecution. This influential priest was pleased to report the success of his punishment of Buddhists, Hindus, Manichees, and Christians. As Kartir informed the king, "images are destroyed, the lurking places of demons demolished, and the abodes of angels preserved."

This stress on orthodoxy had an impact on warfare since the protracted struggle between the Romans and the Sasanians came to be seen in religious terms. This was perhaps inevitable after the Roman emperor Constantine converted to Christianity and moved the empire's capital in 330 to the Greek city of Byzantium, located on the Sea of Marmara midway between the Mediterranean and Black Seas. Not only did Constantine wish to sever the imperial regime's links with pagan Rome, but he saw how the wealth of the empire now lay in the eastern Mediterranean. The Germans' overrunning of Rome's western provinces a century later has given rise to a tendency among historians to refer to the surviving eastern provinces as belonging to the Byzantine era, a name that signally fails to recognize the continuity of the later Roman Empire. The Greek-speaking inhabitants of Constantinople, the new capital founded by Constantine on the site of Byzantium, always called themselves Romans and their state Romania.

By the reign of Constantine, the Christian church possessed a coherent and homogeneous structure and body of agreed belief, but the emperor discovered there were still unresolved issues concerning the nature of Christ. Determined to establish Constantinople as the center of the Christian world, Constantine was in no mood for unnecessary disputes, and so he decided that the feuding bishops would settle their differences at the Council of Nicaea, modern Isnik in Asia Minor. The emperor himself presided over the crucial debates, guiding discussion toward a satisfactory conclusion. "Internal strife in the Church of God," he declared, "is far more evil and dangerous than any kind of war or conflict." Just how aware Constantine was of the profound theological shift he oversaw in 325 we have no way of knowing, but his intervention established an orthodoxy no less strict than that of Shapur I.

Some Christian groups, of course, resisted the identification of their faith with the Roman Empire. They simply could not accept it was the image of the heavenly kingdom, despite Constantine's calling himself the thirteenth apostle.

Yet a pangloss such as Eusebius of Caesarea, a favorite bishop of the emperor, could insist that "it was not just a result of human effort that the greater part of the world should be under Roman rule at the precise moment Jesus was born. The coincidence that our Savior began his mission against such a background was undeniably part of a divine plan."

Thus the scene was set for a final showdown between two state-sponsored religions: Christianity and Zoroastrianism. Before this climatic clash happened in the reign of Emperor Heraclius, however, periodic quarrels over Roman holdings of territory in the ancient Middle East were a sufficient cause of war. Ardashir had made it clear to the Romans that they should withdraw at the very least to Syria. In order to forestall any Roman advance into Mesopotamia, the Sasanians occupied the upper Euphrates-Tigris valley, notably the fortified cities of Carrhae and Nisibis. At this time the Roman legionaries were so keen to have emperors to their liking that they raised and pulled down twenty rulers in as many years.

It was a perfect opportunity for a Sasanian invasion of Syria, and Shapur I easily captured Antioch, the Roman seat of power there. Over 60,000 people were carried off into captivity. When Valerian arrived to restore the eastern frontier in 260, he was taken prisoner, the only Roman emperor to suffer such an indignity. At Naqsh-i-Rustam in southern Iran, a huge rock carving celebrates the event. It depicts a life-size Shapur I seated on horseback, while in front of him two Roman emperors acknowledge his supremacy. Tribute-paying Philip kneels in submission, and Valerian holds the king's horse, as Kartir contentedly looks on. The inscription tells us how "the Mazda-worshipping king" lords it over lands as far distant as Mesopotamia and India. Defeated rulers were regarded as the victor's slaves from the Assyrian Empire onward. One ex-king was obliged to run alongside the wheel of Tiglath-pileser III's chariot. This form of public humiliation still remained popular in Sasanian times, since Valerian acted as Shapur I's footstool whenever he mounted his horse.

Persia triumphant. A famous celebration of Rome's humiliation at Naqsh-i-Rustam.

Shapur I's capture of Antioch was not untypical of war along Rome's eastern frontier. Essentially pastoralists, the Parthians lacked the capacity to undertake sieges, but such was not the case with the Sasanians, who had settled down as farmers in a more urban-based society. Despite retaining a preference for mounted warfare, the Sasanians conducted numerous sieges of Roman strongholds, developing an enviable reputation in this field of military technology. That they were able to do so was most likely a result of their copying of Roman technics, even to the extent of using captured siege equipment. The Sasanians also proved adept at the construction of fortifications. In response to the spread of Sasanian fortifications, several Roman emperors built forts and military roads to link them together as a defense in depth against any repeat of Shapur I's assault on Antioch.

Ever since the reign of King Philip of Macedon, there had been a steady development of siege craft. Philip realized that the Macedonian army would only achieve limited objectives if it could not reduce cities as well as win battles. Alexander the Great's far-flung victories would have been impossible without this capacity. In their struggle against Macedon, the Romans were forced to improve their own skills in conducting sieges. They developed armored siege towers, massive iron battering rams far larger than any that had come before, large iron hooks to dislodge masonry from city walls, powerful catapults, covered platforms to protect miners and assault teams, and drawbridges to deliver attackers from the tops of towers. Once the Romans were committed to a siege, it was only a question of time before the invested city fell. The Jewish historian Josephus relates how, at the siege of Jerusalem in 67, Roman artillery pieces were able to hurl one-hundred-pound stones over four hundred yards, a weight of shot that thoroughly intimidated the city's defenders.

The striking force of the Roman army was always its heavy infantry, the legionaries. The tactical proficiency and killing power of these soldiers was unsurpassed in ancient times, especially when they wielded the *gladius*, an exceptionally sharp sword. Apparently adopted from the Celtic peoples of Spain, this weapon terrified the spearmen of Greek armies. Legionaries were armed with a shield, two javelins, a dagger, and a sword. The javelins were thrown to disrupt enemy formations before the Romans closed to attack with their swords. A skirmish between a unit of legionaries armed with the *gladius* and Macedonian infantrymen in Thessaly prior to the Battle of Cynoscephalae in 197 BC dramatically revealed the advantage in close combat enjoyed by the Romans. So as to stiffen the resolve of the Macedonian phalanx the day before the battle proper, an elaborate funeral was arranged for the men who had fallen in the skirmish. But the plan backfired as the Macedonian rank and file were appalled by the damage inflicted by the legionary swords. Instead of the neat wounds resulting from a spear thrust, they saw injuries that looked like the work of a meat cleaver.

Despite their dismay, the Macedonians came within an ace of defeating the Romans the next day. The massed charge of one phalanx—an unnerving sight, even for battle-hardened legionaries—overcame a legion, but a second phalanx overreached itself, lost formation, and fell victim to another legion. The battle hung in the balance until the more versatile tactics of the legionaries told at close quarters. When the Macedonians raised their pikes as a sign of surrender, the Romans either misunderstood this gesture or decided to ignore it. Cynoscephalae was the first Roman victory over a Greek army in a major pitched battle.

Yet, as the Romans first discovered at Carrhae and then in later engagements in Mesopotamia, getting to close quarters with either the Parthians or the Sasanians was far from easy. As Ammianus Marcellinus points out, the Romans found themselves confronting a very different kind of enemy. An eyewitness of action against the Sasanians, this Roman historian tells us that all their lancers

> were clad in mail; their bodies were covered with plates so closely fitting that the stiff joints of the armor conformed to the shape of the limbs underneath, and the armor was so skillfully fitted to their heads that the whole person was clad in metal scale. The only spots where a weapon could lodge were the tiny holes left for the eyes and nostrils, which allowed some degree of vision and a scanty supply of air. . . . Close by, the archers, practiced from the very cradle in a skill in which that people especially excel, were bending their flexible bows.

Ammianus also mentions elephants, "whose awful aspect and gaping jaws inspired unbearable fear, and whose noise, smell and strange appearance terrified our horses even more than ourselves."

Notable in its absence from Ammianus's description is any reference to infantry, a branch of combat to which neither the Parthians nor the Sasanians gave much attention. Both these Iranian peoples recruited foot soldiers, but they were appendages to the main attacking force, the lancers and the archers. To counter this unusual challenge, the Romans fielded a greater variety of combatants, with a significant increase in the numbers of mounted archers and heavy cavalry. Workshops were even set up in Syria and Cappadocia in order to manufacture cavalry equipment.

The accession of Aurelian in 270 ended the military anarchy that had engulfed the Roman Empire for over three decades. He reunified the empire, ringed the city of Rome with strong walls, and reduced Palmyra to obedience. This oasis kingdom had used the withdrawal of Shapur I from Antioch and the temporary weakness of Rome in the eastern Mediterranean to extend its authority beyond Syria. But Palmyra could only flourish in the absence of Roman and Sasanian forces, as Queen Zenobia soon found to her personal cost.

Following the death of Shapur I in the same year that Aurelian became emperor, the Sasanians gradually lost the gains that this energetic king had made. As a result of pressure from the Kushanas on the eastern frontier, the Sasanians ceded to Rome both northern Mesopotamia and Armenia. One Sasanian king married a Kushan princess in a vain attempt to promote peaceful relations in the east. Out of this chaos, however, arose one of the most powerful figures in Sasanian history, Shapur II. Promoted though he was by a discontented aristocracy, Shapur II quickly established himself as a monarch unprepared to broke opposition to his commands. And his military prowess enabled him to win back all the recently lost territories. The Kushanas were brought under control, the Huns restricted to the Central Asian steppe, and the Romans put on the back foot.

Shapur II's successful siege of Amida, a Roman stronghold on the upper Tigris, provoked a full-scale invasion of Mesopotamia in 363. Neither the Romans nor the Sasanians could destroy each other militarily, since their centers of power were too far distant, in the Mediterranean basin and on the Iranian plateau, respectively, but this did not stop them from an endless contest in the ancient Middle East. Both peoples felt compelled to dominate this region, which explains Shapur II's desire to reopen hostilities. It began with the siege of Amida. Having stabilized the Rhine frontier, the Roman emperor Julian decided that the eastern frontier needed his attention. It was even suggested that Julian saw himself as a second Alexander the Great.

Julian was an experienced general, but his opponents had all been of one kind—tribal peoples, brave and resourceful, yet rarely united when faced by Rome. Across the Rhine he had repeatedly exploited the superior mobility and striking power of his troops by making deep thrusts into enemy territory and sweeping pincer movements against isolated German tribesmen.

A war against Sasanian Iran was another proposition altogether, a fact that Julian was slow to grasp. Even more, his plan to replace Shapur on the throne with his brother Prince Hormizd was unrealistic, to say the least. The Sasanians were unlikely to accept Hormizd, who had long been an exile among the Romans. Ignoring all advice, Julian pressed on with his Mesopotamian campaign, which at first went well. Marching down the bank of the Euphrates, the Romans took what they needed from the narrow belt of cultivation and set fire to the rest. There was hardly any contact with the enemy, although Sasanian patrols were never far away. Approaching Ctesiphon, the Romans were obliged to besiege well-fortified settlements such as Porisbora, the second-largest city in Mesopotamia. Only when the Romans moved up a great tower on wheels, equipped with catapults and rams, was the garrison persuaded to capitulate. Both the city and its citadel were then destroyed.

Not long afterward three squadrons of Roman cavalry patrolling near the burnt-out city were surprised by a similar force of Sasanians. A few of the Romans were killed and a standard captured. Infuriated by the reverse, Julian cashiered the two surviving officers of the defeated patrol and put to death ten soldiers under their command. Whether this exemplary punishment was intended to restore discipline or showed a loss of nerve on the part of Julian is impossible to decide. Ammianus states that the Roman army acquiesced in the emperor's action, which was accompanied by a "sober speech, which steered a middle course between indulgence and severity," and that the soldiers "returned to their tents and recruited their strength by a night's sleep and such food as was available."

But the campaign had so far not brought about the decisive encounter that Julian wanted, for Shapur II was content to wear the invaders down with harassing tactics like mounting sudden attacks by mounted archers and flooding the route of their advance. Every day lost by Julian was a day gained by Shapur II. Yet, under the walls of Ctesiphon, the Roman emperor achieved his goal: in an engagement before they retired into the city, he slew over 2,000 Sasanians with a loss of just seventy men. Then, "at a conference of the general staff about the siege of Ctesiphon, the day was carried by those who were sure it would be a rash and foolish undertaking: first, because the location of the city made it impregnable, and, second, it was believed that the Sasanian king would soon arrive with a formidable host."

Evidently the Romans had not appreciated the strength of the Sasanian capital. Julian himself may have hoped that some of its inhabitants would betray the city. Doubtless Hormizd had adherents inside, but nothing happened. There was no alternative but to fall back to Roman territory. During the retreat toward Syria, Julian fell in a skirmish, and in order to shake off the pursuing Sasanians, his successor, Jovian, agreed to give up all the land along the Tigris as well as the whole of Armenia. The Armenians resisted stubbornly, but as they now lacked Roman support, Shapur II was able to incorporate them into a Sasanian province. According to Ammianus, Jovian was a lazy and incompetent staff officer who had no stomach for fighting. "It would have been better to fight ten times over the territories," Ammianus thought, "than surrender any of them." As it was, Nisibis and Singara were handed over to Shapur II without their inhabitants; the garrisons of surrendered Roman fortresses also made their way to Syria.

Notwithstanding Armenias remaining a disputed territory, the eastern frontier of the Roman Empire was remarkably undisturbed during the fifth and sixth centuries. Both the Sasanians and the Romans were preoccupied with problems on their northern frontiers, triggered by the movement of Central Asian peoples. Most of the energy of the Roman emperor Justinian, for instance, was directed at the reconquest of north Africa from the Vandals and Italy from the Goths, two of the German peoples who had settled in the western provinces of the Roman Empire. A devastating outbreak of the plague in 542, which resulted in an enormous loss of life, also weakened the military capacity of both Rome and Sasanid Iran.

Conflict only resumed in earnest during the seventh century. So hard-pressed were the Romans in 626 that the city of Constantinople was threatened by the Avars as well as the Sasanians. The Avars took advantage of the absence of Emperor Heraclius and his army in Asia Minor, where he was attempting to hold back a Sasanian advance. Just 12,000 men under the command of Bonos, whom Heraclius had appointed as regent, remained to defend the capital. The Avars destroyed buildings in the western suburbs, constructed a palisade to hem in the city's inhabitants, and built wooden towers to assault the walls. One Roman eyewitness relates how the Avars and their Slavic allies were "the most frightening sight to behold, and to see it was to derange the senses. For against each one of our soldiers there were a hundred and more barbarians, all dressed in breastplates and helmeted, bringing every war machine. The sun from the east with its rays accentuated the iron, and made them appear frightful and shook the viewers."

As a sign of supernatural support against this threat, the patriarch Serios carried an icon of the Virgin around the city walls and through the city streets. But the ability of the small garrison to withstand Avar assaults, other than a grim determination not to yield, really depended upon the landward defenses that Theodosius II had built in the fifth century.

These defenses comprised three lines of obstacles: on the outside edge was a deep ditch some eighty yards wide, sections of which could be flooded if required; inside the ditch was a low breastwork, protecting an open space in front of the outer towers; behind this wall was the final defense, a formidable inner wall that was studded by towers rising twice the height of the outer wall. The Theodosian wall was pierced by a number of gates, some used by the general public, others reserved for the army.

The turning point of the Avar siege appears to have been the bloody repulse of an all-out attack on the Theodosian wall that coincided with the Roman defeat of the Sasanian fleet on the Sea of Marmara. By sinking these ships with some 4,000 horsemen on board, the Romans prevented a linkup with the Avars on the European shore. Afterward the Avar khan burned his wooden assault towers and withdrew—a tremendous psychological triumph for the Romans. The siege and its defeat were strictly military actions, but the inhabitants of Constantinople saw the event as nothing less than a Christian miracle. Already a growing belief in the efficacy of religious images, not to say holy relics, was anticipating the conflicts of the Middle Ages, especially the Crusades.

In an irony of history, the duel between Heraclius and Khusrau II, the Sasanian king, arose from Roman political turmoil. In 590 Khusrau II had been driven into exile by a rebellious aristocracy, but he found in the Roman emperor Maurice someone prepared to restore him to the throne. In return for ceding a large part of Armenia, Maurice dispatched an army and reinstated Khusrau II as the Sasanian king. For Maurice, a peaceful eastern frontier was priceless. So short of money was the imperial treasury that he cut the rations of his troops, whose inevitable mutiny led to Maurice's overthrow in 602. Even though Heraclius restored order in Constantinople a decade later, Khusrau II remained unconvinced that this second coup was anything more than continued Roman intrigue, and so he remained intent on avenging the murder of Maurice.

By 619 Khusrau II had overrun Syria, Palestine, and Egypt. Once the Sasanians advanced into Asia Minor, Heraclius knew that a critical moment had arrived for what was left of the Roman Empire. The loss of so much territory made meeting the army payroll impossible, but the emperor got the church to furnish a massive loan instead. He also appreciated how his troops needed a program of intensive training, because the survival of Constantinople depended now upon military versatility. With a limited pool of manpower, the Roman army could not afford to waste the lives of its soldiers. Like their modern

The late Roman emperor Heraclius and his son Constantine III.

counterparts, and unlike most medieval warriors, Heraclius's men were trained to fight in different ways, according to specific tactics adapted to the terrain and the enemy at hand.

The Avars were at first allies of the Romans but fell out with Heraclius when he refused to let them settle within the empire. The Romans thought they were much like the Huns, who had earlier arrived from the Central Asian steppe. But as one Roman general remarked, setting them apart was a "concern for military organization, which makes them stronger than other nomads when it comes to pitched battles." The Avars could handle effectively the lance as well as the bow through the use of the stirrup, which was immediately adopted by the Roman cavalry. When added later to the built-up saddle, another Asian innovation, it laid the basis for knighthood in Europe.

It was fortunate for Heraclius that the Avars lacked the skill and patience to invest Constantinople for long, because it was more important for the Roman emperor to carry the counterattack into the Sasanian heartland, which seemed possible now that he was pushing Khusrau II's forces steadily eastward. Heraclius's sense of timing and his willingness to combine battle with diplomacy had put the Sasanians on the defensive. In frustration, the Sasanian king dismissed Shahrbaraz, his best commander. Even worse, the Romans intercepted a letter from Khusrau

II ordering Shahrbaraz's execution. When shown the correspondence, the commander stopped fighting the Romans altogether in Asia Minor, leaving Heraclius free to retake Syria and Palestine.

Although he received no Sasanian military assistance, Heraclius profited from intelligence that Shahrbaraz willingly supplied. The passivity of the disaffected commander and his men indeed permitted the Roman emperor to invade Mesopotamia and capture Ctesiphon almost unopposed. A fifth column, inspired by either Christian sentiment or hatred of Khusrau II, also helped the Romans. Just as critical was an alliance with the Kok Turks, sworn enemies of the Sasanians. Heraclius had to find, create, and seal alliances with peoples who could provide him with additional troops, especially those who were strategically placed or possessed expertise in warfare. One such group was the Kok Turks, whose contribution to the defeat of Khusrau II topped 40,000 men. In Armenia Heraclius came to terms with Yabghu, the Kok Turk leader, at a ceremony that consisted of oath taking, an exchange of gifts, and a celebratory feast. Heraclius even showed Yabghu a portrait of his sixteen-year-old daughter with the intent of securing a dynastic alliance.

The decisive engagement of Heraclius's campaign took place near the ruins of the Assyrian city of Nineveh. There he wanted to exploit his foot soldiers' ability in hand-to-hand combat and close with the Sasanians before they could dominate the battlefield with their bows. So a thick fog covering the battlefield suited the Romans perfectly. It hampered the Sasanian archers and allowed the legionaries to approach their opponents without taking serious casualties from arrows. Once battle was joined, the onslaught of the Roman infantry disconcerted the Sasanians. It also seems that not all of the Sasanian forces were ready to fight at the start of the action, since contingents are reported to have arrived in the middle of the battle. Almost 6,000 Sasanians were slain, with much booty taken after the fighting ceased.

In a panic, Khusrau II tried to flee but was imprisoned by his son Kawadh-Siroy, who then starved his father to death. That the sons of Shahrbaraz participated in this coup, which raised Kawadh-Siroy to the throne, suggests that the commander had come to some agreement with Heraclius. Having restored Roman authority in the eastern Mediterranean, Heraclius must have imagined his work was done. But he was about to face another enemy in the Arabs, who had just begun their raids on Palestine. Although the recovery of the True Cross from the Sasanians seemed to augur well for Christianity, within a decade of Heraclius's victory at Nineveh, the city of Jerusalem surrendered to the Arabs. It was the beginning of a worldwide series of campaigns that saw Arab arms reach Spain and France in the west and India and Central Asia in the east and become the dominant power in the Middle East. The Arabs destroyed Heraclius's old enemy, Sasanid Iran, in 641, the same year in which the Roman emperor died. The process was part of a historical transition from ancient to medieval times, as the reign of Heraclius had straddled both of these distinct eras. Heraclius and his contemporaries exhibited great interest in relics, a new strand of religious belief that even encompassed the emperor himself after his death. Heraclius's belt and other items of dress were coveted: they were used to reward loyal allies. Even his tomb was opened to remove his imperial crown.

The fame of Heraclius rested squarely on military success, for he never gave up a fight. He was no quitter; he could not afford to be one during his troubled reign. That quality made Heraclius the last of the great warrior-rulers of the ancient Middle East and perhaps one of its most notable exponents of warfare.

CHAPTER SEVEN

The Smaller States

HAVING LOOKED AT THE ARMED RIVALRY OF THE GREAT POWERS IN THE ancient Middle East, it is time to examine the experience of five smaller states whose histories illuminate quite separate military events. All five—Troy, Bactria, Judea, Petra, and Palmyra—were important enough to feature in the historical record, although the siege of Troy was celebrated in epic verse rather than documentary detail. Yet Homer's account of the conflict between the Trojans and the Greeks is echoed in the archives of the Hittites, the leading power in Asia Minor. For Bactria there are Macedonian and Indian sources, so great was its impact on northern India. Judea, Petra, and Palmyra were all entangled with the Roman Empire's efforts to strengthen its eastern frontier, against the Parthians first and then the Sasanians. None of them survived as independent kingdoms once it suited Rome to formally annex them to its empire.

TROY AND ASIA MINOR
For over two millennia, the story of the Trojan War has provided the Western world with a heroic ideal of warfare, most memorable in the single combat between the Trojan prince Hector and Achilles, the only son of Peleus, king of Thessaly, and the sea nymph Thetis, daughter of the sea god Nereus. Both Zeus and Poseidon, the chief marine deity, wished to have a child by the beautiful Thetis but were warned that her son would be more powerful than his father. Hector alone dared to meet Achilles beneath the walls of Troy. "Fate," we are informed, "for her own evil purposes, kept Hector in front of the Scaean Gate." But when Hector

saw Achilles face-to-face, "he began to tremble. . . . No longer with the heart to stand his ground . . . he left the gate, and ran away in terror." What follows is a nightmarish pursuit on foot in which "the pursuer cannot overtake nor the pursued escape." As only the gods could settle this contest, Zeus held up "his golden scales, putting death sentences in each pan, one side for Achilles, on the other side for horse-taming Hector. When the balance began to tilt towards Hector, his fate was decided. Apollo immediately abandoned him, while the goddess Athena let Achilles know of his forthcoming success."

Thus Achilles's spear drove into Hector "between his collar bone and his neck." The combat over, the Trojans should have been permitted to recover Hector's body as custom dictated, but instead Achilles subjected "the fallen prince to a dreadful humiliation. He slit the tendons at the back of both his feet, inserted leather straps, and made them fast to his chariot, leaving the head to drag. . . . Then he whipped his horses, who galloped off. Behind a naked Hector raised a cloud of dust, his once handsome head dragged ignominiously through the Trojan soil."

Though he finally allowed Hector's body to be handed over to the Trojans, Achilles had behaved in appalling fashion. Without the aid of the goddess Aphrodite, who rubbed on "ambrosial oil" to slow down the process of decomposition, the corpse would have been in a terrible state, for Achilles had chosen to add insult to injury by driving in his chariot round the city of Troy while Hector's body twisted and turned in the dust behind him. Achilles himself was in fact slain by Hector's younger brother Paris, none other than Helen's lover, whose arrow the archer god Apollo guided into the Greek champion's heel. Thetis had dipped the baby Achilles into the river of Hades, the Styx, so as to make him invulnerable, but since she had to hold him by the heel, this spot remained unprotected.

Because of the involvement of the gods in *The Iliad*, Homer's account of the Trojan War, there was skepticism about the authenticity of the conflict before the German archaeologist Heinrich Schliemann in the late nineteenth century identified present-day Hisarlik in northeastern Asia Minor as the site of the Trojan capital. Until this discovery, the war was regarded as myth, not history. Excavation at Hisarlik revealed almost

A sixth-century BC vase depicting Achilles's pursuit of Hector.

continuous occupation of the settlement from the fourth millennium BC onward. And a destruction level dated to around 1200 BC rather neatly corresponds to Homer's timing of the Trojan War.

That Homer tells us Apollo was the only god who consistently sided with the Trojans signals the non-European heritage of this people. Besides assisting Paris in slaying Achilles, Apollo showered the Greek camp with plague-tipped arrows from a bow he must have acquired from Resheph in Cyprus, where the Phoenicians appeased this plague god and, more importantly, linked him with Apollo himself. Homer seems to have sensed that the Greek-Trojan contest was as much a clash of cultures as a struggle between two ancient military powers. By Homer's lifetime, Apollo had become a thoroughly Greek deity, the owner of the greatest oracle of all at Delphi, but not every aspect of his original character was lost. He remained the mainstay of the chariot-riding Trojans, the god who delighted in guiding the arrows they fired from their composite bows.

A real king of Mycenae may well have led the Greek armada to Troy, but Agamemnon's leadership has been absorbed into a tale of divine rivalry, of gods and goddesses settling their personal disputes by backing either the Greeks or the Trojans. Yet even with Helen, the cause of the war, we are dealing with a goddess rather than a wayward queen. Hatched from an egg, this daughter of Zeus was probably a tree goddess whose cult encompassed abduction as well as rescue. Her abandoned husband Menelaus had no choice but take Helen back to Sparta at the end of the ten-year siege.

Hisarlik was known to the Hittites as Wilusa and to the Greeks as Wilios, later Ilion. The Hittites called the "land of Wilusa" Truisa, which can hardly be distinguished from the Greek Troia. Archaeological finds also show that the city of Troy was once a royal residence and trading center whose prosperity is evident in an increasing population and an expanding settlement. Troy's importance was a consequence of its exceptionally favorable economic and strategic position in Asia Minor, which afforded the closest control over maritime trade between the Aegean and the Black Sea. The city thus served as a commercial harbor, storage facility, manufacturing center, marketplace, and terminus for products from the interior. Its wealth obviously attracted the Greeks, whatever the specific reason for their famous assault on the city. Hittite texts reveal that during the thirteenth century BC, Troy suffered a number of attacks that might have involved Greek marauders since we are aware that they were interested in the Aegean coastline of Asia Minor. The Cretan foundation of Miletus, Millawanda to the Hittites, was for a long time a Greek stronghold.

Yet Homer's account of the actual fighting beneath the walls of Troy is unrealistic. He was of course a poet and not a military historian. As a result, Homer dwells on the prowess of individual warriors locked in single combat or the struggle of a lone hero pitting his strength against several assailants rather than on the tactics of the opposing forces. Unaware of the role of the charioteer and the chariot archer during the Trojan War, Homer celebrates the glory of dismounted fighters. This is really his heroic theme in what is a very circumscribed poem. The whole story told in *The Iliad* unfolds in less than two months, with armed combat measured in days, not weeks. When the Greeks and the Trojans clash on the plain between the city of Troy and the Greek camp, the various engagements are at locations within a few miles of each other.

Despite his best efforts to give the chariot a role in the narrative, Homer describes no massed chariotry attacks, and the vehicle is presented as a battle taxi, delivering warriors to the action. Possession of a chariot marks out the owner as an important person, but the use to which it is put in *The Iliad* has no parallel at all in the ancient Middle East, where at this period it dominated the battlefield. Yet Xanthus, one of Achilles's chariot horses, rebukes the Greek hero for his lack of trust in the chariot team and warns him of his approaching death. In anger at this prophecy, the Erinyes, the furious spirits of justice, at once strike the immortal horse dumb. Their intervention probably reflects a desire to see events run a normal course, undisrupted by any warning of a future event. Not that "Achilles of the nimble feet" cares a hoot: He tells Xanthus he is doomed to die at Troy. It seems likely that the divine horses of Achilles were imported from the ancient Middle East, where they were worshipped in Syria.

Another blank in Homer's understanding of early warfare concerns his treatment of Paris's slaying of Achilles with a composite bow, the

Achilles harnesses his chariot horses.

weapon of the chariot archer. The Greek poet is entirely ignorant of its method of manufacture. No matter the expertise of its maker, such a bow as Homer describes—"two horns of an ibex [fitted] together, made all smooth, [with] a golden tip at the end"—would have been far too stiff and unyielding for practical use. Homer did not appreciate that the extra velocity of a composite bow derived from adding strips of horn and sinew to wood. By the time *The Iliad* was composed, the composite bow's pivotal role in combat had been forgotten, not least because the nature of warfare had completely changed. Infantry engagements now took the place of chariot battle as Greek communities moved from citadels to city-states. Chariot-riding aristocrats no longer ruled from fortified palaces and instead fought alongside their fellow citizens on foot. Another reason for the lack of archery in *The Iliad* could well be a disdain on the part of Homer for missile weapons. It is almost as if Achilles, the terror of the battlefield, is killed by an underhand method, a sneaky arrow.

A curious tradition relating to the Trojan War is the Romans' belief that one of their ancestors was Aeneas, the son of the goddess Aphrodite and Anchises, a member of the royal family of Troy. Aeneas is an important warrior in *The Iliad*, second only to Hector, but his significance lies in the events that supposedly took place after the Greek sack of Troy, when

A Mycenaean depiction of warriors.

The coin Julius Caesar struck to underline his own descent from Aeneas.

he led a remnant of his people to Italy. The Romans regarded Aeneas as the beneficiary of both destiny and providence, since the success of his epic voyage westward depended upon the goodwill of the Fates.

The story of Aeneas's arrival in Italy was in existence well before Virgil made it the theme of *The Aeneid*, which celebrates Rome's greatness under Augustus, its first emperor. As the great-nephew of Julius Caesar, Augustus was delighted with the poem because his family claimed descent from Aeneas. To emphasize this divine lineage, Julius Caesar had struck coins showing Aeneas carrying his aged father from the burning city of Troy.

BACTRIA AND INDIA

The campaigns of Alexander the Great brought Macedonian rule to large territories in Central Asia and northwestern India. One of these kingdoms, Bactria, appeared a miracle of fertility based on oases and extensive pasturage. It was bounded in the north by the Oxus river, in the northwest by the Pamir mountains, and in the south by the Hindu Kush. Under the Seleucids, Bactria and nearby Sogdiana formed a single province, but as the power of the Seleucids declined, Bactria broke away as an independent kingdom.

King Antiochus III was the last Seleucid king to exert any real authority over Bactria. In 208 BC he launched an expedition to reassert Seleucid authority in the east, besieging the Bactrian capital, present-day Balk, for three years. But the standoff ended with concessions, Antiochus recognizing the value of Bactria as a buffer state against intruders from the Central Asian steppe. He allowed the de facto ruler Euthydemus to call himself king, and taking the Bactrian elephant corps with him, Antiochus descended into northwestern India, where he renewed his friendship with Subhagasenus, a local Indian dynast. Subhagasenus may have been a semi-independent ruler on the edge of the Mauryan Empire.

The reign of Euthydemus saw significant expansion of Bactria, both to the southwest and to the southeast toward India. This king's freedom of action was undoubtedly enhanced by the Parthian ruler Arsaces, who had created a kingdom of his own between the Seleucids and the Bactrians. Even Antiochus was obliged to accept the existence of an independent Parthia.

It used to be thought that Demetrius I, Euthydemus's son, was responsible for the extension of Bactrian power into India, but now the architect of the Indo-Greek era of Indian history appears to have been Demetrius II. Around 150 BC this Bactrian king issued coins showing himself wearing an elephant-scalp headdress, symbolizing his conquests in India. The period in which Greek kings ruled northern India lasted 150 years, the same length of time that the Normans dominated England.

Neither the remnants of the once mighty Mauryan Empire nor the Sunga dynasty that replaced it in northern India could resist the expeditionary forces that Demetrius II dispatched from Bactria. Whether or not Candragupta was inspired to found the first Indian empire through a meeting with Alexander the Great at Taxila in 326 BC, as Plutarch would have us believe, this native ruler put together territories spread right across the Indus and Ganges valleys, after the Macedonian king headed back to Mesopotamia. The refusal of the Macedonians, the core

Multilingual coin issued by King Agathocles of Taxila, with Greek and Indian scripts.

of Alexander the Great's army, to do more than subdue the Indus valley provided an opportunity for conquest. The sheer size of India, the scale of its kingdoms and their populations, baffled these hardened soldiers as much as Alexander himself, for Aristotle, the king's tutor, had said that the subcontinent projected eastward into the great ocean that surrounded the lands of the world in the same manner as the Chersonesus, the Gallipoli peninsula, fitted into the Aegean Sea.

Four years after Alexander left India, Candragupta founded the Mauryan Empire in the undisturbed Ganges valley and then moved eastward to conquer the states and cities loyal to the Macedonians. Megasthenes, the Seleucid ambassador who attended Candragupta's court, was amazed at the professionalism of the standing Mauryan army. It was organized under a committee of thirty senior officers, divided into subcommittees that controlled the infantry, chariotry, elephant corps, navy, and supply train.

Candragupta was assisted, however, by more than able commanders. He discovered in the brahman Kautilya a minister of outstanding worth. The surviving writings of Kautilya show him as a profound political and economic thinker. The minister's linking of taxation, administration, and military power was crucial in the establishment of India's first large, centralized state. Yet, at the same moment the political landscape was undergoing this far-reaching change, another transformation thoroughly reshaped religion. Two beliefs, Buddhism and Jainism, were then making startling headway. Traditional religious practices were being challenged by the teachings of the Buddha, who had died in 479 BC, and the Jain savior Mahavira, his contemporary. No less open to their influence than his subjects was Candragupta himself. Finding that he could not save his empire from the ravages of a terrible famine, he abdicated in 297 BC in favor of his son Bindusara and traveled to southern India where he became a Jain recluse. A bas-relief at Sravana Begola records Candragupta's life, including his final act of renunciation, the Jain rite of fasting unto death.

Jainism has its roots in the most ancient stratum of Indian belief: it holds that karma, the sinful trigger of rebirth, is present in matter itself and pollutes the immaterial soul. Unlike Buddhists, who consider inten-

Seleucid coin showing the elephants given by Candragupta around 300 BC as part of the settlement of the Indian frontier.

tion as the fundamental issue to be overcome in the pursuit of enlightenment, a Jain ascetic was so worried about accidental contamination that he carried a broom to sweep his path, lest his feet crush minute creatures. This idea is located at the impersonal end of the spectrum of ancient belief, far removed from Western notions about the survival of the personality. Only through an act of sustained self-renunciation could the soul escape the sufferings of the world. Hence the bewilderment of Alexander's men in 324 BC at Ecbatana, on their return from India, when the holy man Kalanos chose to cremate himself on a pyre. He was almost certainly a Jain who had accompanied the Macedonian king on his journey westward.

Perhaps because Candragupta—as a usurper of power over an extensive area of land that had previously been a patchwork of squabbling kingdoms—was such a new phenomenon in Indian politics, he could safely indulge his own preference for Jainism. Despite the suffering caused by the famine that had prompted him to abdicate, Candragupta handed over to his eldest son Bindusara a well-established empire. Yet Bindusara did not espouse the nonviolent doctrines of Jainism; on the contrary, his belligerent foreign policy earned him the title "slayer of foes." Religious scruples would trouble Bindusara's successor, Asoka, however. Although he did not abdicate like his grandfather Candragupta, Asoka became the world's first Buddhist ruler. It seems that the unprecedented bloodshed involved in a campaign in Kalinga, a part of modern Orissa, proved a turning point, for afterward Asoka suffered a crisis of confidence in Mauryan aggression. To pull himself together, this third Mauryan emperor embraced Buddhism, and for the rest of his life he endeavored to conquer through righteousness rather than warfare. In the process Asoka turned Buddhism into a pan-Asian religion two and a half centuries after Buddha's death. He even sent envoys to the eastern

Mediterranean urging the belligerent successors of Alexander to abandon aggression and follow the Buddha's gentler ways.

Although several kings in India were sympathetic to the Buddha's teachings during his lifetime, there was no systematic effort to adhere to the principles of behavior that he preached. Not that this worried the Buddha in the least, because he predicted that at a future date a great ruler would establish a Buddhist world order. This ruler, Asoka came to believe, was none other than himself. As he said of the rock-cut edicts that he caused to appear throughout his territories: "They are not everywhere yet, because of the extent of my dominions. But I shall have more prepared so that people may know how to behave." Carved on tall pillars, sometimes on rock faces, the edicts of Asoka employed many languages, including Aramaic as well as Greek. Inscriptions in these two languages, discovered in 1958 by archaeologists in southern Afghanistan, were intended to propagate Buddhism among the peoples Alexander had settled in cities there.

Greek musicians depicted at the Buddhist site of Sanchi.

There were of course descendants of Macedonian and Greek veterans in the Indus valley as well. Alexander had left the Punjab under the rule of Porus and Taxiles as subordinate kings, but Taxiles was toppled in 321 BC by Eudamus, whom Alexander had left in military command of the area. Eudamus went on to assassinate Porus too. Candragupta swiftly exploited the ensuing confusion to extend his empire northwestward, but he stopped short of invading Bactria. The subsequent border agreement with Seleucus I left Candragupta in control of the Indus valley, and Greeks and Indians did not face each other in battle again until two centuries later.

Already Agathocles, the son of the Bactrian king Demetrius I, had become the king of Taxila, where he issued a multilingual coinage that featured images of Indian deities. Yet the decisive thrust into the subcontinent was made by Demetrius II and his son Menander. The result of their

Demetrius II of Bactria, whose elephant headdress records his Indian conquests.

campaigns, especially those of Menander, which penetrated the Ganges valley, was that Demetrius II became the ruler of the most extensive Indo-Greek realm yet—larger than any Alexander the Great had ever ruled in India. These remarkable conquests were facilitated by the decline of the Mauryan Empire after Asoka's death in 232 BC, which has been blamed on his ardent support for the Buddhist doctrine of nonviolence. But this idea ignores the fact that if he had been an out-and-out pacifist, there would have been no executions during his reign. Whatever the reason for Mauryan weakness, the dynasty ended in a palace coup when, in 185 BC, Pusyamitra killed the last Mauryan ruler and declared himself the first Sunga king.

Menander was the most significant of the Indo-Greek kings. He is remembered in the Indian record not least for his starring role in the Buddhist work the *Milindapanha*, or the "Questions of King Milinda." These questions were put to Nagasena, who believed that monasteries were not the sole property of monks as their chief function was to facilitate contacts between monks and the laity. Otherwise Buddhist monks might as well conduct their spiritual exercises in the depths of a forest. Nagasena's willingness to answer the questions of Milinda, as Menander is rendered in the text, rests on the firm conviction that the duty of the monastic order was the spreading the Buddha's teachings across society at large. It explains why lay Buddhists were so zealous in building monasteries and seeing them prosper and multiply.

Menander was probably the first Greek king to be drawn personally to Buddhism, as the coins of Agathocles carried Buddhist symbols as well as Indian deities. But Menander's adoption of Buddhism may have also been a way of rallying support against the Sunga dynasty. Only under the Sungas would the brahmans begin to occupy the highest social rank, which they thought was rightfully theirs. The Sunga kings were indeed brahmans themselves. Within four more centuries, the rigidity of the

The Bactrian king Menander, the only Greek ruler known to have become a Buddhist.

caste system had fully evolved, as the law-giver Manu argued that Indian society was properly divided into four hereditary classes. He also reduced the status of women, who, like the lowest caste and outcastes, were henceforth ineligible to hear the scriptures.

The Buddha had rejected this point of view outright. He said that people should be judged by how they behaved, not by the family into which they were born. This viewpoint appealed to the individualist Greeks as much as to the Indians whom brahmanical

theory downgraded socially. A tradition that Menander built a Buddhist stupa at Pataliputra, the old Mauryan capital, seems to refer to a second campaign in the Ganges valley when he was himself the Bactrian king. Then the Sungas were forced to move their capital to Vidisa, on the northern edge of the Deccan. A lone sandstone pillar at Besnagar, the site of ancient Vidisa, boasts an inscription carved at the behest of Heliodoros, the ambassador of Antialcides, who ruled in the Indus valley around 100 BC. The column was raised in honor of Krishna, an incarnation of the preserver god Vishnu, whose emerging cult fascinated the Bactrian Greeks. The youthful Krishna's ability to kill a series of monsters sent against him by the tyrannical ruler of Mathura had already led to his identification with the Greek hero Herakles.

Hardly surprising then is the Buddhist column raised by Menander in the Ganges valley, because pillar dedications were then in vogue. In his inscription Menander refers to himself as "the Great Savior, Just and Invincible," who was "King of Kings." These grandiose titles did not stop him from becoming a Buddhist and, after entrusting the throne to his son, abdicating like Candragupta before him. It was believed that Menander attained enlightenment.

Greek power in Bactria and northern Indian was shattered by the Sakas, the Central Asian cousins of the Scythians. These pastoralists overran Bactria, only to be ejected in turn by the Da Yuezhi. A factor that indirectly brought about these invasions, which were to trouble India for centuries, was the unification of China by Qin Shi Huangdi, its first emperor,

Serpent tamer Krishna, in whose honor Heliodoros erected a pillar at ancient Vidisa.

in 221 BC. The consolidation and expansion of the Chinese Empire, most dramatically demonstrated in the construction of the Great Wall, put pressure on the peoples living on the Central Asian steppe. Two of them, the Da Yuezhi and the Hunnish Xiongnu, to use their Chinese names, waged a fierce war for control of the pasture lands north of the Great Wall. When the Da Yuezhi were soundly defeated in 165 BC, they migrated westward to the border of Bactria. Pushed along by the Da Yuezhi, the Sakas were driven to invade Bactria and then move on to northern India. Though some of the Da Yuezhi were content to settle down in Bactria, one of their clans, the Kushanas, followed the Greeks and the Sakas into India, where they adopted the Buddhist faith.

Like Asoka, the Kanshan king Kaniska is celebrated as a great patron of Buddhism. The extent of Kaniska's kingdom in northern India remains a matter of dispute, although he appears to have held sway over the Indus valley and that of the Ganges as far west as Pataliputra. His control of large areas to the north of India allowed him to profit from the diversion of the Silk Road from China through the Khyber Pass and down the Indus valley, whence merchandise went by sea to the head of the Persian Gulf.

Kaniska may have suffered a severe defeat by the Chinese general Ban Chao, who was ordered to punish a Kushan king for having the temerity to demand the hand of a Chinese princess in marriage. Ban Chao's western advance was in fact probably a response to the intimidation of China's Central Asian allies. From his headquarters in Kucha, an oasis city in the Turfan depression, Ban Chao marched in AD 90 against the Kushanas, defeated them somewhere in Bactria, and then advanced all the way to the shores of the Caspian Sea, the closest a Chinese army

Kushan warriors.

has ever gotten to Europe. The intervention did not have a lasting effect on the Kushanas, who in India were well on their way to becoming naturalized. Almost as eclectic as the Mauryans, they showed an interest in all the subcontinent's beliefs, while on their coins they reveal an even wider spiritual outlook because European as well as Mesopotamian deities are often represented alongside Indian ones. It was at Kaniska's command, however, that a gathering known as the Fourth Buddhist Council met to discuss doctrinal differences. Attending were representatives of no fewer than eighteen Buddhist sects.

JUDEA AND SYRIA

Although ethnic revolts within the Seleucid Empire were nothing new, the successful independence movement of the Jewish people was totally unexpected, not least because of its proximity to Syria, the seat of late Seleucid power. It also came as a surprise to Jerusalem's upper-class minority, whose members were more than willing to embrace Greco-Macedonian manners in order to preserve their own social position. The emergent Jewish state differed little from that of Parthia, except that under Judas Maccabeus's leadership, the uprising drew more powerfully upon religious sentiment.

As far as the Macedonians were concerned, Jerusalem was just another city-state that had control over Judea. Alexander spent little time on Palestine, having other objectives in mind, and to his Seleucid successors Judea was simply a border territory wedged uncomfortably between themselves and their rivals, the Ptolemies, based in Egypt. The tug-of-war between the Ptolemies and the Seleucids resulted in pro-Ptolemaic and pro-Seleucid factions forming in Judea itself. Not until 201 BC would the Ptolemies cease to dominate the area. In that year Antiochus III inflicted a crushing defeat on Ptolemaic forces at Panion, near the headwaters of the Jordan river, in a whirlwind campaign that brought the Seleucid king to the frontier of Egypt. It was about this time that the Romans advised Antiochus to refrain from invading Egypt, which was not his immediate intention, since he was more interested in subduing Palestine and attacking Ptolemaic holdings in southern Asia Minor, along the coast from Caria to Cilicia.

Correctly deducing that the Roman warning did not constitute any desire to go to war with him but rather reflected a wish to stabilize Ptolemaic-Seleucid relations in the eastern Mediterranean, Antiochus reached an amicable agreement with Ptolemy V over Palestine and even married his daughter to the young king. For all intents and purposes the Jews were now Seleucid subjects. Their new masters missed, however, the growing power exercised by the high priest, whose hereditary office let him behave like a petty monarch. This official's sacerdotal authority, backed by a council of elders and centered on the Temple, had led to a strict adherence to the scriptures. Such an approach to belief was quite unlike that of the Jews resident in Alexandria, who, having lost the use of both Aramaic and Hebrew, relied instead on a Greek translation of the Old Testament.

Initially the Seleucid takeover was welcomed in Jerusalem because Antiochus provided sacrificial animals, oil, wine, wheat, flour, salt, and incense for use in the Temple. It is unlikely that this Seleucid king knew or cared much about the Jewish way of life, but he undoubtedly appreciated the value of a lasting political settlement. This meant, of course, that the pro-Seleucid faction in Jerusalem came into its own. As the current high priest, Simon the Just, seems to have been the leader of this faction, no attempt would have been made to Hellenize the Jewish people then.

Yet, within thirty years Antiochus IV launched an all-out attack on Judaism in a complete reversal of his father's policy of tolerance. What caused this sudden change? Antiochus was a complex character, although not the monster he appeared to be to the Jews. More of an eccentric, he liked to stroll through his Syrian capital, Seleucis-in-Piera, alone or with one or two attendants, distributing largesse as the fancy took him. He also enjoyed drinking parties and, like the Roman emperor Nero, fancied himself a great actor. His proscription of outmoded Jewish customs may well have had the support of high-ranking Jews who had fully embraced Greek culture. Perhaps in reaction to the increasing Parthian threat, Antiochus thought such a policy would help to shore up his crumbling empire.

The Seleucid king could not have chosen a worse time. The accommodating high priest Simon the Just had just died and been replaced by the pro-Ptolemaic Onias II, a strict conformist. A large bribe persuaded Antiochus IV to remove Onias II and install Jason, Onias's brother, as high priest. The ease with which the purchase was agreed is an indication of the financial problems facing the Seleucids, still struggling to service the punitive indemnity imposed by Rome after Antiochus III's defeat at Magnesia in 189 BC. With a more compliant high priest in post, Antiochus moved to Hellenize Jerusalem. A gymnasium was built on the Temple hill, and crowds of Jewish youths participated Greek style in naked athletics. One problem for the competitors was apparently their circumcision, which had to be disguised somehow by artificial means. Antiochus's proscription of ritual practices meant in the longer term that circumcision became a hallmark and a test of faith. After the parting of the ways between Christianity and Judaism, the rite of circumcision would inevitably become optional, despite heated argument on the subject among the apostles. Today, only the Christians of Ethiopia continue the practice, circumcising their children between the third and eighth day after birth.

Yet, even Jason, Antiochus's protégé, could not bring himself to permit the Seleucid confiscation of the Temple treasury. In the end Antiochus stormed Jerusalem in 169 BC, aided by the treachery of his Jewish supporters, who opened the city gates for him. His soldiers were instructed to spare no one, neither young nor old, not man, woman, or child; they were also given permission to loot the city. Eighty thousand of its inhabitants were killed in three days. "Raging like a wild beast," Antiochus was on his way back from Egypt, where the Roman envoy Popillius Laenas had just humiliated him by forcing him to abandon his war against the Ptolemies.

Having apparently dealt with the Jewish problem, Antiochus was ready to march against the Parthians. Like Alexander, he could not afford to leave unfinished business behind him when he embarked on an eastern campaign. But in 165 BC Antiochus IV died on the march eastward: among his final acts, the dying king rescinded his degree of persecution of Judaism. This volte-face came too late to save Seleucid rule in Palestine as Judas Maccabeus and his brothers were already at the head of a Jewish revolt. They could never forgive the Seleucid persecution, which included throwing mothers of circumcised boys from city walls with their babies strung around their necks and forcing the consumption of pork and unclean cattle.

The insurrection was ignited by Mattathias, a priest living in a village north of Jerusalem. A Seleucid official arrived to enforce non-Jewish sacrifice on the part of the villagers. Not only did Mattathias prevent this from happening, but he also slew the official and overturned his Greek-style altar, declaring, "Let everyone who is zealous for the Law, and would maintain the covenant, follow me." Then he and his five sons—John, Elezar, Simon, Johnathan, and Judas, who was later called Maccabeus, "the Hammer"—took to the Judean hills. There they learned of the deaths of thousands of Jews who had refused to defend themselves on the Sabbath, and they resolved to fight all seven days of the week.

Once Judas Maccabeus assumed command, following the early death of his father, the uprising turned into a full-scale war of independence. His guerrilla tactics outwitted the Seleucid generals sent to crush the rebels. At this point Antiochus's belated abandonment of the assault on Judaism was irrelevant because Judas Maccabeus's goal was nothing short of Palestine's separation from Syria. Political ambition and religious fer-

The Seleucid king Antiochus IV, whose anti-Jewish policies provoked the great rebellion led by Judas Maccabeus.

vor combined to make him an unstoppable leader. Once he had entered Jerusalem and set about restoring and rededicating the Temple, his message was clear: his quest was the reinvigoration of national Jewish belief.

The subsequent contest pitted Jew against Hellenized Jew and set off serious disagreements on the Seleucid side as well. Only a heavy defeat of the Seleucid army in 161 BC ended the conflict, after which Judas Maccabeus petitioned Rome, this now being the acceptable mark of international recognition. The Romans warned the Seleu-

cids against further military action, and taking advantage of this, the Jews elected Simon, the surviving son of Mattathias, as their leader and high priest on condition he would bring the bloodshed to a close, which he did by negotiating with the Seleucids their independence. He also founded the dynasty that produced King Herod.

Impatient with Jewish unrest following Pompey's settlement of the eastern Mediterranean, Rome acknowledged Herod as ruler of a kingdom that encompassed all of Palestine as well as territories beyond the Jordan river valley. But this realm was not at all what proponents of continued Jewish independence wanted because, as a client king, Herod took his orders from the Romans. The first Roman emperor, Augustus, understood that Herod's Judaism was superficial through a personal attachment to Greek culture. Besides building a Greek-style city on the coast at Caesarea, Herod also introduced both a theater and an amphitheater to Jerusalem. The nude athletes who competed in games held there shocked traditional Jews, whose ability to object was effectively blocked by the mercenary forces backing Herod's rule. Because of family quarrels though, Herod had to alter his will many times, and his death in AD 4 or 5 caused further disputes, which Augustus settled by dividing Palestine between his three sons, none of whom was entitled to be addressed as a king.

Roman administration in Palestine was introduced in stages. As client kingdoms were already considered part of the Roman Empire, there was no need to rush to annexation. The presence of Pontius Pilate in Jerusalem during the arrest of Jesus is explained by his supervisory role as prefect. He strove to avoid entanglement with Judaism, only reluctantly bowing to the demand of "the high priests" that Jesus should be crucified. But Pilot was prepared to act when Rome's interests were at stake, and in 37 he was replaced after harshly suppressing a Samaritan uprising.

Throughout the period of Roman domination, popular Jewish resistance alternated with provocations by the authorities. The third Roman emperor Caligula's desire to be treated like an eastern Mediterranean monarch, which he believed included deification, was bound to provoke a violent reaction. At Alexandria in 38, members of the large Jewish community became involved in street fighting against the Greek majority of inhabitants, who rejected the Jews' claim to full citizenship of the city. This conflict resulted in the first serious pogrom known in history, during the course of which Greek gangs forced their way into synagogues and set up statues of the deified emperor. In 40, each of the two parties sent delegations to Rome to plead its case. The Jews tried to explain to Caligula that, although their religious belief made it impossible for them to sacrifice to him, they were always ready to sacrifice for his well-being, which they regularly did. The emperor replied that failure to recognize his divinity seemed not so much criminal as lunatic. But then more news reached Rome of ominous events taking place in Judea, where enraged Jews had destroyed an altar set up by Greek residents in honor of the emperor. At once Caligula decreed that the province's places of worship should all be converted into shrines of the imperial cult. So instructions were sent to Publius Petronius, the governor of Syria, to commission a statue of the emperor as Jupiter, the Roman equivalent of Zeus, and put it in the Temple at Jerusalem. It was perhaps fortunate for the governor that Caligula was assassinated in 41, since fulfilling the order would have met with widespread resistance in Judea.

Even those upper-class Jews who had gained most from collaboration with the Romans were now disturbed by the authorities' growing indifference to Judaism. The inevitable revolt that broke out in 66 is the most famous of all Jewish rebellions because of its consequences: the destruction of the Temple and the abolition of the high priesthood. The ensuing settlement did not immediately provoke another uprising as the extent of the disaster of 66 to 70 deeply shocked the Jews. But subsequent confiscation of land and its redistribution to soldiers and other foreigners meant that the new owners hired Jewish laborers, an affront to a traditional society of landowning peasants, whose discontent provided most of the recruits in Simon bar Kokhba's great revolt, which between 132 and 136 established a separate state that many Jews viewed as the start of a messianic age. Bar Kokhba was prepared to use strong-arm measures to compel wavering Jews to fight, but the vast majority were fully behind him, for at first the Romans fared badly. Once the Roman army mastered the rebels, however, the province was reduced to a wilderness, and Jerusalem became a Roman colony for veterans. Jews were forbidden on pain of death from entering the city, except for one day each year during the feast that commemorated the Temple's destruction. This prohibition remained in force for centuries, thereby depriving the Jewish people of the most holy place in "the promised land."

PETRA AND ARABIA

Today the ruins of Petra, the capital of the Nabatean Arab kingdom, are the highlight of any visit to Jordan. Its splendid rock-cut tombs are a reminder of a once prosperous state, small though it was in comparison with other ancient Middle Eastern kingdoms. And the site of Petra, a secluded valley approached by narrow wadis carved out of solid rock, explains how it managed to remain independent for so long.

Petra's unusual location must also explain the veneration given to rock itself. The Nabateans were eclectic in their beliefs: They worshipped gods of pre-Islamic Arab origin such as Dushara, who lived in the mountains and presided over natural phenomena, regulated the seasons, and, last but not least, protected the royal dynasty. The principal female deity was Uzza, the goddess of life and love. She was equated with Aphrodite and Venus. Her temple at Petra was decorated with winged lions, a reference to her power over animals as well as human beings. As Nabatean deities were not anthropomorphic, their presence was indicated by geometric shapes either in temple decoration or on solid rock cubes. The goddess Uzza is represented by no more than eyes, nose, and mouth carved on flat panels. At places of worship on hilltops around Petra, the only signs of sacrifice are obelisks cut out of the solid rock. Non-Nabatean deities such as the Greco-Egyptian healer god Serapis appear in human form with curly hair and beard, since Petra was willing to absorb the most important cults in the eastern Mediterranean, despite the nonrepresentational approach to its own pantheon.

Because of the absence of Nabatean inscriptions, we have to rely on Greek and Roman sources. In 321 BC Antigonus, one of Alexander the Great's most ambitious successors, decided that a natural complement to his conquests in Syria and Palestine would be an extension of his power into "the land of the Arabs who are called Nabateans." Four thousand infantry and six hundred cavalry were dispatched to subdue them. Even though the attack took the Nabateans by surprise, they rallied and counterattacked, destroying most of the invaders. A subsequent invasion by

Demetrius, Antigonus's son, was abandoned, and the Nabatean kingdom was left alone.

Though the heartland of the Nabateans was arid and best suited to pastoralism, the inhabitants of Petra managed to grow enough crops to feed themselves by means of an ingenious system of water conservation. Along the wadis running down to the valley in which the city stood, channels carved into the sides of the rock carried rainwater down to storage facilities. The wealth of Petra, however, rested upon trade routes that brought frankincense and myrrh from Arabia as well as spices from India.

The successful development of Petra as a capital seems to have a changed Nabateans' attitudes, especially when their kings drew them together as a united people and began to expand by arms the territories in which they could settle. Although never hit-and-run raiders like the Arab tribesmen who descended on settlements around the Syrian desert, the Nabateans are known to have committed acts of piracy in the Red Sea. Quite possibly these attacks on ships bound for Egyptian ports were an attempt to block the seaborne trade in Indian perfume and spices, for during the first century the overland traffic through Petra had declined. But the Ptolemies and then the Romans effectively suppressed Nabatean efforts to disrupt this new east-west trade route.

The steady decline of the Seleucids and the Ptolemies, prior to the arrival of the Romans, gave the smaller states of the ancient Middle East an opportunity to expand their power. The Nabateans pushed northward, clashed with the newly independent state of Judea, and under King Obadas I reached the Golan. By fomenting internal divisions among the Jews, Obadas I was able to take control of land east of the Jordan river valley. King Aretas III, who came to the throne in 86 BC, was strong enough to invade Palestine, but this meddling in Jewish affairs had an unexpected consequence because it brought Nabatea into direct contact with Rome. An officer of Pompey told Aretas in no uncertain terms to leave the city of Jerusalem alone or risk becoming an enemy of the Roman people. Farther north Pompey was then winding up the Seleucid kingdom. His decision to add Syria to the Roman Empire in 64 BC was in large measure due to the power vacuum created by the final decline of Seleucid authority. Elsewhere Pompey was content to leave the political situation as it was: Judea and Nabatea could continue as independent kingdoms. Such an arrangement permitted the Romans to rely on experienced native regimes at no cost to themselves.

The Nabatean king who reigned during the period of the Roman civil wars, which began with Caesar's crossing of the Rubicon in 49 BC, was Malichus I, whose name actually means "king." Amid the constantly shifting fortunes of the rival commanders, it was not easy for a neighboring state to decide to which Roman leader it should lend support. During his reign, Malichus I had a choice between Caesar and Pompey, between Caesar's murderers and Mark Antony, and between Antony and Octavian: Since one of Caesar's former commanders invited the Parthians to assist in punishing the tyrannicides, the Nabatean king even found a Parthian army dangerously close to Petra in 40 BC. Worse still, Antony later gave parts of Phoenicia, Judea, and Arabia to his lover, Egyptian queen Cleopatra. But her attempt to annex all of Judea and Nabatea came to nothing when, at the Battle of Actium in 31 BC, Octavian, the future emperor Augustus, triumphed.

Only a year after that, Cleopatra allowed a poisonous snake to bite her. Though of Macedonian descent, Cleopatra had adopted the Egyptian belief that a snake bite from a cobra, the sacred symbol of the pharaohs, conferred immortality. With her death the once great kingdom of the Ptolemies became a Roman province. After the defeat of Antony and Cleopatra at Actium, a shrewd operator like Octavian was able to see that a king who had remained faithful to an enemy would prove to be a more reliable client than one who was prepared to switch loyalties as circumstances changed. As a result, both Herod's Judea and Malichus's Nabatea survived intact.

By the time of Augustus's death in AD 14, Judea was no longer a client kingdom but a Roman province, and the Nabatean kingdom had reached a cultural apex under King Aretas IV. Described on his coins as "a lover of his people," Aretas IV ruled a prosperous and artistically accomplished kingdom. Petra itself blossomed into an attractive city with a theater, colonnades, parks, and temples. El Khazneh, "the Treasury," remains Petra's most impressive building, its colossal rock-cut facade incorporating both Nabatean and Greek motifs. Dramatically sited at

El Khazneh, the impressive front of King Aretas IV's rock-cut tomb at Petra.

the end of the Siq, the narrow passageway leading down to Petra from the present-day town, El Khazneh still stuns the visitor with its elegant proportions. Archaeological exploration during the first decade of this century has established that it was actually King Aretas IV's own tomb. This ruler presided over the final move away from pastoralism since further advances in water conservancy allowed other Nabatean settlements to house most of his subjects.

Despite the Jewish revolt against Rome in 66, the Nabatean kingdom was undisturbed until in 107 the emperor Trajan made it into a province. A single legion detached from the Egyptian garrison was reckoned to be adequate for its defense, although it is not impossible that existing Nabatean units were added to the Roman army as auxiliaries. The annexation of Nabatea could be seen as the culmination of Rome's control of the Mediterranean, the completion of its hold over all the lands close to the shoreline. An inscription on a triumphal arch in Petra records how the city welcomed Trajan as its new overlord. In return the emperor granted Petra the title of metropolis.

PALMYRA AND EGYPT

Unlike the Nabatean kingdom, Palmyra was annexed in 273 after an all-out war against the Romans. Located midway between the Syrian coast and the Euphrates river valley, the oasis city of Palmyra was the focus of the caravan trade carrying eastern goods to the Mediterranean. Its name, Palmyra, derived from the clusters of palm trees that greeted weary travelers as they approached the city across the Syrian desert. Originally called Tadmor, it had once been an Assyrian possession since its strategic location could not be ignored by an ancient Middle Eastern power intent on dominating Syria.

Pompey left Palmyra independent when he established the Roman province of Syria, and it enjoyed a large degree of independence during the early Roman Empire, even though Roman military units were often stationed in the city. A great boost to Palmyra'a fortunes came when Petra was annexed along with the rest of the Nabatean kingdom. Though Petra remained a hub for overland trade, the commercial center of gravity shifted northward to Palmyra, which enjoyed a closer relationship with the Roman stronghold of Antioch.

Trajan's successor, Hadrian, reverted to the previous Roman policy of a balance of power in the ancient Middle East. Mesopotamia was restored to the Parthians, and Palmyra became once again an outlying bulwark of the eastern Roman frontier. In 129 Hadrian actually visited the city and was welcomed so warmly that he confirmed the free status of its inhabitants: this led to a marked increase in the caravan trade, the profits of which were ploughed into civic buildings. The conduct of business, an activity dear to the Palmyrenes, was balanced by a passionate belief in their city gods, and nearly all their building works were devoted to enhancing temples. Mostly derived from the Mesopotamian pantheon, the deities worshipped in Palmyra were concerned with fertility and martial strength. Even the fertility goddess Allat, revered by the Palmyrenes as well as the Nabateans, was readily identified with the warlike aspect of Athena, helmeted and with one hand holding a spear, the other resting on a shield.

The political circumstances of Palmyra altered dramatically in the 260s, when Rome was in a state of shock from its humiliation at the hands of the Sasanians. The Roman emperor Valerian had been taken prisoner by the Sasanian king Shapur I, and it looked as if a resurgent Iran would now rule the ancient Middle East. During these uncertain times, Udaynath, or Septimus Odenathus to the Romans, rose as leader of the Palmyrenes. Apparently Odenathus mustered an army of Syrian farmers, transformed them into an effective fighting force, and attacked the Sasanians as they headed back to the Euphrates after sacking the city of Antioch. Odenathus may have harassed the Sasanians all the way back to their capital, Ctesiphon. He is even credited with preventing an attempted usurpation of the imperial throne by a Roman officer stationed in Syria.

If all this is true, Odenathus was instrumental in restoring Roman prestige, which could explain his appointment as *Dux Romanorum*, "Commander of the Romans," and *Dux Orientis*, "Commander of the East." The question is whether he received these grandiose titles during his lifetime or they were only attached to his name for propaganda purposes after his death. It is not impossible that his widow, the ambitious Zenobia, invented them in order to strengthen the claim of her son

Vaballathus to rule Palmyra. With Rome weakened by internal strife, Odenathus may have been playing a double game at securing full sovereignty for his city-state. The Roman emperor Gallienus, the son of Valerian, was hard-pressed to hold on to power: on average, he faced one usurper for every year he held office between 253 and 268.

The situation Gallienus faced can only be described as daunting. Besides the rivals he had to face down within the empire, the German tribes were joining in a mass onslaught along the entire length of the northern frontier. In 258 the Alamanni reached Italy, and although Gallienus defeated them at Mediolanum, today's Milan, it was realized that the city of Rome now needed stronger defenses. They would be constructed in due course by Aurelian, who started to build a new city wall round the capital in 271.

Despite Gallienus's troubles, the first signs of a recovery from the military crisis were visible. This busy emperor gave a new flexibility to the Roman army. The Romans had long employed mounted archers and javelin men but not the heavy cavalry that Gallienus developed. These armored horsemen may well have assisted in his crushing defeat of the Goths in the Balkans after they had ravaged Greece. Ambushing their booty-laden column at Naissus, present-day Nis in Serbia, the Roman army fought the bloodiest battle of the century, gaining a complete victory and slaying over 50,000 of the enemy. This success definitely signaled that the military tide had begun to turn in Rome's favor. Gallienus was, however, assassinated in 268. Even though he was popular with the troops, his political opponents used his interest in Greek culture to undermine his position, since they regarded Gallienus as insufficiently warlike for the role of Roman emperor.

The reason for this harsh outlook was that the balance of power between outside pressure and Roman resistance had changed, and the initiative now lay with enemies beyond the empire's borders. No longer isolated events, attacks were almost continuous and more widespread. The demands of defense reinforced the military character of imperial authority, and the political influence of the Roman aristocracy declined. Emperors were now created by the army and deposed by the army. Lacking the legitimacy of the earlier constitutional arrangement, they sought to compensate by surrounding their persons with ceremonial, often borrowed from Sasanid Iran.

The accession of Aurelian as emperor in 270 marked the real start of Rome's recovery, even though he inherited a threefold division of power. He himself held Italy and the central provinces, the usurper Tetricus ruled the west from Trier, and the whole of the east was controlled by King Vaballathus of Palmyra and his mother Zenobia. Aurelian's aim had to be the reunification of the empire, which he achieved prior to his own assassination in 275.

How Palmyra came to gain control of Rome's eastern provinces is the subject of the rest of this section. There is no doubt that Zenobia was responsible for this brief triumph of arms. She exploited the complex diplomatic relationships that she inherited from Odenathus, playing Sasanid Iran off against Rome. Zenobia's own elevation in Palmyra took place shortly before the murder of Gallienus, and her reign spanned those of three Roman emperors: first Gallienus, then Claudius, who lasted only two years, and finally her nemesis Aurelian.

The Palmyrenes seem generally to have accepted Zenobia's installation of her son Vaballathus on the throne of Palmyra as his father's successor. As she served as regent, Vaballathus could have been no more than ten years old at the time. Quite possibly Zenobia would never

have agreed to hand over power to her young son once her reputation grew along with her conquests. Vaballathus was still barely fifteen when his mother's meteoric career came to an abrupt end.

Well informed about the confusion in Roman affairs, Zenobia embarked on a deliberate policy of expansion, ordering her general Zabdas to invade the Roman province of Arabia. An inscription over the entrance of the temple of Jupiter at Bostra,

A coin struck to signal Queen Zenobia's temporary military triumph over Rome.

the legionary base there, states that it was rebuilt after being "destroyed by Palmyrene enemies." This attack during the reign of Claudius must have taken place as Zabdas advanced on his real objective, Egypt. It would appear that Zenobia's intervention coincided with an Egyptian rebellion against the Rome, which went virtually unchecked because the Roman governor was then away from the province, trying to clear the eastern Mediterranean of pirates.

So a Palmyrene army of 70,000 men marched into Egypt more or less unopposed. Seizing this Roman province by force was about the most provocative thing that Zenobia could have done. Egypt had been directly administered by the emperor since its annexation by the emperor Augustus. Even more, it was a vital source of Rome's food supply, with its annual fleet of corn ships sailing to Ostia, that city's port. In addition, the province provided a large amount of tax that a hard-pressed military treasury simply could not afford to lose. Zenobia may have visited Egypt herself as a liberator, claiming a family connection with Cleopatra, the last of the Ptolemies to rule the country.

So important was Egypt to the Romans that Zenobia might have imagined she was in a strong-enough position negotiate a peace settlement, which would establish her credentials not as an enemy but as a worthy partner of Rome. Strengthening Palmyra's international standing was evidently part of her strategy because, without active Sasanian support, Zenobia knew she could not hope to resist Rome for long.

Another direction in which Palmyrene arms were directed was Asia Minor, where they reached the southern shore of the Black Sea. This advance, like the one into Egypt, seems to have enjoyed a degree of popular support. Yet most of the cities in Asia Minor were quick to side with Aurelian when he finally advanced eastward in 272.

The city of Tyana in Cappadocia, however, shut its gates against him. A ten-year gap in Roman military activity could have made its inhabitants believe that Palmyra was now the best bet for their survival. Betrayed by one of its citizens, the city was about to be sacked when an apparition frightened Aurelian: it was said to be the ghost of Apollonius, a famous sage who had lived in Tyana. This Pythagorean philosopher was said to have "surpassed human nature in wisdom." So the city's inhabitants were spared but not its dogs, because the emperor had already sworn that once he captured Tyana, not a single dog would be left alive within its walls.

When Aurelian finally faced Zabdas in battle near Antioch at Immae, the Palmyrene general at first got the better of the Romans. But in the end, he was outmaneuvered and outfought. Aurelian ordered his legionaries to fall back when charged by the heavily armored Palmyrene cavalry, then wheel around and attack their pursuers when the heat and their armor began to take their toll. The tactic worked, and Zenobia fled to Emesa to make another stand, with a large force already assembled there. Once again the Romans won, and Zenobia found herself under siege in Palmyra. Success or failure for Roman armies was decided by their better discipline against less-controlled opponents. Palmyra's formidable defenses supposedly held the Romans at bay for a while, although the city was in fact not properly fortified until a later date. Zenobia may well have been in contact with the Sasanians, hoping that a relief force would arrive to save Palmyra. Desperate to escape Aurelian and allow the Palmyrenes to surrender without suffering a sack, Zenobia fled to Mesopotamia, but she was captured on the way.

Having gained his objective, Aurelian was disposed to be merciful. Except for a small group of the queen's supporters who were taken prisoner, the rest of the Palmyrenes remained free, although a small garrison was left to keep order in the city. But on his way back to Rome, Aurelian learned of an uprising in Palmyra and the massacre of the garrison he had installed. He hastened back to the oasis city, which he then razed to the ground. As there is no archaeological trace of this destruction, we cannot be sure of exactly what happened.

At Aurelian's triumph in Rome, he paraded Tetricus, the breakaway ruler of the western provinces, and Zenobia, the conqueror of the eastern provinces, as a sign of his restoration of imperial unity. We are told that the Palmyrene queen was so weighed down with jewels and golden shackles that she stumbled on several occasions during the triumph. Afterward Zenobia was beheaded in the traditional fashion. Yet two other versions of her end are perhaps worth noting. Both suggest that Zenobia lived on to enjoy an honorable old age, either as the wife of a prominent Roman or as a widow in a villa near Rome presented to her by Aurelian himself. It is hardly surprising that the life story of such an unusual person as Zenobia should be embroidered with fantastic details.

CHAPTER EIGHT

Famous Sieges

Siege craft and artillery were developed in an attempt to deal with the fortified city, the stronghold of the earliest kings. Though the first fortified settlement appeared at Jericho in the eighth millennium BC, only much later at Uruk can we be absolutely sure that the city's walls were built for a military purpose. Gilgamesh had made the people living in Uruk construct a wall nearly ten miles in length. This tyrannical ruler was determined to protect his city from the aggressive attentions of rival Sumerian kings, and Uruk's defenses proved extraordinarily effective.

Fortified cities put attackers at risk. Safe behind the city walls, the defenders could provision themselves for months at a time, while attacking armies were obliged to live off the land until hunger, thirst, and, more often than not, disease forced the abandonment of a siege. Because invaders could not afford to bypass fortified strong points, lest they were subject to surprise attacks from the rear at a time of the enemy's choosing, the success of a campaign depended on the reduction of fortified cities. As a result, all kinds of methods were devised to overcome fortifications: battering rams to break down walls and city gates, earthen ramps to access the tops of walls, as well as wooden siege towers. The Assyrians were the first to master siege craft, their skills not being surpassed until Roman times. That the Assyrian army had a specialist corps to conduct its sieges explains this early advance.

Besides mobile battering rams for weakening city walls and the construction of earthen ramps to allow the use of scaling ladders, the Assyrians deployed groups of archers and slingers to keep down the

An Assyrian siege machine.

heads of defenders on ramparts. Behind a wall of large infantry shields, the archers and slingers were able to maintain an almost constant rate of fire. Perhaps the oldest missile weapon in the world, the sling could fire a variety of lead and clay shot, the heaviest being capable of hitting a target at two hundred yards. Short-range shot, often plumb shaped and made of lead, was designed to have increased penetrating capacity. Xenophon noted that these missiles inflicted horrible wounds when he marched into Persia with the Ten Thousand. And we should not forget how just one of "the five smooth stones" that David had gathered from a brook was sufficient to incapacitate Goliath, the Philistine champion. It struck Goliath in the forehead so that "he fell upon his face to the earth." When the Philistines saw David cut off the head of their prone champion, they fled.

But the bow dominated long-range fighting. Craftsmen tried to increase its killing power by varying its shape without any great success. Then, in either Sumer or Akkad, they hit upon the design of the composite bow. The increased velocity of the composite bow's arrows made it more deadly than the ordinary bow; this extra strength derived from adding strips of horn and sinew to the wood. Either on foot or in a chariot, this short bow was the weapon of choice. The Persians were particularly fond of the composite bow, with the result that boys from age five upward were required to practice archery. Probably as a legacy of their pastoralist heritage, the Persians expanded in their fighting

Assyrian archers and slingers during a siege.

235

formations the role of mounted archers to the extent that they lacked in their army an adequate number of heavy infantry. This made them dependent on Greek mercenaries.

The Assyrian army always relied on a mix of units acting together, although infantry remained the primary shock force in battle. The introduction of the shoulder quiver increased the fire power of archers, who fought on foot alongside spearmen, by bringing a supply of arrows within easy reach of the bowmen. Assyrian soldiers wore leather for protection,

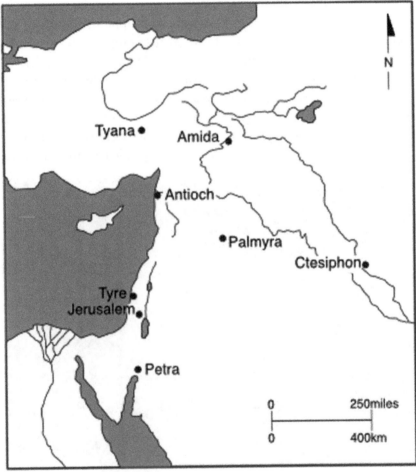

Ancient cities that were besieged.

except among the higher ranks, which had scale armor. The large shields carried by spearmen provided a degree of protection for the archers.

HAMMURABI OF BABYLON'S CAPTURE OF LARSA

The Elamite-led invasion of Mesopotamia in 1765 and 1764 BC soured relations between Babylon and Larsa, a city located to the south of Uruk. King Rim-Sin of Larsa was lukewarm about offering military assistance during the invasion because he told the Babylonian king, "the enemy plans to move off to some other country." Evidently unwilling to make any practical contribution at all, Rim-Sin preferred to await events.

The seriousness of the situation for Babylon, however, can be judged by the emergency measures that King Hammurabi introduced. He called all able-bodied Babylonian men to arms and also freed slaves who were willing to join his army. Still, Rim-Sin held aloof from the conflict. The withdrawal of the Elamites and their allies, which saved Hammurabi, was the prelude to the siege of Larsa.

Apparently the successful Babylonian defense of northern Mesopotamia did not impress Rim-Sin. "Now the man of Larsa," said Hammurabi, "has disturbed my kingdom through pillage. Since the great gods have removed the grip of the Elamites, I have shown favours to the man of Larsa but he has not repaid me with any sign of friendship." Hammurabi at first limited his anger to breaking off diplomatic relations with Rim-Sin, but he really wanted to attack Larsa as soon as he had secured a guarantee of success from the gods. He did not even presume to gather his forces together until his diviners approached the gods, who approved the attack. As Hammurabi commented, "Now I have asked Shamash and Marduk, and they have both answered yes. So I have embarked on this invasion with divine approval."

Because the outcome of all military operations was believed to depend entirely upon the will of the gods, Hammurabi paid close attention to the reports he received about auspicious signs occurring in his kingdom, for these would certainly be an indication of what the gods intended. The Babylonian king also adopted a systematic approach to consulting oracles before and during military operations. We are aware that his diviners always accompanied him, answering questions that he put to the gods and reporting their own daily consultations with the divine realm. The Greeks and Romans adopted the Mesopotamian practice of examining the entrails of sacrificial animals in order to determine the will of the gods. Famously, Alexander the Great resolved a strategic dilemma in India by the same method in 326 BC. The outcome of the consultation allowed the Macedonian king to announce his decision to abort an unpopular invasion of the Ganges river valley.

A successful assault on Larsa in 1783 BC would need to start with the capture of Mashkan-shapir, a city close to the Tigris. Only after overcoming this outer defense of Rim-Sin could Hammurabi safely lay siege to Larsa itself. He told his troops that their target was occupied by betrayers who had "disobeyed their oath to Shamash and Marduk." Such a statement reveals how the Babylonians regarded the expedition as almost a holy war. Even so, Hammurabi wanted his men to show mercy to the enemy, thereby suggesting that they had been forced into military action by Rim-Sin's indifference to properly sworn oaths of alliance.

Although we possess no details of the fall of Mashkan-shapir, the garrison of several thousand soldiers appears to have capitulated fairly quickly. The prologue to the law code of Hammurabi celebrates the surrender of this city, whose principal temple was Emeshlam, "the house of the netherworld warrior" Nergal. The fall of Mashkan-shapir meant that a large part of the kingdom of Larsa passed under Babylonian control. Afterward the inhabitants of the entire area rallied to the side of Hammurabi, a switch in loyalty that turned his campaign into something of a popular movement. Traditional hostility between Mashkan-shapir and Larsa can in part explain this abandonment of Rim-Sin, but it must also reflect general discontent with Rim-Sin's rule. Reinforced by these volunteers and additional forces sent by his allies, Hammurabi laid siege to Larsa for six months.

The city of Larsa could withstand such a prolonged siege due to the strength of its defenses. The siege may indeed have lasted much longer than Hammurabi expected, but at least he enjoyed the bonus of popular disdain for Rim-Sin. There was no likelihood of either a relief column arriving at Larsa or any interference with the conduct of the siege. So Hammurabi blockaded Larsa and awaited the exhaustion of its food stocks. Once the grain reserves were consumed, Rim-Sin was forced to give in, and Hammurabi took possession of the defeated king's territory.

We are told that "once the Babylonian troops entered Larsa, they occupied the citadel. The next morning the entire army went into the city." As for Rim-Sin, he was spared and removed with his family to Babylon, where presumably he died as a captive. Hammurabi destroyed the fortifications of Larsa, leaving its temples and houses intact. One of his most urgent actions, however, was repairing the irrigation system of southern Mesopotamia, which had become unable to provide enough water for the cities of Nippur, Eridu, Ur, Larsa, Uruk,

King Hammurabi of Babylon. It was customary in the ancient Middle East to damage the statues of opponents, as this example shows.

and Isin. Possible crop failure connected with the neglect of water control and a consequent collapse of the economy could have contributed to Rim-Sin's downfall. The prosperity of a kingdom was viewed as the responsibility of a ruler, and with rainfall so poor in Sumer, maintenance of canals was a duty that a Mesopotamian king neglected at his peril. An inscription unearthed at Sippar, a city to the north of Babylon, records Hammurabi naming a new canal after the goddess Aya as an expression of gratitude to her. As the wife of the sun god Shamash, she was greatly venerated at Sippar. "The lord of heaven and earth," Shamash was the god of justice, whose view of Hammurabi's conduct was of critical importance to the Babylonian monarch. The bas-relief at the top of the column on which the king's famous law code is inscribed shows Hammurabi in the company of Shamash, who beams approval at the comprehensiveness of the regulations. There was no doubt in Hammurabi's mind that his conquests brought peace and prosperity to Mesopotamia. As he put it at the end of his law code,

I am Hammurabi, the noble king. I have not been careless or negligent towards the men whom Enlil has entrusted to me and whom Marduk gave me to nourish. I have found peaceful places for them to live . . . made enemies disappear and I have put an end to conflicts. . . . I have embraced the people of Sumer and Akkad and they have prospered in safety. I have protected them through my wisdom.

Hammurabi was the good shepherd who acts justly and leads his people along correct paths. Other Mesopotamian kings placed emphasis on their strength, especially in battle, but Hammurabi seems to have desired above all else the accolade of just ruler, the earthly equivalent of Shamash. The rays and flames emerging from the sun god's shoulders in the depiction of his meeting with Hammurabi at the beginning of the law code are a reminder that here we witness a privileged encounter with the divine.

THE ASSYRIAN SACK OF BABYLON

Completely different in outlook was the Assyrian king Sennacherib, who razed the city of Babylon to the ground. He regarded war as a vocation and took delight in confronting his enemies. An inscription of his relates,

I raged like a lion. I put on a coat of armor; I placed upon my head the helmet, the ornament of fighting. I quickly mounted my splendid battle chariot, which smashes my enemy, in the heat of my anger. I seized with my hands the mighty bow, which the god Ashur had given me; I grasped the life-ending arrow. Against all the hosts of wicked foes I raised my voice like a thunderstorm; I roared like the storm god Adad. At the order of Ashur, the great god, I charged like a hurricane. With the weapons of Ashur, and my furious onslaught, I made the enemy break ranks and flee in confusion under a shower of deadly arrows.

This ideal of a reckless, heroic, and ever-victorious Assyrian king was certainly royal propaganda by Sennacherib's reign and not the description of any monarch's actions on the battlefield. A courtier even advised the son of Sennacherib, the hesitant Esarhaddon, "not to go into the midst of a battle." It was better to leave the actual fighting to Assyrian generals, the battle-hardened aristocrats who understood how to deploy troops best.

But Sennacherib's inscription is an accurate expression of Assyrian attitudes toward military conflict. War was both good and necessary for the Assyrians, as they claimed the right to world domination on behalf of their supreme deity, Ashur. They believed that only through the proficiency of the Assyrian army were the forces of chaos kept under firm control. Under Tiglath-pileser III, who came to the throne in 744 BC, the Assyrian Empire seemed to justify this claim, since it encompassed then nearly the whole of the ancient Middle East.

A perennial worry for the Assyrians was Babylon, whose periodic raids on Assyria reflected its relative strengths and weaknesses. But civil unrest in Babylon was as much a problem as encroachment on Assyrian lands, obliging Tiglath-pileser III to intervene when an uprising threatened the very existence of the city. He triumphantly entered Babylon in 729 BC and was crowned its king. This practice continued down to Sennacherib, who reigned from 704 to 681 BC.

Assyrians flaying prisoners alive.

Since the time of Hammurabi, the city of Babylon had experienced periods of prosperity and poverty; yet in the early centuries of the first millennium BC, its fortunes declined markedly. Despite the prestige of the deities living in the city's temples, Babylon endured an economic collapse. Long stretches of watercourses, the essential means of irrigating fields, were abandoned or had fallen into disuse. The king of Babylon tried to assert his authority, but the independent actions of larger cities and tribesmen spread across the countryside limited his power. So ineffectual were the weaker monarchs that the disruption of trade routes forced the Assyrians to become more involved in Babylonian affairs. As the hereditary principle for monarchical succession had almost disappeared, there was a rapid turnover of rulers prior to Sennacherib's attack in 689 BC. Most of these Babylonian kings ruled for less than four years.

Despairing of Babylon, Assyrians undertook a variety of initiatives, including campaigns in rural areas against truculent tribes, alliances with neighboring cities, and the installation of pro-Assyrian rulers on the Babylonian throne. Deportation was another technique much in favor with the Assyrians: it was used to deport insurgent tribesmen and import more docile inhabitants from other lands. Almost half a million people were removed, the majority of whom were Chaldeans. For many years they had been moving northward from the Persian Gulf and settling in Mesopotamia. But this policy failed to achieve a satisfactory result because, in 721 BC, a Chaldean king by the name of Merodach-baladan sat on the Babylonian throne. And he stirred up anti-Assyrian feeling not only in Babylon but also in Elam, northern Arabia, and Judah.

Despite being a usurper, Merodach-baladan was able to rule Babylon through a temporary weakness in Assyria caused by the violent ends suffered by two of its kings. Shalmansesr V was toppled by a revolution in 722 BC, and Sargon II died on the battlefield in 701 BC. One of only two Mesopotamian rulers to have been killed in combat, Sargon II suffered the indignity of having his body left unburied on the battlefield as well. At the start of his reign in 704 BC, Sennacherib abandoned the newly completed capital of Dur Sharruken, moving the seat of imperial government to Nineveh, the ancient cult center of the goddess Ishtar, where it remained until the city was overwhelmed by the Medes and the

Babylonians in 612 BC. Because the death of Sargon II was regarded as "a divine punishment," Sennacherib did everything he could to distance himself from his unfortunate father: he abandoned the new capital that Sargon II had built at Dur Sharruken and never mentioned him in any of his own inscriptions.

The absence of Assyrian interference for two decades allowed Babylon to recover some of its strength, even with a Chaldean on the throne. Merodach-baladan behaved like a Babylonian king, repairing and endowing temples as well as keeping the traditional tax exemption enjoyed by the inhabitants of the city. For Sennacherib, however, the Babylonian question seemed an insoluble problem, which he finally settled by the capture and destruction of the city of Babylon itself.

Sennacherib's offensive actually began with an attack on the Chaldean allies of Merodach-baladan. These tribesmen were routed and their settlements devastated. Merodach-baladan himself fled by ship to the Persian Gulf, eventually dying as an exile in Elam. Ashur-nadin-shumi, Sennacherib's son, was placed on the Babylonian throne instead. But the Babylonian question was far from resolved. In 694 BC the Assyrian king had to confront Babylonian rebels along with their Elamite allies and continued fighting them right down to the sack of Babylon six years later.

In order to destroy the Elamite base of the fugitive supporters of Merodach-baladan on the shore of the Persian Gulf, Sennacherib sent for shipwrights from Syria to build craft of Phoenician design. Having been constructed in northern Mesopotamia, the vessels were brought down the Tigris by sailors recruited from Tyre, Sidon, and Cyprus. An unexpected setback happened on the Persian Gulf when large waves buffeted the Assyrian king's fleet, since the seamen were accustomed to the virtually tideless Mediterranean. But at last the seaborne expedition was able to sail and, after a difficult landing, defeated the Chaldeans. Loaded with loot, the expedition returned to Sennacherib, who praised the thoroughness of the operation.

Yet the Assyrian king had been outwitted. While he was busy in the Persian Gulf, the Elamites had marched on Babylon, where Ashur-nadin-shumi was handed over to them. His place on the throne was taken by Nergil-usherzib, a candidate of the pro-Elamite faction. The new ruler was able to take Nippur, but in a battle with Sennacherib near that city, the new king was defeated and taken prisoner; he was executed at Nineveh following a victory parade. The last great battle between the Assyrians and the Elamite-Babylonian coalition was fought in 691 BC at Halule, close to the Tigris; both sides claimed a victory, but Sennacherib was left in possession of the battlefield.

Having prayed for victory, the Assyrian king armed himself for battle. As he described it, "I cried bitterly against the enemy like a demon. I roared like the storm god Adad. . . . I blew against the enemy on long and short sides like the attack of a terrible storm." Another source tells us, in simple terms, that this maneuver "bored through" the enemy ranks and scattered the Elamite soldiers in every direction. The result was that Sennacherib managed to capture a number of Elamite nobles but did not succeed in capturing or killing the leaders of the Elamite-Babylonian forces confronting him. It appears that, at Halule, even though the left wing of the Assyrian army was pressed backward, its right wing smashed through the enemy's left wing with such power that it threatened to surround Babylonian troops who were getting the

The Assyrian king Sennacherib's war chariot.

best of the struggle on the Assyrian left. According to Sennacherib, "The king of Elam, together with the king of Babylon, and their Chaldean allies, were overcome by the fear of my demon-battle. They abandoned their tents, and in order to save their lives, they trampled over the corpses of their own men in an eagerness to escape." Their ability to avoid capture was in fact a consequence of the Assyrian right wing's failure to swing far enough around behind the enemy and to reach the bank of the Tigris. This left an escape route open. The Assyrian tactic of assaulting the flank of an opponent did not work out as well at Halule as in other battles. Sennacherib's cavalry and infantry archers "bored through" the enemy left wing without much difficulty, but they were unable to cause the total collapse that was intended.

Not until two years later, in 689 BC, was Sennacherib ready to lay siege to Babylon, so the most his enemies gained from the Battle of Halule was a brief respite. No detailed account of the siege survives, although we know it lasted for well over a year. Starvation and death stalked the streets of Babylon, but the inhabitants still refused to surrender. Finally taken by storm, the city was put to the sword, so greatly did Sennacherib

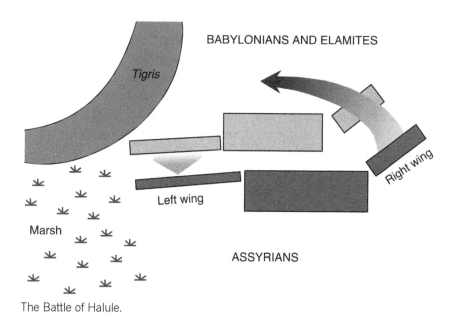

The Battle of Halule.

harbor hatred for the Babylonians. Then he destroyed the city; water was diverted from its canals to flatten buildings, and his soldiers carried off everything of value. The Assyrian king could neither forget nor forgive the treatment of his son Ashur-nadin-shumi. Perhaps it is to be expected that in Sennacherib's inscriptions there are more details of siege techniques than in other Assyrian royal records. By his reign the Assyrian army had become a master of siege craft, as the capture of so great a city as Babylon demonstrates.

NEBUCHADREZZAR II'S DESTRUCTION OF JERUSALEM

Next to Babylon the most important area in Sennacherib's foreign policy was Palestine, particularly the kingdom of Judah, whose king, Hezekiah, had been drawn into intrigue with Merodach-balaban. Encouraged by Egypt, Hezekiah had even renounced his alliance with Assyria. Something clearly had to be done about such defiance, lest other western states should follow Judah's example.

Our problem in understanding what happened when Sennacherib moved against Jerusalem is a consequence of a confused record of events, since his earlier Palestinian campaign of 701 BC has got mixed up with this new one. It would seem that during Sennacherib's first campaign, all the fortified cities of Judah were taken by force, except Jerusalem. The timely submission of Hezekiah and the payment of tribute satisfied Sennacherib then. In the Bible we are told how "Hezekiah handed over all the silver that was found in the house of the Lord, and the treasures of the king's house. At that time did Hezekiah cut off the gold from the doors of the temple of the Lord, and from the pillars which Hezekiah had overlaid, and gave it to the king of Assyria."

During subsequent years, while Assyria was busy with other problems, Hezekiah resolved to resist any future Assyrian demands. He strengthened Jerusalem's defenses and devised a plan to secure the city's water supply and deny water to an enemy. Accordingly, the Bible explains that Hezekiah "made a pool, and a conduit, and brought water into the city." He also blocked the flow of water outside the city wall, cutting a tunnel to bring the water into Jerusalem. It survives today.

So it was that Jerusalem defied Sennacherib's second advance against Judah. The biblical narrative adds that an epidemic decimated the Assyrian army. "That night the angel of the Lord went forth and slew a hundred and eighty thousand in the camp of the Assyrians." Whatever took place, Sennacherib was obliged to raise the siege, leaving the Judean capital intact, just as the prophet Isaiah had assured Hezekiah he would. The Temple of Solomon may have been less splendid in its ornamentation, but miraculously the Assyrians were unable to sack it. Because the prophecy came true, a feeling spread among the Jews that Jerusalem was inviolable. This article of faith was to receive a rude shock in 587 BC when King Nebuchadrezzar II of Babylon destroyed the city.

Again, Egypt encouraged Judah's defiance of a Mesopotamian power. After the collapse of the Assyrian Empire, Babylon had assumed the leadership of the ancient Middle East. The Egyptians tried to take control of Palestine and Syria, but in 605 BC Nebuchadrezzar drove them south. During the course of his forty-two-year reign, this Babylonian king not only revived his city's military fortunes but, even more, rebuilt Babylon itself so that it was acknowledged as a wonder of the world. Herodotus was most impressed by the size of the city, the largest Mesopotamian settlement ever, and by its double set of defensive walls. He also marveled at its ziggurat, "a solid central tower ... with a second tower on top of it and then a third and so on up to eight." Begun by Nabopolassar, who freed the Babylonians from the Assyrian yoke and passed the throne to his son Nebuchadrezzar, Marduk's ziggurat took forty-two years to complete. In due course the massive structure inspired the Jewish myth of the Tower of Babel. According to Genesis, Yahweh confounded the speech of the workmen building a tower that would reach heaven. The resulting incomprehension and strife thwarted the project and broke up the original unity of humanity. The word "babel" means confusion, and there is no mention of the legendary Nimrod, but a recently discovered Sumerian myth attributes the end of a golden age to the water god Enki's diversification of language.

This story and the splendor of Babylon's other great buildings shows how Nebuchadrezzar's reconstruction of the city following the Assyrian sack dazzled the ancient Middle East. Such a determined king was unlikely to tolerate Judah's disobedience for long. Throughout Syria and Palestine his campaigns were directed against pro-Egyptian factions in their cities. Near Gaza, a strategically important coastal city, Nebuchadrezzar defeated an Egyptian expeditionary force, effectively ending any future domination by Egypt. In 597 BC the Babylonian king captured Jerusalem. The city was not destroyed on this occasion, although much plunder was taken, some of its inhabitants deported, and Zedekiah appointed as a compliant ruler. The aim of this appointment of a member of the royal family must have been political stability through the continuation of the monarchy in Judah.

At this time the prophet Jeremiah called for a revival of traditional Jewish worship, placing emphasis on the First Commandment: "Thou shalt have no other gods before me." Jeremiah was in fact warning the Jews that they could no longer take for granted Yahweh's presence in the Temple. Henceforth his protection would depend upon whether or not they were faithful to him. Righteous behavior is here juxtaposed with cultic ritual. Only if they obeyed divine commands would Yahweh continue to protect Jerusalem.

The small number of Jewish deportees in 597 BC indicates that the Babylonians wanted to see Judah recover its strength as a client kingdom. Perhaps the deportation was equal to 10 percent of Judah's population of around 110,000 people. The exiles were transported to uninhabited territory that had been devastated during the final struggle between Assyria and Babylon. More pragmatic in their use of deportation than the Assyrians, the Babylonian purpose was twofold: to secure Babylonian rule in the deportees' homeland and to resettle areas laid waste by recent warfare. And the Judeans, as well as other western deportees, were settled as a separate community, which allowed them to preserve their own identity while in exile. Even after Judah ceased to exist as an independent kingdom, throughout the two generations leading up to the Persian conquest, the exiled Jews remained a coherent community.

Yet Babylon itself was not without its problems. In 594 BC there was a revolt in the city by "numerous high officials," while Nebuchadrezzar was dealing with a threat from the east of the Tigris. The

Babylonian army encamped on the bank of the river a day's march from the enemy, whose king panicked and retreated without any engagement taking place. This may well have been a planned diversion at the time of the revolt in Babylon, but Nebuchadrezzar soon gained the upper hand for the king captured the rebellion's leader personally. Along with others, this functionary was found guilty of breaking his official oath and condemned to death.

That this unrest coincided with a resumption of Egyptian interest in Palestine caused Nebuchadrezzar to change his policy toward client states. He became less willing to countenance disloyalty, and so a new pact between Judah and Egypt made him take action. Already he had moved against rebellious Phoenician cities: Sidon and Tyre were attacked and turned into Babylonian provinces.

King Zedekiah of Judah now became the focus of opposition to Babylon. Despite warnings from the pro-Babylonian faction, for which Jeremiah was spokesman, Zedekiah remained firm in his stand against Babylon. Nebuchadrezzar had had enough: he decided to conquer the remaining petty kingdoms so tempting to Egypt and incorporate them into a directly administered province. Despite the biblical account of Jerusalem's destruction as the result of Jewish reluctance to fully embrace the commands of Yahweh, the Babylonian response to Zedekiah's rebellion was nothing other than a move designed to end Judah's chronic tendency to disloyalty. The Babylonians simply wanted to create a province that no longer looked to Jerusalem as its capital, with all the religious tensions concentrated in that city.

Zedekiah refused to heed Jeremiah's warnings about the unlikelihood of Egyptian military support against the Babylonians. As a consequence of this stubbornness, "came Nebuchadrezzar and his army against Jerusalem and besieged it." For two years Jerusalem held out until, in the summer of 587 BC, battering rams breeched the northern wall of the starving city. The Bible relates how the king, with some of his guards, "fled, and went forth out of the city by night, by way of the king's garden betwixt the two walls, and he went out the way of the plain." The Babylonians gave chase and apprehended Zedekiah on the road to Jericho. He was escorted to "Nebuchachadrezzar king of Babylon at Riblah in the land of

Hamath, where he gave judgment upon him. Then the king of Babylon slew the sons of Zedekiah: also the king of Babylon slew all the nobles of Judah. Moreover, he put out Zedekiah's eyes, and bound him in chains, to carry to Babylon." A month after the fall of the city, the Babylonians "burnt the house of the Lord, the king's house, and the houses of the people . . . and broke down the walls of Jerusalem."

The reason for the destruction, according to Nebuzaradin, the captain of the Babylonian king's guard, was that "the Lord thy God hath pronounced this evil upon this place." The prophet Jeremiah agreed. The thoroughness of the sack accords with archeological evidence revealed in excavations of the site. Additionally, the exile of the Jewish people afterward confirmed Nebuchadrezzar's policy of suppression: picked out for deportation were those likely to stir up trouble in the new Babylonian province. The Bible gives the impression that the entire population was deported, but it refers to the inhabitants of Jerusalem and not other parts of the kingdom. The phrase "Thus Judah was carried away captive out of its land" cannot be taken at its face value, because we know that a certain Gedaliah was appointed by the king of Babylon as "governor over the cities of Judah." We are also informed that Jeremiah went to Gedaliah and "dwelt with him among the people that were left in the land." That Gedaliah had previously held a high-ranking post in the Judean administration was a guarantee for Babylon that he knew how to govern properly.

ALEXANDER THE GREAT'S SIEGE OF TYRE

After his victory over the Persians at Issus, in present-day Turkey, Alexander the Great decided, instead of pursuing the Persian king Darius III farther east, to secure the coastline of the eastern Mediterranean. The decision was a wise one, for when, in 332 BC, he marched south to Tyre, the most important naval and commercial port in Phoenicia, Alexander was met by envoys from that city who proposed an alliance with the Macedonians but really intended to hold Tyre for the Persians. The city itself must have believed it possible to defy the Macedonian king, since it stood on a rocky island half a mile offshore, protected by great walls that, on the landward side, rose to a height of 150 feet. Point-blank the envoys refused to surrender, perhaps with the intention of giving Darius enough time to raise another army. They also dared to tell Alexander that he could not enter the city when he asked permission to worship at the temple of Melqart, the Phoenician deity equated with the Greek hero Herakles, whom the Macedonian king counted among his ancestors.

Infuriated by this refusal, Alexander dismissed the envoys with dire threats. On returning home they advised their king to think twice before taking on so formidable an opponent. But the Tyrians had confidence in their city's defenses because of the channel between its defensive walls and the mainland and the fact that the Macedonians lacked ships to launch a seaborne assault.

Melqart, the city god of Tyre.

Our main source for these events is Arrian, who wrote his history of the Macedonian conquest of Persia in the first century. Apart from his own experience as a military commander and a governor of a Roman province in the ancient Middle East, Arrian brought to his narrative a desire to establish the truth about Alexander's exploits. He read all the works then available and gave priority to the accounts of eyewitnesses. The amount of detail Arrian included in his own history is staggering, which means that the siege of Tyre is one of the best-known ancient investments. Above all, he wanted to explain why things happened as they did. Arrian's strong religious faith, however, led him to emphasize divine signs as a trigger for action. The dream Alexander had of Herakles inviting him to enter Tyre is credited with persuading the senior Macedonian commanders to agree to a siege. "The dream was interpreted by Alexander," according to Arrian, "as signifying that Tyre would be taken, but with much labor, because labor was characteristic of all that Heracles accomplished." The siege indeed proved to be the most grueling military operation of the Macedonian king's entire career. Not only was the whole Macedonian army involved but all able-bodied men from the surrounding towns and villages found themselves drafted into a vast labor force, numbering "many tens of thousands."

According to Arrian, Alexander's

plan was to construct a mole across the stretch of shallow water between the shore and the city. In-shore there were patches of mud with little water over them, the deepest part of the channel, about three fathoms, being close to the city wall. There was an abundant supply of stones, which could be used for the foundation of the mole, and plenty of timber, which they packed down on top. It was an easy matter to drive piles into the mud which itself acted as a binding material to keep the stones in place. The men worked with a will as Alexander was always on the spot giving precise instructions as to how to proceed, with many a word of encouragement and special rewards for conspicuously good work.

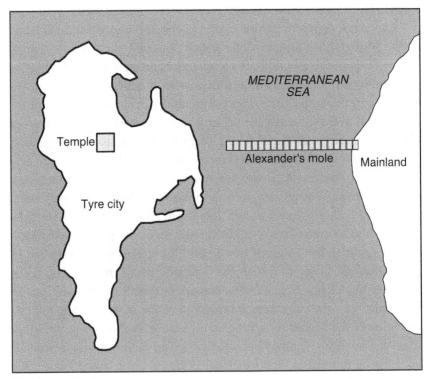

The siege of Tyre.

There was little difficulty in constructing the in-shore section of the mole, but closer to the city troubles mounted. The Macedonians "were in working clothes and not equipped for battle, and the Tyrians used their superiority at sea to make constant raids on various points along the mole, thus making the continuation of the work slow. To counter these raids, the Macedonians built two towers on the mole and mounted artillery on them; they faced the towers with skins and hides to prevent damage from incendiary missiles." When the Tyrians tried to harass the men extending the mole, they were showered by "missiles from the towers and easily driven off."

That the Macedonians could contemplate such a major undertaking as the siege of Tyre was a result of the advances in siege craft under Alexander's father, who early in his reign employed only traditional siege equipment such as battering rams and scaling ladders. But Philip soon realized that he needed new weapons, such as catapults, as he had to lay siege to more and more Greek cities. The construction of 120-foot-high siege towers also allowed the Macedonians to top city walls as well as to fire torsion catapults at the defenders. Alexander's own engineers contributed a number of new ideas as well. One was a hook mounted on a lever suspended on a vertical frame, which was used to dislodge the parapets of city walls. They also invented a primitive crossbow that fired a wooden bolt on a flat trajectory along a slot in the aiming rod. These new weapons were quite large and provided with wheels so as to improve tactical mobility.

"But the Tyrians," Arrian recounts, "soon had an answer to the towers. They filled a boat with dried brushwood and various sorts of timber ... plus pitch, sulfur, and anything else which would burn fiercely." Once the blazing vessel had set the towers on fire, "the Tyrians in the city came swarming out, leapt into boats which ran upon the mole at various points, and soon succeeded in wrecking the palisade made to protect it and setting fire to all the war machines which had escaped the blazing boat."

Undaunted by this setback, Alexander gave orders to build new towers and artillery and directed that the mole be widened further. Yet he realized that only an amphibious assault stood any real chance of success, and so other Phoenician cities were required to supply ships. Engineers

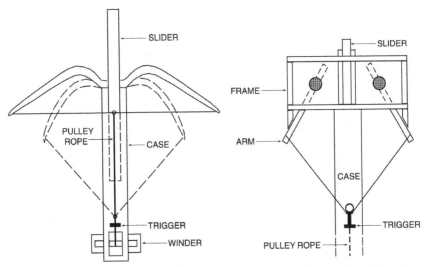

Siege weapons developed by the Macedonians: mechanical bow on the left and a catapult on the right.

were also set to work mounting siege artillery on barges and old transport vessels. Once the fleet was ready, Alexander the Great embarked an adequate number of soldiers in the expectation that "in the coming engagement close fighting would be the order of the day rather than naval tactics."

The Tyrian admiral's first thought, on hearing of the fleet's approach, was to seek a battle. But when he saw the size of the opposing fleet, far larger than he anticipated, he put about and raced for Tyre's two harbors. The Tyrians just managed to squeeze through the harbor entrances in front of Alexander's leading vessels. By jamming the bows of his ships across the harbor mouths, the admiral blocked any further pursuit. This thwarting maneuver, however, effectively bottled up Tyre's navy and handed to the Macedonians command of the sea.

Now Alexander was free to press on at full speed with the mole, his workmen protected from attack by a defensive screen of ships. There was, however, another reason "why it was difficult for Macedonian transports and warships to work in close to the city with their artillery, and this was the fact that blocks of stone in large numbers had been thrown into the water in order to obstruct their advance." Arrian adds that Alexander was

> determined to remove them, but the task was far from easy because the men had only the unsteady ships' decks to work from, but also because the Tyrians in specially armored boats managed to cut their anchor cables, so that it was impossible to remain on station. Alexander, in reply, sent a number of thirty-oared galleys with similar armor, mooring them broadside-on ahead of the warships' anchor ropes. . . . But the Tyrians, not to be outdone, sent down divers to cut the cables as before. Once the Macedonians replaced the ropes with chains, the Tyrians could do no more, and finally, from the mole, large cranes were able to clear away the obstruction of stone blocks.

Still unwilling to give up the fight, the Tyrians sallied out of the northern harbor and attacked the blocking squadron outside. Learning of this, Alexander immediately sailed around the island of Tyre and engaged the enemy squadron. Although the Tyrians suffered few casualties, as the sailors of damaged ships were able to swim ashore, this ended "all hope of protection by their navy."

Alexander now proceeded to launch the ancient equivalent of a saturation barrage with catapults brought up to the end of the mole. At the same time, no less vigorous an assault was being pressed from the seaward side with battering rams positioned on a large platform mounted across two barges. Arrian relates how

> a considerable length of wall began to give way under the assault and a breach was made, though not a large one. . . . Once a breach of sufficient breadth was made, Alexander withdrew the artillery carriers and ordered up two vessels with gangways which he proposed to throw across the breach. . . . No sooner were Alexander's ships under the city wall and the gangways lowered than the Macedonians sprang upon them and pressed powerfully into the breach with Alexander himself in the thick of the fighting.

Not to be outdone by this attack, the ships blockading the city's southern harbor

> *smashed a way through the defensive booms and made short work of the shipping inside, ramming some vessels where they lay afloat and driving others ashore; and the northern harbor, which was not even protected by booms, presented no difficulty at all. The warships sailed straight in and quickly gained control of that part of the city. The main body of the defenders abandoned the city wall once they saw it was in the enemy's hands, and withdrew to the shrine of Agenor, the founder of Tyre. There Alexander was soon upon them: some fell fighting, others fled, the Macedonians in hot pursuit.*

The savagery of the Macedonians was dreadful. Besides their frustration at the stubbornness of the defenders, "another action . . . roused them to rage. The Tyrians had dragged the few prisoners they had taken to the battlements, cut their throats in full view of the Macedonian army, and flung their bodies into the sea." The killings may have been intended as a sacrifice to a Tyrian god, since the Phoenicians were known to offer human sacrifices in times of peril such as war, plague, or drought. Whatever the idea behind this cruel display, the Macedonians were not going to overlook it.

Sieges were always likely to end badly for the besieged. A timely surrender was an extremely important matter for the inhabitants, as capture of a city by force often entailed rape, brutality, and enslavement. Despite the initial slaughter, Alexander pardoned the Tyrian king Azemilicus and visitors from Carthage who had come to the mother city to pay honor to Herakles. Everyone else was sold into slavery, some 30,000 in total.

"After the victory," Arrian notes, "Alexander offered sacrifice to Herakles and held a ceremonial parade of his troops in full battle equipment; the fleet also took part in the review in the god's honor, and there were athletic contests in the temple enclosure and a torch race. The piece of artillery which had made the breach was dedicated in the temple, and the Tyrian ship sacred to Herakles, which had been captured in the naval action, was solemnly presented to the god."

After the Macedonian army marched southward to Egypt, the mole was gradually covered by sand from the nearby dunes; today, it firmly links the city of Tyre to the mainland. Its ancient stone core remains in place, but the surface now boasts a road and apartment buildings.

ROME'S CAPTURE OF JERUSALEM

We are fortunate in having an eyewitness account of the Roman siege of Jerusalem provided by Flavius Josephus, a Jewish commander captured at the fortified town of Jotapata in AD 67. The Roman general Vespasian spared his life apparently at the request of his son Titus, but just as Vespasian was about to send Josephus off to Rome to stand trial before the emperor Nero, the Jewish captive requested an interview with the general. At this meeting, he prophesied that one day Vespasian would be proclaimed emperor, as in turn would Titus. Initially skeptical, Vespasian learned that Josephus's previous predictions had proved correct, and so he allowed him to remain in custody. When two years later in 69 Vespasian was raised to the purple by the Roman soldiers in Egypt and soon afterward acknowledged by those in Syria as well, he remembered the prophecy and released Josephus, whose chains were severed with an axe so as to expunge the indignity of imprisonment.

The Roman emperor Titus, son of Vespasian.

Afterward Josephus attached himself to Titus and witnessed the siege of Jerusalem. This event was the culmination of the great Jewish revolt against Roman rule. The unrest in the province of Judea had arisen from a number of causes. The local ruling class did not command respect and was seen to be in league with mostly inept or corrupt governors. And a marked decline in the economy during the two years prior to the revolt's breaking out in 66 only served to increase the general unease. Specific provocations included the high-handed treatment of Jews by Roman soldiers in Caesarea and other cities. The first flash point occurred in Caesarea, where a building site impinged on land belonging to a synagogue, closely followed by another in Jerusalem when money was forcibly taken from the Temple treasury, perhaps to make up for tax arrears. Gessius Florus, the procurator of Judea, was obliged to quit Jerusalem in haste, leaving behind a few Roman soldiers to protect the high priest. They proved insufficient to maintain order as a vicious struggle between revolutionary and moderate factions soon convulsed the city. The violence in Jerusalem coincided with a massacre of Jews in Caesarea, and reprisals across the province soon meant that there was no way of avoiding a full-scale rebellion.

The small size of the province did not lead Nero and his advisers to underestimate the potential seriousness of the Jewish uprising, which had to be prevented from spreading elsewhere. It may not have threatened the survival of Roman authority in the eastern Mediterranean, as Josephus claims, but it could draw in the support of Jews living beyond the Euphrates and encourage the Parthians to take advantage of the unrest. Jewish communities elsewhere in the Roman Empire were also likely to become targets if there was a prolonged war in Judea.

So Nero dispatched the experienced general Flavius Vespasian to Syria to put down the revolt. "At Antioch Vespasian concentrated the Roman forces and large allied contingents provided by neighboring kings," Josephus tells us, "while Titus went to Egypt to fetch another legion." Meanwhile initial Jewish enthusiasm had led to an assault on Ascalon, a coastal city with a small Roman garrison not far from Jerusalem. As Josephus points out, the action was ill-judged because

> when the raw Jewish recruits were confronted by veteran troops . . . undisciplined individuals by regulars who fought as one, men with nondescript weapons by fully armed legionaries, men guided by passion rather than reason, by men who instantly respond to every signal, the issue could never be in doubt. . . . After the front ranks of the attackers were disordered, they were routed by cavalry . . . and scattered all over the plain. This was large and ideal for cavalry tactics, a fact which weighted the scales in favor of the Romans and led to frightful carnage on the Jewish side. . . . so that the struggle continued to dusk, by which time 10,000 Jewish men had fallen along with their two commanders, John and Silas. . . . Roman casualties in this encounter amounted to a few wounded men.

Josephus adds that "far from being broken-hearted by this disaster, the Jews were stimulated to still greater determination."

At this point in the uprising, Josephus was in charge of the defense of Galilee, which would bear the brunt of Vespasian's southern advance. Realizing how important fortification was, he oversaw the improvement of the existing defenses, including those of his own base at Jotapata. Even though a premature attack on this town was repulsed, Josephus was prepared to contemplate surrender on terms if there was no way of resisting a concentrated assault. But for forty days Jotapata withstood everything the Romans threw at it, even breaking off the iron head of their battering ram. Eventually the attackers succeeded in overcoming the depleted garrison, and Josephus was taken prisoner. He gave himself up after two score of his companions killed each other in a suicide pact, Josephus having drawn the lot to die last. Some 40,000 of the town's inhabitants were slain, with just over 1,000 women and children sold into slavery. "The Romans," Josephus comments, "recalling what the siege had cost them, showed no mercy or pity for anyone."

Though Vespasian appreciated that the Jewish revolt would not be fully crushed until Jerusalem had fallen, he knew that he had to subdue other centers of resistance first. While this campaign was in progress, however, great events were taking place in Rome. The senatorial aristocracy deposed an increasingly demented Nero, and with the passing of Rome's first imperial dynasty, three other military commanders attempted to seize power before Vespasian secured the throne for himself. Though the senators gave their approval to his usurpation, Vespasian chose to date the start of his reign from the acclamation of his troops. This was a frank admission on the part of the new emperor that he owed his elevation to them and a reminder to the senators that not they but the army now constituted the real basis of political power.

That Vespasian was the first emperor to be succeeded by his own son, Titus, only served to underline the point. Their joint triumph in Rome in 71, a year after the capture of Jerusalem, was splendid but still an anomaly in being the only triumph ever to celebrate a victory over a provincial people. As a first-generation senator, Vespasian had no inherited social prestige to draw on, and so urgent steps had to be taken to enhance his public standing. In a sense the joint triumph represented the new dynasty's foundation myth.

While Vespasian began his reign in Rome, Titus besieged Jerusalem. A detachment was detailed to improve the quality of the road leading to the city so that the siege train and the baggage wagons could move more easily. A number of sailors, protected by light-armed troops, carried out this task ahead of the main column. Titus's army was also well protected against ambush: it possessed a strong vanguard and rearguard as well as scouts sent out to inspect the terrain on each side of the line of march. This scout cavalry was assisted by local guides.

Although Vespasian would have preferred to starve Jerusalem into submission, fearing heavy losses in an outright attack, Titus had other ideas for overcoming its fortifications. He had, in addition, the advantage of turmoil within Jerusalem itself. Josephus informs us that the situation in the city was made worse when

> the leaders of the various gangs of bandits had had enough of plundering the countryside [and] came together and formed a single pack of rogues. They infiltrated Jerusalem, a city without military command, where by age-old custom anyone of Jewish birth was admitted without scrutiny, and where at this juncture everyone thought those who were pouring in all came out of kindness as allies. It was this very thing, quite apart from the faction fighting, which ultimately wrecked the city; for a useless and idle mob consumed supplies adequate for the defenders, and in addition to war they brought on themselves faction and starvation. Other bandits from the country slipped into the city and, joining forces with these desperadoes within, gave themselves to every imaginable crime. They did not limit their insolence to theft and brigandage but went so far as to commit murder, not by night or secretly or against the common people but openly by day, beginning with the most eminent.

Against this divided city "seething with discontent," Titus advanced. The entire city was already a battleground, so "old men and women prayed for the Romans to come and looked forward to war without, which would free them from the miseries within." They were relieved therefore when "the warring factions for the first time put an end to their incessant strife in view of war suddenly descending on them from without in all its fury."

Having temporarily settled their differences, they decided to surprise the Romans, who were building strongholds around Jerusalem. A sudden sortie against one legion engaged in construction work threw its men

into disorder. Leaving their tasks some retreated; many ran for their weapons but were struck down before they could turn and face the enemy. . . . It is likely that the entire legion would have been in danger had not Titus, hearing of the situation, at once gone to the rescue. Denouncing their cowardice in no uncertain terms, he rallied the runaways; then falling on the flank of the Jews at the head of picked men who were with him, he killed many, wounded more, routed them, and drove them into a ravine. On the downward slope they suffered severely, but when they had crossed, they turned about and, with a stream between them, they put up a determined resistance. So it went on until a few minutes after noon, when Titus lined up the reinforcements he had brought and . . . sent one legion to resume their fortification work on the ridge.

Despite this impressive showing against experienced Roman soldiers, the Jews thought that they had suffered a serious reverse, and again "internal faction raised its head." One group even occupied the Temple and set about the worshippers there. With no further sign of Jewish activity, Titus closed in on Jerusalem. "To deal with any sorties, he posted what he considered an adequate body of horse and foot, instructing the rest of his forces to level the ground as far as the city walls."

Jerusalem's defenses comprised three walls, except where it was shut in by ravines; there a single rampart was enough. The Temple itself stood on a separate hill, surrounded by steep slopes. Yet, as the Romans moved closer to the outer wall, the defenders continued to fight each other. "At the time of the first sortie," Josephus relates, "they momentarily recovered their wits, but their frenzy had quickly returned, cooperation was at an end, and the internal struggle resumed as if their one desire was to play into the hand of the besiegers."

The Romans' first assault on the city walls revealed the effectiveness of their artillery. "The engines were masterpieces of construction ... with powerful spear and stone throwers. . . . The stone missiles weighed half a hundred weight and traveled four hundred yards or more; no one who got in their way, whether in the front line or far back, remained standing." Finally Titus brought up siege towers, from which the Jewish defenders were pelted with arrows and sling shot. Nearby the outer wall was giving way to a battering ram, and when the legionaries entered the breach, the Jews fell back to the second wall.

Josephus says that Titus then offered terms for the surrender of Jerusalem, which would have spared the Temple, but "the war party mistook humanity for weakness and believed it was through an inability to take the city that Titus made the offer." Since the Romans knew that famine was ravaging the inhabitants as much as civil strife, they could afford to temporarily suspend military operations. When Josephus was sent to explain how a rejection of Titus's offer would result in a massacre of the city's inhabitants, he was "greeted by howls of derision and execration, sometimes by stones." So the Romans tightened their grip by establishing

Loot from the Roman capture of Jerusalem in 70 depicted on the Arch of Titus in Rome.

a total blockade with a trench and a wall all around the city. Once the second city wall was breached and the remaining defenders hemmed in the Temple compound, the Roman soldiers attacked with fire and sword. Titus is reputed to have tried to prevent the destruction of the sanctuary, although it is hard to imagine why he would have been keen to spare the Temple. His arch in Rome bears a depiction of the Temple's destruction as well as the prominent display of the gold menorah and offering table during the triumph through the city streets.

THE SASANIAN SIEGE OF AMIDA

Whereas Flavius Josephus reports the siege of Jerusalem from the perspective of the attackers, Ammianus Marcellinus describes the Sasanian investment of Amida from the point of view of the besieged. This senior Roman officer's account of the siege in 359 is available because, with two companions, he managed to slip out of an unguarded postern gate as the city was overwhelmed.

The fortified city of Amida, located on the upper reaches of the Tigris, was part of the Roman defenses along the frontier with Sasanid Iran. Such strongholds became ever more important in the wars between the Romans and the Sasanians because they served a number of purposes. First, they acted as refuges for soldiers when threatened by a stronger enemy force. Second, they functioned as staging posts for campaigns since they were well stocked with supplies and weapons. Third, they protected the local population against sudden raids and provided a safe haven in times of war. According to Ammianus, the fortification of Amida primarily served as a refuge for the farmers living nearby.

When Shapur II invaded the eastern provinces of the Roman Empire in 359, this Sasanian king intended to bypass the fortified cities along the frontier and advance straight to Syria. But he was instead provoked into attacking Amida after an arrow fired by one of that city's crack shots killed the son of one of his principal allies. The young man had approached too close to Amida's walls in order to inspect its defenses.

"When the body of the young man had been burned and the bones enclosed in a silver urn to be taken home and buried as his father decreed, a council of war was held," Ammianus reports, "and it was decided to propitiate the spirit of the deceased by destroying the city." Since an immediate Sasanian assault on Amida failed, Shapur II had to settle down for a regular siege. During the investment an epidemic occurred in the city. Ammianus relates how "the number of corpses lying in the streets was too great to allow them to be buried, so that our troubles were increased by an outbreak of plague, fermented by the rotting worm-eaten bodies, the humid heat, and the feeble state to which the inhabitants were reduced.... But one night a fall of rain dispelled the thick and stifling air, and we regained our health."

Meanwhile the Sasanians had not been inactive, and "high towers faced with iron were going up. On the top of each one was placed a piece of artillery to drive the defenders from the ramparts."

Toward the end of the siege, a dramatic incident happened. Ammianus's description is a reminder of how dangerous unguarded entry points could be. He explains how

> in a remote part of the southern wall, which commands the river Tigris, there was a tower rising to a great height . . . with an underground passage cut through solid rock. . . . Through this water could be carried secretly from the bed of the river. . . . So steep was this dark passageway that it was left unguarded, and through it one night a treacherous inhabitant of the city conducted seventy Sasanian archers who occupied the tower. . . . From the third story of the tower in the morning they displayed a scarlet cloak, which was the signal for battle to begin, and seeing their own forces rushing towards the city on every side, they discharged their arrows with great skill. Soon all the massed forces of the enemy were assaulting the city far more furiously than before. We were divided in mind whether to direct our resistance to the threat from above or on the host mounted on scaling ladders. . . . So we shared the work and moved five of the lighter engines to positions opposite the tower. These kept up a rapid fire of wooden projectiles, some of which transfixed two of the enemy at once; part of the force fell seriously wounded, while others in panic at the noise of the artillery threw themselves down headlong and were dashed to pieces.

> *The engines were then restored to their usual places, and our united
> efforts enabled us to defend the walls with more confidence.*

Although a daring night attack by Gallic legionaries on the Sasanian
camp came close to killing Shapur II, this made little difference to the
progress of the siege. The Sasanians even deployed elephants to intimidate the defenders.

Having tried a whole series of assaults with scaling ladders accompanied by heavy artillery bombardment, Shapur II constructed a siege
ramp. Amida was eventually captured because Roman efforts to counter
this ramp were unsuccessful. Apparently the Sasanian king was so beside
himself with frustration that,

> *though never obliged to fight in person, he rushed forward into the
> thick of the fighting like a common soldier. This was a most unusual
> event. The number of his suite made him a conspicuous target even
> at a distance, and he was the target of a hail of missiles. After losing
> many of his companions he withdrew, passing through the lines of his
> disciplined troops, and at the end of the day, undaunted by the ghastly
> sight presented by the dead and wounded, he at last allowed a brief
> interval of rest.*

Ammianus adds that "for a long time the outcome of the siege hung
in the balance as the unremitting courage of the besieged set death at
defiance." But the collapse of the Roman counter ramp decided the issue,
for "suddenly the mound, on which we had spent so much labor, fell
forward as if struck by an earthquake . . . and presented the enemy with
a level surface over which they could advance unhindered." A general
massacre ensued in which "soldiers and civilians were slaughtered like
sheep without distinction of sex."

"As it was getting dark," Ammianus tells us, "and while a group of
our men was still keeping up the fight, hopeless though it was, I and
two others hid in an obscure corner of the city and escaped through an
unguarded postern under the cover of darkness. My acquaintance with

the desert and the pace kept up by my companions brought me at least ten miles from the city." Yet they would still have perished if they had not stumbled upon a deep well. "Though we possessed no ropes," he says, "we tore our linen clothes into long strips and made a great line, to the end of which we attached a cap which one of us was wearing under his helmet. We let this down and it sucked up water like a sponge, so that we were able to quench our raging thirst."

Ammianus was lucky to get away as all the Roman officers who fell into the hands of the Sasanians were crucified. Shapur II's anger is easy to understand. The siege of Amida had detained him for seventy-three days, diverted him

The Sasanian king Shapur II, the successful besieger of Amida.

from his objective, and consumed the lives of 30,000 of his men. The loss of this frontier stronghold was a setback for the Romans, who belatedly came to realize that the city could have been saved by the timely dispatch of reinforcements. A failure to appreciate the sheer determination of the Sasanian king cost the Romans dearly.

FURTHER READING

CHAPTER 1 SUMER AND AKKAD
Cotterell, A., ed. *The Penguin Encyclopaedia of Ancient Civilisations*. London, 1988.
Dalley, S. *Myths from Mesopotamia: Creation, the Flood, Gilgamesh and Others*. Oxford, 1989.
Foster, B. R. *The Age of Agade: Inventing Empire in Ancient Mesopotamia*. Abingdon, UK, 2016.
Liverani, M. *Uruk: The First City*. Translated by Z. Bahrani and M. van De Microop. Sheffield, UK, 2006.

CHAPTER 2 INTERNATIONAL RIVALRY
Bryce, T. *The Kingdom of the Hittites*. Oxford, 1998.
Charpin, D. *Hammurabi of Babylon*. London, 2012.
Cotterell, A. *Chariot: The Rise and Fall of the World's First War Machine*. New York, 2005.
Sanders, N. K. *The Sea Peoples*. London, 1978.

CHAPTER 3 THE GREAT MESOPOTAMIAN POWERS
Cotterell, A. *The First Great Powers: Babylon and Assyria*. London, 2019.
Finkel, I. L., and M. J. Seymour, *Babylon: Myth and Reality*. London, 2009.
Olmstead, A. T. *History of Assyria*. London, 1923.

CHAPTER 4 THE PERSIAN EMPIRE
Briant, P. *From Cyrus to Alexander. A History of the Persian Empire*. Translated by P. T. Daniels. Winona Lake, IN, 2002.
Herodotus. *The Histories*. Translated by A. de Selincourt. London, 1954.
Stoneman, R. *Xerxes: A Persian Life*. New Heaven, CT, 2015.
Xenophon. *The Persian Expedition*. Translated by R. Warner. London, 1949.

CHAPTER 5 THE MACEDONIAN SUPREMACY
Bosworth, A. B. *The Legacy of Alexander: Politics, Warfare and Propaganda under the Successors*. Oxford, 2002.
Buckler, J. *The Theban Hegemony, 371–362 BC*. Cambridge, MA, 1980.
Hamilton, C. D. *Agesilaus and the Failure of the Spartan Hegemony*. Ithaca, NY, 1991.

Hammond, N. G. L. *Alexander the Great: King, Commander and Statesman*. London, 1981.

———. *Philip of Macedon*. London, 1994.

Hanson, V. D. *The Western Way of War: Battle in Classical Greece*. Berkeley, CA, 1989.

Livy. *Rome and the Mediterranean*. Translated by H. Bettenson. London, 1976.

Plutarch. *The Age of Alexander*. Translated by I. Scott-Kilvert and T. E. Duff. London, 1973.

Xenophon. *A History of My Times*. Translated by R. Warner. London, 1966.

CHAPTER 6 THE IRANIAN REVIVAL

Bennett, J. *Trajan: Optimus Princeps*. London, 1997.

Fyre, R. N. *The History of Persia*. Munchen, 1983.

Goldsworthy, A. K. *The Roman Army at War, 100 BC–AD 200*. Oxford, 1996.

Plutarch. *The Fall of the Roman Republic*. Translated by R. Warner. London, 1958.

Polybius. *The Rise of the Roman Empire*. Translated by I. Scott-Kilvert. London, 1979.

Sartre, M. *The Middle East under Rome*. Translated by C. Porter and E. Rawlings. Cambridge, MA, 2005.

CHAPTER 7 THE SMALLER STATES

Bowersock, G. W. *Roman Arabia*. Cambridge, MA, 1983.

Bryce, T. *The Trojans and Their Neighbours*. London, 2006.

Stoneman, R. *The Greek Experience of India: From Alexander to the Indo-Greeks*. Princeton, NJ, 2009.

Winsbury, R. *Zenobia of Palmyra: History, Myth and the Neo-classical Imagination*. London, 2010.

CHAPTER 8 FAMOUS SIEGES

Ammianus Marcellinuus. *The Later Roman Empire (AD 354–378)*. Translated by W. Hamilton. London, 1986.

Arrian. *The Campaigns of Alexander*. Translated by A. de Selincourt. London, 1971.

Josephus. *The Jewish War*. Translated by G. A. Williamson. London, 1959.

INDEX

About the Author

Arthur Cotterell was formerly principal of Kingston College in London. Having lived and traveled widely in Asia, he has spent much of his life writing about its history and culture. In 1981 he published *The First Emperor of China*, whose account of Qin Shi Huangdi's remarkable reign was translated into seven languages. Among his recent books, *Western Power in Asia: Its Slow Rise and Swift Fall, 1415–1999*, was described by the *Japan Times* as "three dimensional historiography at its best," while Professor Anthony Milner of the Australian National University called *Asia: A Concise History* "an extraordinary achievement." Milner added that in this first-ever coverage of the entire continent, "modern Asia is given its true place in a very long, rich history—and amazingly that history is told in a way that will stimulate both students and general readers."

The last two books he published, *The Near East: A Cultural History* and *The First Great Powers: Babylon and Assyria*, indicate a shift of interest westward. It was in fact the research undertaken for these two publications that persuaded Cotterell of the urgent need for a general survey of ancient conflict, since organized warfare first arose in the Middle East. As a result, *Where War Began* reveals how such violence became an integral part of human society. The surge in military proficiency led to fighting on a scale unrepeated before modern times. As Cotterell points out, it is a sobering thought that, short of cyber weaponry, the ancient soldier experienced almost everything his present-day counterpart does.

Arthur Cotterell's previous study of ancient warfare, *Chariot: The Rise and Fall of the World's First War Machine*, was, according to the *Wall Street Journal*, "not aimed at your average subscriber to the History

Channel. It is instead—thank goodness—a wide-ranging cultural tour, via chariot, of the major civilizations of the ancient world, from Egypt, Greece and Rome to Persia, India and China. There is as much in *Chariot* on the *Iliad* and the *Ramayana* as on battlefield tactics. Still, there is also the nitty-gritty of war."